CW01066631

Headship Matters
conversations with seven secondary school headteachers

Peter Ribbins and Michael Marland

LONGMAN

Contents

1 Headteachers matter

An introduction to the text and to the cast

A prelude to the text

The theme of our text is that headship matters. Its justification is that we know surprisingly little about headteachers as people. Why this should be so, why it should matter and how we might go about filling this gap in our knowledge are amongst the subjects of this opening chapter. It also attempts to set the subsequent chapter by chapter reports of our conversations with seven very different headteachers of a wide range of state secondary schools in context. In doing so it presents a brief pen portrait of each of the contributors to the book and draws upon our conversations with these seven interesting people to examine how and why they became headteachers and what they think of headship.

A case for a new approach to the study of headship

Over time various opinions have been expressed as to how much schools matter. For some, their contribution in determining levels of pupil achievement is modest when compared with the influence of more general contextual variables. So, at least, it has been claimed in studies reporting on research in the United States (Coleman et al., 1966; Jenks et al., 1972). More recently, such findings have been challenged and the data they present has been subjected to sweeping reinterpretation. As Thomas Greenfield (1993) has pointed out 'in multiple regression analysis, subjective decisions such as the order in which variables are input significantly affects the result. In Coleman's study of equal opportunities, for example, the order of entering the variables shifts the value of in-school factors from virtually everything to almost nothing' (p. 236). It could be schools do make more of a difference than these pioneering studies initially supposed.

Certainly, subsequent research conducted within the United Kingdom has been more optimistic on this issue (Rutter et al., 1979; Mortimer et al., 1988).

If doubts remain as to how much schools matter, few outside the Netherlands (see Creemers and Scheerens, 1989; Creemers, 1992) dispute that heads matter. This belief is widely shared, not least amongst heads themselves. It is also commonplace amongst policy makers. Some rate its significance more highly than the 'contextual variables' accorded such prominence in the research from the USA discussed above. Kenneth Baker (1993) has claimed that:

> all too often educationalists (want) to explain away the poor performance of, say, an inner-city school by reference to the socio-economic circumstances of the area in which the school was located. Certainly one should not discount such factors entirely ... On the other hand, even in these areas there can be very good schools with a high level of achievement. It depends essentially upon the leadership of the Head and the quality of the teaching (p. 199).

John Patten is also reported as saying that he could not:

> stress too strongly how important the quality of leadership is in any school. Time and again inspectors conclude that the single most important factor in a school's success is the quality of leadership provided by the head and his or her senior colleagues. A poor one — and mercifully there are few of them — can seriously damage its success (SHA, 1993).

In reflecting upon these comments it may be worth remembering that the Secretary of State made them in a speech to the Annual Conference of the Secondary Heads Association in April 1993. He did so at a time when his personal popularity amongst teachers and headteachers was at a low ebb and when he was trying to persuade the latter to resist pressures on them to abandon Key Stage 3 testing in English and other subjects. But whatever his motives, what he said may well reflect accurately the views of many parents, pupils and, perhaps, even teachers.

It also mirrors the findings of many of the committees of the great and the good which have examined aspects of schools and schooling. Thus Elton (1989) concludes that:

> visiting different schools left us with the strong impression that the attitude and motivation of their headteachers and staff were decisive influences on their atmosphere. This impression is confirmed by the research evidence. Heads manage schools in different ways ... Research shows that differences in the ways

in which schools are run are associated with different standards of work, behaviour and attendance among their pupils (p. 90).

The report stresses that the nature and quality of a school's atmosphere is determined by the way in which all its major features combine. However, in identifying these features, it lists 'the quality of leadership' first. The National Commission on Education (1993) also gives priority to 'strong, positive leadership by the head and senior staff as the first of ten characteristic features of the successful school' (p. 142). It suggests that this view has been 'emphasised time and time again, both by the Inspectorate and by researchers and by practitioners' (p. 229). In addition, it argues that this:

> has always been the case, particularly in Britain where heads have a powerful role, but the major changes which are affecting schools will make even more significant demands. This is affecting all senior staff in schools, but is felt most by heads, whose roles and responsibilities have increased most of all.

Finally, it notes that 'Government has stressed that successful implementation of its reforms depends on leadership of schools by experienced, dedicated and highly motivated heads. We agree with that judgement' (p. 229).

It is not surprising, then, that no other management role within the British education system has been the focus of so much attention over such a long time as that of the headteacher. This interest dates back into the last century when it took the form of accounts of the careers and views of some of the foremost headmasters of the day including Arnold of Rugby, Butler of Shrewsbury, Moberly of Winchester, Keate of Eton and Thring of Uppingham. In the post-war era, they and other Victorian headmasters (Castle, 1967) and even some Victorian headmistresses (Pedersen, 1975, 1981; Dyhouse 1987) have continued to attract the interest of researchers.

In 1956 Baron published a paper on 'Some aspects of the "Headmasters Tradition"'. This looked back but it also suggested a need to look forward. Since then the study of the contemporary headteacher has become a growth industry. The literature contains numerous *surveys* (Hall et al., 1986; Hughes, 1972, 1973; Jones, 1987; Lyons, 1976; Morgan et al., 1983; Weindling and Early, 1987), *autobiographical statements* from heads and former heads (Barry and Tye, 1975; Dawson, 1981; John, 1980; McKenzie, 1970; Neill, 1960; Poster, 1976; Rae, 1993; Toogood, 1984; Watts, 1977), *biographies* (Gronn, 1986, 1992) and *case studies* of schools which to a greater or a lesser extent are concerned with the role of the head of the secondary school (Ball, 1980; Berg, 1968; Best et al., 1983; Burgess, 1983; Hargreaves, 1967; Lacey, 1970; Richardson, 1973).

In addition, papers *surveying the field* continue to be published in numbers (Holmes, 1993; Hughes, 1990; Weindling, 1990; Busher and Saran, 1994). Given the existence of this rich and varied literature, what is the case for yet another study of headship within the secondary school? We would offer two reasons for this.

First, because much of the literature on headship draws upon research which was conducted in the 1970s and before — and times, as the National Commission on Education (1993) has noted, have changed and much of this has dated badly. Given this, as Reynolds and Parker (1992) have pointed out, 'it would be very surprising if the effective headteacher of the 1990s bears more than a very superficial relationship with the effective headteacher as we now describe him or her' (p. 178). In developing this view Reynolds (1994) questions whether much of the research which was conducted in the last decade is helpful. He suggests that the

> effective headteacher of the 1980s got his school moving in the context of the absence of any external pressure for change; the effective headteacher of the 1990s has to somehow broker the external change agenda to his or her staff, a very different and complex task. The 1990s headteacher has to relate to parents, be a public relations person, cope with uncertainty, motivate staff in the absence of substantial instrumental rewards, has to be a financial manager and be able to cope with rapid changes. The sorts of headteacher that stand out in the 'old' school effectiveness literature are unlikely to be those that really 'work' in the 1990s (p. 23).

Reynolds and Parker (1992) conclude:

> the complexity of the contemporary situation in which he or she is likely to be, the overload of pressures — all these are likely to call for a style of effective headteacher very different from the one-dimensional creatures that stalk through the present day literature within school effectiveness (p. 178).

The same can be said of most of the accounts of headship more generally currently available. What we 'know' of effective headship relates to a bygone age. But there is another sense, we would suggest, in which heads have tended to be presented as 'one dimensional creatures'. It is this contention which leads us to our second reason for yet another study of headship.

This is derived from our belief that it is the methods used to study headship in the past which have tended to lead to the depiction of heads in monochrome. Rae (1993) seems to share a similar view. His book, he claims, aims 'to explore, through my own experience, the role of the English public school headmaster' (p. 11). He knows that biographies and autobiographies of heads exist but claims that they 'do not tell you much about what it is really like to do the job' (p. 11). Indeed, in Rae's view:

fiction has been more successful in entering the headmaster's mind. I am not thinking of the most famous cases, Thomas Hughes's portrait of Dr Arnold in *Tom Brown's Schooldays*, but of a more recent and less well known novel. *The Rector of Justin* by Louis Auchincloss. Other novelists have tried to create or recreate the character of a headmaster: sometimes he is at the centre of the novel as in Anthony Trollope's *Dr Wortle's School* or G. F. Bradby's *The Lancaster Tradition*; sometimes he is a supporting player as in Samuel Butler's *The Way of all Flesh* . . . or Hugh Walpole's *Mr Perring and Mr Traill* (p. 11).

This list is by no means comprehensive. To it might be added such more recent classics as Ralph Delderfield's *To Be With Them All My Days* and the many portraits of headteachers to be found in a growing number of films and on television over the last forty years. A journey which would take us from *Mr Chipps* to *Grange Hill* and even to *Coronation Street*. What is particularly interesting about the latter cases is that they focus upon *headmistresses* and are located within *state comprehensive schools*. However, if fictional portraits can sometimes offer a technicoloured view of headship, they can still be one-dimensional. Rae (1993) concludes:

Auchincloss is the only author who understands how the master's personality influences the way he will play the role *and* how the demands of the role draw out particular aspects of his personality . . . What makes the life of a public school headmaster interesting is not just how he did the job but what the job did to him (pp. 11, 12).

Such views may well have as much relevance to the study of headteachers working in state secondary schools as they do to those in public schools. Furthermore, what might be of equal interest in both cases is the ways in which the personality of a headteacher shapes how he or she interprets and plays the role.

To answer these and related questions about the role of the contemporary headteacher requires not just more research, but new methods of research. What these methods might look like was the subject of a keynote paper which one of us gave at the Annual National Conference of the Association for Australian Educational Administration and the Association of Australian Secondary Principals held in Adelaide in late September 1993. This set out six propositions for the study of headship during a period of radical educational reform. The sixth stated that 'we need to augment existing methods with a new approach for the study of headship in the 1990s. An approach which enables the production of an account of headship which contextualises in three main ways'.

First, as a *situated perspective*. Many accounts of headship are based upon surveys which typically claim to some extent to be more or less representative of the views of headteachers as a whole. From these surveys the researcher extracts composite glossed accounts of key issues which may represent more or less accurately the views of the sample as a whole or the ideas of a particular headteacher on one or more topics. In extreme cases, the data from such research seems to be simply *raided* to demonstrate the validity of a thesis to which the researcher was committed before undertaking the study. But even where the data is treated with respect, it is still hard to see how such an approach can possibly offer a rich and comprehensive understanding of the *perspectives* and *styles* which heads bring to their work. For this to be possible the reader must be offered a much fuller access to the *views* and *actions* of the headteachers involved across a representative range of *issues* and *events*. Such an approach would present a series of portraits of individual headteachers each of which is reported in some depth. It might take a number of different forms. Mortimer and Mortimer (1991), for example invited a small number of headteachers to respond *in writing* to a set of issues specified by the researchers. In preparing for this book we have relied upon a series of *face to face* interviews using as our model the approach used so effectively by Kogan in his interviews with ministers of education (1971) and chief education officers (1973). Before describing how these interviews were conducted we need to say something more about the second form of contextualising.

Secondly, as a *contextualised perspective*. Traditional reports *decontextualise* in the way described above but also in-so-far as they do not attempt to locate what heads say within a context of the views of *significant others* (senior and other staff, pupils, parents and governors) in the *community of the school*. A contextualised perspective would seek to give the reader access to such information.

Thirdly, as a *contextualised perspective in action*. Few studies explore what heads say (as this has been described above) in the context of what they do. To offer a contextualised perspective in action the researcher must do four things. First, to observe heads as they enact their role in relevant situations. Secondly, to discuss with heads what they are trying to do and why. Thirdly, to set these accounts against the views of significant others. Finally, to compare and contrast the available evidence in the hope of producing the kind of enriched portraits of individual heads and of headship identified earlier.

It is possible, and worthwhile, to engage in research into headship in each of these ways. It is also possible to regard them taken together as amounting to a comprehensive research programme made up of *three levels* in which the second level subsumes the first level and the third level subsumes the second and the first levels. Since 1989 Peter Ribbins has been involved in just such a programme of research. Initially, this focused upon an examination of the way in which Great Barr, a large comprehensive school in north Birmingham, was responding to the agenda of reform set out in the 1988 Educational Reform Act and refined and revised in subsequent legislation. It began as the kind of modified ethnographic study he had undertaken in a number of secondary schools over the past fifteen years. But as the research progressed he became increasingly interested in the role of the head as an interpreter and enactor of change. With the headteacher, Brian Sherratt, he has been trying to develop a 'novel' approach to headship based on the ideas outlined earlier (see Ribbins and Sherratt, 1992).

In this book we report upon a 'first level' study of headship. It would be possible to build upon the discussions with our seven headteachers and by doing so to engage in second or even third level studies of the kind described above. Each of the seven chapters which follow, reports separately on a one-to-one conversation which one or other of us has had with Sue Benton, Valerie Bragg, Peter Downes, Elaine Foster, Michael Marland, Brian Sherratt and Harry Tomlinson. In these discussions, the first of which took place on the 27th April 1993 and the last on the 21st December 1993, they answer a series of questions on aspects of their early life and schooling, their reasons for becoming teachers and for seeking headship, and the way in which they interpret and enact their role as secondary headteachers. We do not claim the seven are in any sense a representative sample. Instead, we have tried to select people who we believed would be interesting, who worked in a wide variety of comprehensive secondary schools, who were at diverse points in their careers as headteachers, and who were different in terms of their life experience and their views. We will say something about each of them below and they will say a good deal more about themselves in the chapters which follow.

The list of topics which we wished to raise was prepared and sent to each of our respondents in advance of our discussion with them. Our preliminary interview schedule contained sixteen sets of questions (Appendix 1). An advantage of an interview-based approach is that it is possible to revise and renegotiate the agenda of discussion as a natural aspect of the dialogue. In practice this did happen and we were challenged once or twice to show how a particular follow-up question could be justified in terms of the agreed interview schedule. Every head was interviewed at least once and we talked to some twice. The interviews were of between two and three hours in length and were tape recorded, transcribed and edited. Each of our respondents was sent a transcript of their interview to propose such revisions as they might wish to see included in a final script. Some made much use of this opportunity, others less. There was always a risk that the advantages of allowing respondents prior sight of our interview schedule and enabling them to comment subsequently upon a draft script of our conversation with them might be gained at the price of some loss of spontaneity. This was a price which we felt that we had to pay. In retrospect we do not feel that the conversations as we have reported them are lacking in either authenticity or colour. In examining what they say we have restricted our preliminary analysis to a brief examination of two broad themes: preparing for headship and professing headship. Before turning to these themes we will introduce the members of the cast and contributors who have worked together over the last year and more to make this book possible.

A note on the cast

The idea of using the concept of a cast as a metaphor to introduce the eight contributors to this book is not as fanciful as it might at first seem. Not least because several stressed the importance of the arts in general and of music and the theatre in particular to their lives. At least two — Brian Sherratt and Michael Marland — might be regarded as semi-professionals. Sherratt comments that 'because I had a reasonable voice I was fortunate enough to be successful in voice trials for a cathedral choir school. In a sense one felt one was a professional musician'. He stressed that 'I listen to music at home as often as I can but of course this is mostly during the school holidays. During term it is mostly what I can snatch from Radio Three or cassettes whilst driving the car'. Marland tried to make a career in the theatre and his family has had many connections with the world of music — his father as 'a very successful dance band pianist and composer. He was Henry Hall's pianist and arranger' and one of his sons has been a musical director for Tina Turner.

Others attest to the importance of the arts in their lives. Harry Tomlinson, for example, admits that he stayed on at university after his first degree 'in great part' because 'I wanted to ... produce Ibsen's *Master Builder*. I had acted in it and it has always been a play I think about quite a lot ... The PGCE was, I fear, an opportunity to stay in Oxford for another year and to do this'. He stresses the continuing significance:

throughout my life of the theatre ... About once every two or three weeks I try to go to the theatre. I suppose that is about trying to understand what life is like. I am not as interested in the other arts. For me the theatre is the art that most relates to real life. It is, in a sense, about education and it is about education in the best way. I like the psychologist to tell me about myself and I like to learn from the dramatist about myself and life.

Sue Benton and Peter Downes also comment, rather less fully, on the place of the arts within their lives. At university, Sue Benton 'took up Art as a subsidiary. It was, in fact, an Art History course. That started off something which has become a life long interest'. Peter Downes, in commenting upon the ways in which he tries to deal with the stresses of headship, talks of the need to make time for other things as he struggles to cope with a working week which runs to between 75 and 80 hours. Teaching is listed amongst his 'recreations' on the grounds that it enables him to 'do one thing for sixty minutes without any interruption'. Another might be thought of as rather more conventional — 'during term I try to have one night a week off, playing in a local orchestra'.

In the next section the cast and contributors are introduced in alphabetic order. The reader will learn much more about each of them in the chapters that follow but we felt that a preliminary note on each might be useful.

Sue Benton is headteacher of Newlands School in Berkshire. Newlands is a girls' comprehensive school with about 1,100 pupils including a sixth form of some 200. This is her first headship. At the time of the interview she was nearing the end of her third year. As such, she is one of the least experienced of our heads. She remarks 'I had my children very young. This had some advantages from my point of view because I did not have a career pattern which was then interrupted. I was able, in effect, to start a normal career pattern, but later. And go for the top without time out'. The early years of her career was made up of 'a whole series of part-time jobs'. Her crucial career move, Sue believes, was to Bicester School in Oxford. She spent 13 years there, starting as a junior teacher and ending as a Head of Department, and remembers it as a highly innovative school. In 1985 she studied an MSc in educational management at the University of Oxford where her research was on new heads and how they changed their schools. Shortly afterwards she was appointed as a deputy head of an 11–16 school and a few years later moved to Newlands.

Valerie Bragg has been head of the City Technology College at Kingshurst, Birmingham since 1987. The CTC is co-educational and

currently has 1,300 pupils, It was the first school of its kind to be set
up and she was the first head of a CTC to be appointed. On reading
Kenneth Baker's plans for CTCs she remembers thinking that 'they
seemed like the schools of the future'. She did not intend to apply
but a variety of reasons, not least an article which said 'the *headmaster's* first job would be to appoint the staff and *he* would be
planning the curriculum', led her to do so. She was appointed in a
blaze of publicity. The school has attracted great media attention
and experienced much hostility from the educational world.
Kingshurst is Valerie's second headship. Her first was in a large
comprehensive high school in Stourport. Before that she was for
seven years a deputy head, encountering a good deal of prejudice
once she started applying for headship. She has many interests.
These have included running an antiques business whilst a deputy.
She is a governor of the University of Central England and a non-
executive director on the Solihull Health Authority.

Peter Downes has for many years been the head of Hinchingbrooke
in Cambridgeshire. Hinchingbrooke is a co-educational comprehensive school with 1,800 pupils of between 11–18. Before that he was
head of Henry Box in Witney. His career began at Manchester
Grammar School, which he also attended as a pupil, where after only
six years, he was given responsibility for setting up a parents' association. He spent twelve years at Manchester Grammar where he was
promoted head of department at the age of twenty-seven. His next
move, also as a head of department, was to Banbury School in
Oxfordshire. There he came under the influence of Harry Judge.
From Banbury he jumped straight from head of department to a
headship. Peter's other interests, in term time at least, tend to be
linked with education. He spent two years seconded for one day a
week to act as an inspector for the LEA. Over the last few years, and
late in his career, he has been much involved with SHA as a member
of its National Council and in other ways. He is a Rotarian, values
his membership of a local orchestra and enjoys his regular summer
visits to France.

Elaine Foster is headteacher of Handsworth Wood (Girls) in Birmingham. At the time of the interview, she had been at the school for
three years. The school is a comprehensive school which was built
for 600 but currently takes just over 800 girls of between 11–16. It is
located on the same campus as Handsworth Wood (Boys). Earlier in
her career, Elaine was for three and a half years a deputy head at the
boys school. She was, for the next three and a half years, a member
of Her Majesty's Inspectorate. It was during this time she definitely
decided she would like to go into headship. Since becoming a head
she has talked to two or three people about becoming a headteacher.
As she points out this 'is a big issue for women, and a big issue for

black women in particular'. She believes that her involvement in 'setting up the African/Caribbean Teaching Unit and the Afro-Caribbean Teachers' Association' has taught her a great deal about this. At the time of writing, she has just resigned her headship and plans to return to the Caribbean

Michael Marland is headteacher of North Westminster School in London and was Honorary Professor of Education at the University of Warwick between 1980 and 1993. He has been a headteacher since 1971, at Woodberry Down (1971–79) and then at North Westminster Community School which he opened in April 1980. North Westminster is a co-educational, multi-ethnic school taking almost 1,800 pupils of between 11–18 and is located on three campuses. Before becoming a head, he worked in two well known comprehensives — first as Head of English at Abbey Wood and subsequently as head of English and Drama and then Director of Studies at Crown Woods. Michael has been a member of many educational and other committees including the Bullock Committee on the Teaching of Reading and the Use of English, the Finniston Committee of Enquiry into Technological Education, and the Education and Human Development Committee of the ESRC. He has also written and edited many articles and sixteen books on a wide variety of themes to do with education and its management. For many years he has been General Editor of the *Heinemann Organization in Schools* series. He has also been General Editor of the Longman *Imprint Books* series. He has broadcast on both radio and television on numerous occasions.

Peter Ribbins has never been a headteacher. This is an oversight he sometimes regrets. His researches in headship and a knowledge of what is expected of his wife, who is a secondary head, has largely cured him of such regrets. He is currently Professor of Education Management and Deputy Dean of Education at the University of Birmingham. Before escaping into higher education Peter worked in secondary schools and as an education officer in the London area. He has written or edited 19 books and manuscripts and numerous articles on management and policy-making in education and is editor of the journal *Educational Management and Administration*. He is to be General Editor of the series *Leaders and Leadership in Education* for Longman. Since 1989 he has been engaged in a study of headship of the kind described above. This has focused, in particular, on the way in which Great Barr Grant-Maintained Secondary School is coping with recent educational change and of the role of its headteacher, Brian Sherratt, in enabling this.

Brian Sherratt has been headteacher of Great Barr Grant-Maintained School since 1984. Great Barr, a co-educational comprehensive with almost 2,300 pupils, is the largest school in the country. Before Great Barr, Brian spent five years as Head of Kirk Hallam, an 11–16

community comprehensive school in Derbyshire. On completing his PGCE, his first teaching post was at Normanton Grammar School. He was appointed despite failing to answer a question in the interview which asked if he had noticed anything about the station at Normanton — it is the longest in the UK! He then went on to be a head of department at Selby Grammar school where, in 1972, he wrote his first book — a study of comparative religion. His latest text was published in 1994 by the Centre for Policy Studies and is entitled *Opting for Freedom: A Stronger Policy on Grant-Maintained Schools* [Study Number 135]. After Selby, for a short time he lectured in comparative religion at Avery Hill College and taught at Kidbrooke School. In 1973 he was appointed to a deputy head post in Tunbridge Wells. Since 1989, he has researched with Peter Ribbins. His commitment to Great Barr is very great — it satisfies, as few other schools could, his passions for comprehensive education, for grant-maintained status and for big schools.

Harry Tomlinson is Principal of Margaret Danyers, a large sixth form college in Stockport. He has been the head or principal of three other schools and colleges. During these years he has had a great deal of practice in the management of reorganisation within individual schools and has been known to talk wryly of his unrivalled experience of the management of closure. Before this, he worked in East Africa and in Kuwait, was a lecturer at Kesteven College of Education and then spent many fulfilling years at Billericay School in Essex, where he came under the tutelage of its headteacher, Arthur Lingard. Harry is treasurer of the Secondary Heads Association and chair of the British Educational Management and Administration Society. He is a Fellow of the Institute of Management, the Institute of Training and Development and the Chartered Institute of Marketing. He has caught the writing bug in a serious way and over the last three years has edited *Performance Related Pay*, *The Search for Standards*, and *Education and Training 14–19*.

Preparing for headship

It was tempting to use, or, perhaps, to misuse, the texts of our conversations to attempt a preliminary sketch for a natural history of preparation for headship. Instead, in interrogating what we have been told by our seven headteacher respondents, we have restricted ourselves to an examination of: the ways in which their attitudes to schooling have been shaped by their experiences of it as pupils; how and why they became teachers; and, how and why they sought to become headteachers.

The making of seven pupils

Before these conversations, our knowledge of the early lives of most of our interviewees was, for the most part, very limited. But we were not surprised to find major areas of difference and some common ground. Some came from relatively comfortable backgrounds economically. Valerie Bragg's 'father was a director at Pilkingtons' and her 'mother is a potter but at the time she was a housewife'. Others were from families less fortunate. Sue Benton recalls that her 'grandfather left school when he was 14 and went to be a miner. In the area in which he lived that was all there was'. Michael Marland's background was rather more exotic. His grandfather was a publican and his father 'made his way by becoming a very successful dance band pianist and composer'. But his mother 'lived in a Manchester slum. She was one of twelve children born, only six of whom survived'. Two, Peter Downes and Harry Tomlinson, were the sons of teachers.

The influence of parents and even of grandparents in shaping and determining the educational experiences of each of the seven is clearly acknowledged. On the whole, the importance of fathers was not emphasised. Valerie Bragg's father was an exception to this 'rule'. She wished to leave school at sixteen but her father told her 'You are going back into the sixth form'. In accounting for this, she remarks that it is best regarded as a consequence of the prejudices of 'typically middle-class parents who felt that their daughter ought to go into the sixth form' and a father who 'wanted to make sure I did what he had not been able to do. He had wanted to go to university but never had, for various reasons, including the war'. In this context, Peter Downes also believes that his 'parents were anxious that I should have the best possible education because they had both been frustrated in their education; they were both quite bright but lived in Salford at the time of the Great Depression and therefore had not been able to fulfil their educational potential. Therefore they wanted me to achieve everything I possibly could'. Similar views, as we shall see, were pressed by yet other parents and grandparents. The influence, both indirect and direct, of grandparents, especially of grandfathers, was mentioned by, amongst others, Brian Sherratt. Sue Benton, in a passage echoing what Valerie Bragg says of her father, recalls that her grandfather had passed the common entrance for grammar school but was forced to leave because his parents could not afford to keep him there. This bred in him 'a sense of frustration along with a strong conviction of the worth of education and the wish to support me in something which (he) had been unable to enjoy'. Notwithstanding the role of fathers and grandfathers and even mother-in-laws, it is mothers who have most often exerted the most compelling example and influence.

Sue Benton remembers the good example of her mother who 'exemplified the grit you need to achieve your educational goals by going to night school and getting the "O" Levels she had not been able to in her youth'. Such 'grit' and such a passion for education in their mothers was vividly recalled by others. As Harry Tomlinson puts it 'my mother was one of those people who was denied a proper education by her circumstances. She was always very ambitious for my brother and myself and put a high value on education. In fact she achieved an Open University honours degree at the age of 72. That kind of spirit was an important part of what drove us on to succeed'.

In these ways and others, the attitude of parents and other relatives seems to have been a powerful force in shaping the way Brian Sherratt and others responded to their schooling. As he puts it 'they certainly were influential in creating the kind of climate in which I was brought up and it was a climate in which the importance of education was taken for granted. It was assumed one was going to work hard. I never knew any other kind of expectation'. Sherratt also acknowledges that 'I owe a great deal to both my schools ... I should like to think that, in years to come, Great Barr pupils will look back with the same kind of affection on their school days'. Sue Benton, asked if she enjoyed the girls grammar school she attended in Sheffield, responded simply 'I loved it'. In retrospect, she identifies its importance in 'forming the values and ideas I hold now. The most obvious influence was the role models we were offered by some of the teachers. They showed us that women could be clever and successful ... We also learnt that girls could do everything. That was important in terms of where I am now'. When pressed, she does not remember everything about her school with affection. Thus, for example, it left her with a deeply grounded belief that she was 'hopeless at maths. I was in the second group of four in a very selective school. When I taught in a comprehensive school I realised that I was wrong; if I had gone to that school, I would have been in the top set. That changed my perspective and has influenced some of the ideas which I have tried to put into practice within this school'. Whatever their reservations, both Sue Benton and Brian Sherratt are generally very positive about their experience of schooling and of most of those who attempted to teach them. This is by no means a sentiment which was shared by all the others.

Harry Tomlinson, for example, was 'not really happy being in a boys' grammar school. It was an aggressive place full of boys acting in a macho way'. Marland also attended a boys' school and he, too, remembers it as 'tough and harsh. You were expected to be good at fighting and at catching and kicking balls'. Both are critical of aspects of the teachers and the teaching which they encountered at these schools. As they say 'It was, at times, an unpleasant place to be

... Some teachers acted in unacceptable ways in terms of violence and homosexuality. There were a number of teachers who behaved like brutes. They were really quite disgusting' [Tomlinson] and 'I don't think the standard of teaching in general was very good. I can remember some awful ill-discipline and some improper goings on' [Marland]. If Tomlinson was appalled by aspects of his experience of secondary school, Valerie Bragg's abiding memory is of being thoroughly bored. As she says, 'I did not like school very much. I did not enjoy it, I was not motivated. I was one of those children who wasted their time and was going to leave school at 16 [...] Most of the time I tended to feel things were boring and uninteresting'. But it is possible to paint too bleak a picture. All seven acknowledged the importance of good teaching and every one, even those who did not remember their school days with affection, testified to the merits of one or more teachers who had, in various ways, managed to inspire them.

For some, such teachers had not only encouraged them as pupils but also influenced their practice when they, in their turn, became teachers. Sue Benton recalled her

Latin teacher ... a funny little Scottish lady who got very cross with people if they did not get their Latin right ... She and my French teacher gave me an image of scholarship in which an important part was that the subject was to be enjoyed. I can remember her giggling to herself as she read the Latin before she translated it to us. She was obviously getting enormous enjoyment out of it. As a teacher I have tried to share with my pupils the same enjoyment in the subject ... There was also the obvious pleasure which such teachers took in our achievements. They were firm ladies who stood no nonsense but were very supportive and helpful and clearly cared a great deal about their pupils.

Brian Sherratt believed that there 'were several very good teachers' at his school. Even so, he singles out one of his English teachers as 'outstandingly good at involving pupils, generating an authentic excitement in literature'. The teachers referred to above worked in secondary schools. Primary school teachers were hardly mentioned. Harry Tomlinson, however, remembers 'two teachers in my primary school. Miss Turpin who taught the first year juniors and Mrs Rhodes who taught the top juniors. The image I have of them is two women who I wanted to work for. They were both very strong and firm ...' The influence of university teachers was referred to several times. Valerie Bragg, for example, describes her professor of Zoology as 'spending the whole day trying to persuade

me to teach'. In the event, he was to be successful. How and why did
the others become teachers?

The making of seven teachers

Valerie Bragg is disarmingly frank about her teaching aspirations.
Or rather, the lack of them. She says simply 'Teaching was the last
thing in the world that I wanted to do'. Her views were to change.
With some misgivings, she decided to try teaching. To her surprise
she 'found it absolutely fantastic ... I think it was about that time
that I first started to enjoy learning, because I began to see how
exciting and interesting it was'. Sue Benton also left school 'not
intending to go anywhere near a school ever again in my life'. However, as she neared the end of her English degree, she, too, changed
her mind and 'decided that I wanted to teach'. For Elaine Forster
'teaching was a second choice'. But, like Valerie Bragg, she can now
say 'I really do enjoy working with children and young people. I
think I enjoy the challenges of education. I love being in the classroom'. Peter Downes, alone, was clear he 'always wanted to be a
teacher. As far back as I can remember I never wanted to be anything else. My parents told me that I played at being a teacher very
early on in my life. When other children were playing cops and
robbers or mummies and daddies, I was playing schools'.
      Given all this, it is not surprising to discover that Downes 'had
been interested in teaching *method* as long as I can remember'.
Others evidently share this interest but several did not undertake
teacher training and some of those who did felt that they had not
gained very much from it. Michael Marland, Valerie Bragg and Sue
Benton, if for very different reasons, did not study for a PGCE.
Marland explains 'in those days you did a PGCE if you wanted
another year in Cambridge to do sports or whatever'. In any case 'at
the time I had not made up my mind to teach. I wanted to direct
plays'. Bragg also feels no compulsion to apologise. As she says 'On
graduating I felt I had had enough education and training and the
sooner I could get started the better. I also wondered what is the
point of doing it anyway. I thought I would try teaching and see if I
liked it. If I had completed a year on the PGCE and then discovered
I did not want to teach that would have been a total waste of time'.
With the 'advantage of hindsight I have rather come to believe that
you can either teach or not'. She has also come to believe that 'In
many ways it might be better for everybody to start teaching to see if
they like it, and if they do perhaps after two or three years then they
might really benefit from training'. It is not clear that these two
beliefs are compatible. Sue Benton's reason for not studying for a
PGCE is also simple. She had applied, but 'there was some confusion

over my papers; they got lost as they were passed from one university to another. By the time it was sorted out everybody had allocated their places. So instead of doing a Cert Ed. I started teaching straight away'. It was, she stresses, easier 'to do that at the time ... Nowadays it is a very different matter and much more difficult to move from your degree straight into a school. I would certainly not recommend such a course to anyone now'.

By no means all those who did undertake a PGCE had done so because they felt the need for professional teacher training. Marland's judgement abut why people took a PGCE at the time was unknowingly vindicated by Harry Tomlinson. He 'wanted to stay in great part because I had decided I would produce *The Master Builder* ... The PGCE was, I fear, an opportunity to stay in Oxford for another year and to do this'. Brian Sherratt had some hopes for his time in teacher training but 'did not enjoy that one year course at all'. As a theology graduate the part which he 'enjoyed least was the RE element. Stupidly, at the time I thought of it as a kind of Sunday School equivalent of the theology faculty. It was quite difficult to take. And this was not just my view. Other people with my background found it so'. One of us works in teacher training and it would have been a consolation to learn that one or two, at least, might have, as a consequence of all this, struggled a bit during their first years of teaching. In fact, this does not seem to have happened. Valerie Bragg might well speak for her six headteacher colleagues when she says of her first year 'I enjoyed it. I had to work incredibly hard ... I think it switched me on. That was when I started to enjoy working. I had to think very hard about how to put things over and how to explain concepts. It all just clicked'. By the end of the year she was beginning to look for her first promotion and felt ready to take the next step along the route to headship.

The making of seven headteachers

Each of our seven contributors talked a good deal about their career as a teacher and a manager and about how this might be regarded as a preparation, planned or otherwise, for headship. In examining what they had to say, we have focused upon four main themes: at what point and why they began to consider the possibility of headship; who they were influenced by in developing their thinking about headship; the ways in which they prepared for headship; and, how they got their first headship.

The idea that they might wish to become heads dawned more quickly on some than others. Valerie Bragg was quickest of all — 'I suspect I knew almost from the beginning — almost as soon as I started teaching'. Most came to this conclusion quite early on in their careers. Sue Benton claims this happened 'once I had decided I was interested in becoming a head of department and became involved, through that, in much wider whole school issues'. Others took their time. One such was Elaine Foster. She recalls that 'I don't think I started out thinking that I wanted to be a head. And I think it was quite a while. In fact it was probably only about five years ago that I thought, this is what I would like to do, at which point I had just come to the end of three and a half years of deputy headship and had started to work with HMI'.

If there was a degree of diversity in the alacrity with which the decision was made, the explanations offered for wishing to be a head were often quite similar. For Elaine Foster, her work as an HMI alerted her to 'the challenges and possibilities of headship'. She began to think that 'if I am reading legislation and educational thinking at the political level right, then headship is the place I need to be. I also realised that a head can actually be very influential in trying to determine the lives and careers of children'. Asked why he wanted to be a head, Harry Tomlinson responded that 'I think it was simply because I had to do that to achieve the things which I felt I ought to achieve. I think it was that I could help children and teachers'. Even after seventeen years of headship he still believes that 'it is the most interesting and useful job there is'. But he also acknowledges the influence of other motives, concluding that 'I should not emphasise that too strongly. It was very much tied up with an ambition to become what I thought I was capable of becoming'.

For most, the key influence for good or ill in shaping the views of our headteachers on headship was, usually, the headteachers they had known as pupils, or, more particularly, as teachers in the schools in which they had worked. Recalling his life as a pupil, Harry Tomlinson remembers his headmaster without much affection. Sue Benton found some of the things which her headmistress said 'risible' at the time but has since learnt to put a higher value on her advice. Michael Marland, asked what he remembered of his head replied 'He was known as "Oily" because he once said to some senior boys . . . "You are the machine and I am merely the oil that helps it work". I had little to do with him'. Marland, and four others spoke, usually more positively, of some of the headteachers with whom they had worked during their careers as assistant teachers.

Taken together, the group, before being elevated to headship, had worked in some of the best known schools in the country — Sue Benton at Bicester, Peter Downes at Manchester Grammar and Banbury, Michael Marland at Crown Woods, Brian Sherratt at Kidbrooke and Harry Tomlinson at Billericay. Several came under the influence of some of the best known heads of recent times. Brian

Sherratt remembers what it was like to work for a famous head-teacher — Dame Mary Green. Harry Tomlinson recalls Arthur Lingard, his head at Billericay, approvingly as 'the kind of head who was prepared to take risks' and Michael Marland regarded Malcolm Ross of Crown Woods as being in some respects 'twenty years ahead of his time'. But it is Peter Downes who speaks of Harry Judge, his mentor at Banbury, in the most glowing terms as 'always an inspiration'. He also claims to 'have learnt from all the heads I have worked for. One tends to admire their strengths and perhaps think that in some ways one would do other things differently'. This hints that what Downes has learnt about headship from some of his former headteachers has sometimes focused upon how not to do things. Valerie Bragg, in commenting upon the four heads with whom she has worked, concludes that 'One tends to learn what not to do rather than what to do. I learnt just how frustrating it can be to work for some heads, which was partly why I wanted to move on. I hope I give space and freedom'. Finally, two mentioned help they had received from other heads. Peter Downes stresses that 'I value enormously what I learn from colleagues' and Sue Benton recalls the support which she got when she studied 'new heads and how they changed their schools'.

Sue Benton carried out this research in part fulfilment of her studies for an MSc in Educational Management at the Institute of Education at the University of Oxford. At the time she had decided that she 'wanted to go for deputy headship and headship and this seemed a good way of preparing'. As such, this takes us neatly into an examination of how our seven heads went about preparing themselves for headship. What can be involved might best be illustrated using particular cases.

Valerie Bragg, asked if she had planned her way to headship, noted:

> I took a very traditional route. I obtained an early promotion to
> head of department, went on to be head of Sixth Form which
> gave me plenty of pastoral contact, then on to a deputy
> headship and then to a headship. I attended carefully selected
> courses on timetabling, curriculum development, pastoral care
> and the like. I suppose the whole thing looks carefully planned
> but I did not have a conscious check list. But I knew I wanted
> to be a head.

There is a warning here that what, in retrospect, can look like a carefully constructed career culminating inevitably in headship, might not, in fact, have been consciously planned. As Harry Tomlinson says — 'in preparing for this interview I have tried to look back on my career. It is easy to impose an *ex post facto* rationale which was less evident at that time'. Peter Downes seemed impervious to the temptation to do this. He says simply 'I don't think I set out consciously to plan a career for headship'. From all this, we conclude that studies of the ways in which individuals attain headship should consider the extent to which this can be regarded as having taken place within the context of a more or less conscious, planned and traditional pursuit of a career.

Peter Downes, in so far as he 'went straight from head of department to headship, missing out on being a deputy', accepted that his route to headship was 'unusual'. He also acknowledged his 'specific preparation for headship was minimal other than . . . trying to read as widely as possible, going on lots and lots of day conferences and being aware of the issues. But in terms of specific training — nothing'. But, whilst at Banbury, he was involved in a major mixed ability/streaming research project and argued 'the outcome of that project in terms of the way schools are managed and organised is directly germane to headship. Now you can rightly say that I have not been specifically trained for headship, but the fact of being involved in a major educational research project was a very good preparation for headship'. He was not the only one whose preparation for headship was 'unusual'. Asked if her secondment to HMI might be usefully regarded as, in part, a preparation and training for headship, Elaine Foster responded 'Yes, I think if you are planning a career, then where you are at any one moment in time should be seen as a stepping stone for something else. So yes, being with HMI gave me those opportunities. I saw at first hand . . . headteachers, deputies, all sorts of teachers working in a number of schools across the country and I was able to . . . pick up some of what I thought were good practices from heads of various schools'.

Another, and perhaps more conventional, way in which some of our heads prepared themselves for headship was by undertaking post graduate training. Sue Benton, as we have seen, took this route. So, too, did Brian Sherratt. Initially he 'followed the part-time Academic Diploma in Education course at the London Institute of Education'. His options were 'Educational Organisation and Administration and the Philosophy of Education'. He was invited to pursue further studies in either at a Masters level. This was a difficult choice. On the one hand his 'whole background lent itself to philosophy' but 'on the other hand [he] saw this as something of an opportunity I think I made a conscious decision then that I was going to do the MA in Organisation and Administration, in part as a preparation for promotion . . .'. Finally, Harry Tomlinson 'did an advanced diploma, mainly on secondary education'. He then 'did the Diploma in Business Administration and in doing so looked at things like organisational psychology, personnel and financial issues'. He concludes that 'I was all the time, I think, training myself for headship. In fact the dissertation I did at Aston University was on the selection and training of comprehensive headteachers'.

Notwithstanding his research into the selection of headteachers, Harry Tomlinson had to work quite hard for his first headship. He recollects making 'over forty applications and was interviewed six or seven times before I got my first headship'. Others had an easier passage. Brian Sherratt, for example, had 'applied for two [headships], was interviewed for both, and was appointed to the second'. It is less clear if Downes and Marland had to struggle for their first headships. They certainly do not mention having to do so. So much for the men. Three out of the seven headteachers we talked to are women. Nationally, there are only a few hundred women headteachers as against several thousand men. Despite their success, each of the women we talked to felt that, other things being equal, it was more difficult for a woman to be appointed to a headship than a man. Valerie Bragg spent seven years as a deputy before she got her first headship. She recalls 'I did get frustrated . . . after four years . . . I started applying for headships but kept coming up against the same problem. I would be told at the end of interviews that I was the best candidate but had a young family and they did not want to take the risk of appointing me'. When finally successful, she remembers feeling 'surprised they appointed me . . . There were few women heads of large comprehensives at that time'. This was twelve years ago but it must be said there are still very few women heads of large co-educational comprehensive schools today.

Although there are now a handful of men who have been appointed to girls schools, this remains an important avenue into headship for women. Sue Benton and Elaine Foster have taken this route. Sue Benton experienced little difficulty. As she puts it 'I was a deputy for three years. I then began to look at headships and put in applications. I thought it might take me several years to achieve this. But in fact I got one straight away'. Even so she has long been involved in issues of equal opportunity which focus in particular on the career prospects of women in education. She was, for many years, a member and then the chair of SWOT [Senior Women Oxfordshire Teachers]. This:

> was a very supportive group. We ran a training programme for younger women whom we had identified within our schools — mainly middle managers who were aspiring to deputy headship and deputies who were aspiring to headship . . . It gave me a perspective on the particular career needs and career paths of women and the problems which they face. It taught me the need to identify and value the experience which women could

bring to senior management roles ... If you can juggle a career and a family successfully then you are exhibiting skills which are of great relevance to the management of schools at all levels ... I have pushed the idea that those years are not wasted years in a woman's career. I think the climate is now changing on this but at the time this had only just begun.

Valerie Bragg shares many of these views. Asked if women manage headship differently than men she suggested that women are generally more caring and compassionate than men. 'I also think women are better than men at coping with a large number of things at the same time. We are used to having to cope simultaneously with problems of the family, food, the hours, etc'. Whilst she believes that 'the number of women reaching headship and other high positions has increased dramatically' she also suggests that 'women are their own worst enemies. If only they would push themselves forward a little more'.

Elaine Foster accepts that white women encounter real problems when they seek appointment to senior management positions in schools but that there are others whose difficulties are greater. Over the last

three years I have probably had two or three people who have been recommended to come and talk with me as a black woman secondary school head about ways into management. I do think it is a big issue for women, and a big issue for black women. For black people in general, because I don't think there are enough of us and I don't think the channels and the opportunities are there for black people, and let me say black women in particular, to map out the path they wish to take. Not in the same way as ... white women and white people have these opportunities, because more times than not my white colleagues will probably have friends who are deputies or heads and very few of my black colleagues probably socialise with white deputies or heads or local authority advisers.

She has responded by, amongst other things, becoming involved in the 'setting up of the African/Caribbean Teaching Unit and the Afro-Caribbean Teachers' Association'. If this is one positive note, another might be that once she decided to seek headship, she was quickly successful. However, it is one thing procuring a headship and another professing it.

Professing headship

In thinking about the professing of headship let us not be too parochial. The international movement bringing a greater exchange of voices across the world of secondary principals, launched at Geneva in 1993, has demonstrated the amazing similarity of challenges and needs which headteachers face even in very different political and social context. Such things as staff leadership, pupil management, curriculum planning resources control, and the school-public relationship, offer remarkably similar challenges from the Ukraine to Australia, from the United States to the United Kingdom. Indeed, trends towards greater within-school control are world-wide across many very different political regimes.

Nevertheless, the traditional independence of the Head of a UK state-maintained school is very noticeable. The voices of the seven heads speaking in this volume bring this to life afresh: UK secondary headteachers are not the 'administrators' of North America, where the School Board procedures dominate and the principal is appointed to the Board's District rather than the school. The varied characters and independent style of most UK schools has a long tradition — perhaps encouraged by the earlier dominance of the public boarding school with its usually powerful headmaster or headmistress.

The administrative vagueness of the Education Act 1944 contributed to this freedom. One of its aims was to readjust responsibilities for decision-making. Before the war, the central government Board of Education had had merely powers of 'superintendence' but in planning for the development of post-war education, the Deputy Secretary declared that 'The prospect of educational reconstruction that lies ahead offers an admirable opportunity for re-establishing the position of the Board as the body competent to lead and to direct the educational system of the country'. This was an ambition never achieved: the local education authorities and the teacher unions ensured that.

Curriculum control was to be located not at the centre but with the LEAs, as Section 18 of the 1944 legislation declared 'The secular instruction to be given to the pupils shall, save insofar as may be otherwise provided by the rules of management of articles of government for the school, be under the control of the local education authority'.

Despite a variety of LEA policies and statements, this was impotent legislation and there was no clear responsibility for curriculum planning. Under the chairmanship of the Labour MP Christopher Price, the Select Committee of the House of Commons reported in 1981 that:

> In our experience the extent of passing powers and the
> responsibilities down the line in education frequently makes it
> very difficult for the ordinary citizen to know just who is held

responsible for many parts of the system, and this is perhaps
especially true of the curriculum. There is, too, a disturbing
tendency in a devolved system for necessary action to be
shrugged off and passed backwards and forward because none
will readily own up to being responsible for action (Select
Committee, 1981, p.xx).

Thus the vagueness of the location of power within the UK in the
forty plus years between 1944 and the Education (No. 2) Act 1986
and its successors as compared with the clarity of most countries
undoubtedly further encouraged the resourceful headteacher to
develop her or his individual leadership of 'my' school. Michael
Marland answered the question 'How far do you see the school as
your school?' typically for many: 'I see it very, very much as my own
school'.

The most striking similarities between these seven voices is their
commitment and deep identification with 'their' school. These are
often significant similarities, and this chapter brings the voices
together theme by theme. Headteachers feel more fully and closely
about the schools they call 'theirs' than do most chief executives.
Each of those we spoke to was very obviously deeply bound up with
all aspects of the life and ambitions of the school. Listening to them
was sometimes like eavesdropping into a family conversation.

The locally managed school

The Taylor Committee was a committee of enquiry set up by the
Callaghan-led Labour government in 1975 into the management of
schools with particular reference to governors. Its findings were not
met with enthusiasm by all, and certain teachers' unions in particular were very critical. The overwhelming thrust was, however, to
increase the responsibilities of governors given that:

> There should be as much delegation of these powers by the
> local education authority to the governing body as is compatible
> with the local education authority's ultimate responsibility for
> the running of the schools in its area, and as much discretion in
> turn granted to the head teacher by the governing body as is
> compatible with the latter's responsibility for the success of the
> school in all its activities (Committee of Enquiry, 1977, p.xx).

Subsequent legislation has increased this step-by-step. Thus the
Education (No.2) Act 1986 firmly places substantial responsibility
upon governors: for appointments, curriculum, exclusion of pupils,
the publication of information, and for annual reports to parents.
Whilst the Education Reform Act 1988 appeared to be centralising

in its important and dominating 'Section 2: the National Curriculum', it did not in fact erode governors' power, and in many ways the legislation of 1992 and 1993, whilst more closely defining the responsibilities of central government and the LEA (e.g. over Special Educational Needs in the Education Act 1993), the roles of governors were further defined and enhanced.

Each of our seven voices clearly relishes this freedom to plan against national criteria. There are therefore inevitable comments on the work of the LEA. The legislation that severely limited the role of the LEA was not preceded by systematic studies or research, and the nineties have therefore seen schools and LEAs devising fresh approaches in a post-legislative high. Sue Benton points to the difficulties 'Coming from Oxfordshire where there was a very strong culture of partnership between the schools and the LEA I will regret the passing of the LEAs should that happen'. But this was not a view shared without qualification by all seven heads.

Brian Sherratt having led the school into grant-maintained status no longer has to be concerned, but remembers the days of what he saw as bureaucratic LEA overload without affection. Clearly, there are still difficulties in LEA role definition. Peter Downes, whilst stressing 'I'm a strong believer in the need for an LEA or some locally accountable body', nevertheless acknowledges that 'at a day-to-day level I enjoy least the errors and the problems that are caused by the way the LEA oversees our finances'. He feels, in this respect at least, that his LEA is in some danger of becoming irritatingly bureaucratic, 'very pernickety' and 'over-legalistic'. And Michael Marland judged that 'the new LEA set up a system which was characterised by too much interference from the centre'.

Heads are evidently looking for a new form of LEA. Hinchingbrooke was a pilot 'Local Financial Management School' in 1982 and Peter Downes supported LMS not 'because I've any grudge against the LEA', but because of its opening of school management scope. Michael Marland summed up the new, post-'88 role of the LEA 'An LEA in the new world of today is to do only those things which only the LEA can do'.

All have relished the re-shaping of the role which came substantially from *The Education Reform Act 1988*: still labelled LMS — 'Local Management of Schools'. It has also had its daunting side. As Sue Benton says:

> Particularly, it takes a lot of time in the first instance. If I think back, for example, to the start of the LMS none of us were trained in managing budgets. None of us had come into teaching expecting that would be part of any role we would have to play as senior managers. Some of us were daunted at

first to find that we had to exercise skills which our previous experience had not prepared us for. But like all these things, it takes longer in the beginning. You have to get your head down and come to terms with it and as you become more familiar with it you become more confident and more efficient. Once that has happened it takes rather less of your time.

Heads have always been deeply concerned about resources, for what is available controls much of the planning. Each of the seven heads has seen the budgetary delegation of 1988 as significant. As Brian Sherratt puts it 'In particular it would be a very strange head who did not have an intense interest in budgetary matters. It is the budget which pretty well drives everything'.

Staff leadership

What is the head head of? Most people outside a school think most often of the headship of the pupils, and this is clearly articulated as the ultimate goal. However, the most immediate and demanding task is leadership of the staff, without which the pupils cannot be adequately cared for. It could be argued that most schools in this country are under-managed and there are inadequate resources for full management.

A repeated theme is that of the management of the corporate work of the school, how to 'head' teamwork. Brian Sherratt, for example, answers the question of 'What do you see as your key task?' 'To me, it is the ability to develop effective teamwork. To work as an ensemble rather than to promote soloists. I do think that gone are the days of the really autocratic head'.

Most of the speakers also see and articulate the paradox that leadership is enabling others to do. Harry Tomlinson puts it strongly 'The ideal head recognises and enables others to contribute to the best of their ability. If you are successful as a head it is almost always mostly because of the work which others do. But it is the head-teacher more than any other who makes this possible'.

Further, the contribution of others is not mainly as individuals, and the head usually sees most matters as requiring a group approach. Part of the effective profession of headship is creating that. Brian Sherratt is typical 'Often the solution to a problem is not just my solution, or a particular deputy's solution, but a team solution'.

This also involves the technical tool of shaping the management structures, for it is clear from these voices that structuring responsibilities and lines of management is one of a head's most influential responsibilities, one curiously under-researched. (Dr Nigel Bennett

is working on a study in the mid-nineties.) As Michael Marland puts
it: 'The first thing I had to do at North Westminster was to create a
new structure'.

The management structures are now considerably more varied
than they were in the past. Valerie Bragg, for instance, has a single
deputy who is 'Director of Administration and Finance':

> I felt that schools are often narrow, so this was an ideal
> opportunity to bring in somebody with a different background
> and experience to its management. One of the criticisms about
> educationalists is that too many of them went to school, went to
> university and then went back to school. I wanted to get away
> from that. So my Director of Administration and Finance, who
> used to be a director for one of Hanson's companies, is my
> deputy. He comes to management meetings and brings a totally
> different viewpoint. This helps him sometimes to challenge our
> fixed assumptions and to put in ideas very different from the
> rest of us, which can be beneficial.

Some solutions are unusual, and it is clear that traditional pat-
terns are being increasingly varied. Valerie Bragg and Harry Tomlinson have devised unusual management structures and teams.
Valerie Bragg, in setting up Kinghurst, decided 'to go for a flat
hierarchy':

> In most schools you have the head, deputies, senior teachers,
> heads of year, heads of department and so on. I rolled all that
> together and created area managers. I gave them administrative
> tasks as though they were deputies, curriculum tasks similar to
> those of a head of department and a pastoral responsibility. I
> tried to set up a system which embraced all these managerial
> tasks without curtailing time in the classroom. Too often, under
> the traditional system, when you wanted to be a deputy you had
> to leave the academic side behind. Here, they retain contact
> with an academic subject and also hold other kinds of
> responsibility. As the college grew so too did the managerial
> structures. I now have ten managers.

This has similarities with the system Harry Tomlinson has set up
at Margaret Danyer. This is:

> Made up of six heads of faculty three of whom are vice
> principals and they are the line managers. Thus the head of
> business and technology manages all the work of all the teachers
> in the business and technology area. Not just their teaching but
> also their responsibilities as tutors and the rest. It is a very
> simple structure: I manage about twelve people and they

manage about twelve each. The vice principals also have a
general responsibility for marketing as a whole, the whole of the
pastoral system, personnel, etc.

It is often claimed that 'management structures' keep senior staff
away from 'the chalk face'. That is clearly not the view of these seven
heads. Elaine Foster, for instance, speaks strongly of the importance
of being close to the classroom — as observer and participant, working alongside other teachers. Furthermore, her decision to 'structure
the school into faculties with each member of the senior management
team having a monitoring role for each of the faculties and therefore
of each member of staff in that faculty' has enabled and encourages
such closeness. Like Elaine Foster, Peter Downes at Hinchingbrooke has sought to ensure that he and his senior colleagues
observe in classrooms more than used to be common. He has also,
for instance, related deputy heads directly to three departments each
and says 'we have got our fingers more directly on the pulse of the
school's curriculum life than we used to have'.

It is clear that this leadership involves professional development
of staff, and that this is both inward-looking, for the benefit of the
school, and moves into career development: Michael Marland, for
example, says: 'I like to see people and help them with this'. Peter
Downes stresses that: 'A very important part of the role of headship
is to identify and train future leaders of schools'.

Staff leadership is also a central focus, and it offers a tension
between 'giving a lead' and 'empowering others'. As Sue Benton
points out 'There is always that two sides to the job. As the head you
have to give the lead. You are the person with whom the buck stops.
You are the person who has to make the ultimate decisions. In that
sense you are a shaping force but you must also be concerned with
empowering other people in the processes by which you achieve your
purposes together'.

Overall, though, leadership is not merely practical and short-
term, but endeavours to build on and encourage deep commitment.
There is very strong conviction and determination. Brian Sherratt
hopes to give his heads of department 'the passion to wish to do their
job successfully'.

Curriculum planning

Curriculum planning was a strange unquestioned activity from 1944
until the 'Great Debate' established by James Callaghan in his Ruskin speech of 1976. Despite waves of innovation, there was a great
deal of similarity, with the inheritance of the old grouped School
Certificate lingering as a 'shadow' national curriculum. Some heads
had had what Brian Sherratt calls the 'idiosyncratic' view of curricu-

lum planning, though clearly it was exercised by only a few. A few schools had a more limited curriculum than was perhaps fully recognised — indeed even LEAs did not always know the curriculum of their schools.

By the mid-nineties many people have seen curriculum planning as essentially a central government matter. For these heads it clearly is an in-school matter, at the centre of their concerns. We now have national requirements, but the fear that the central National Curriculum might 'stifle grass-roots development' as Sue Benton phrases it, is there in most of the headteachers, but they are determined that it should not happen. Thus Elaine Foster speaks of how closely she and her senior colleagues work with heads of departments. Michael Marland declares 'I very much see myself as still a curriculum manager. I do not see the legislation as having greatly affected this'.

The misunderstanding so common, that a school curriculum is the National Curriculum, is demolished in these interviews. Brian Sherratt states 'I certainly do not see it as simply implementing the National Curriculum'.

Indeed, paradoxically, the curriculum aspects of the legislation has, in Brian Sherratt's words, not reduced the school responsibility or planning task but: 'Has sharp focused the minds of heads and staff on those things which they should be doing — which is managing and delivering effectively a curriculum for pupils'.

Their view of the curriculum planning is clearly wide, stretching beyond the National Curriculum components of the 1988 legislation. Brian Sherratt broadens it thus 'A clear interest in enabling the personal development of the pupil through the curriculum and in other ways. In some areas of experience, such as PSME, this is at the forefront. It is there within the pastoral curriculum also which in this school is intended to have a civilising impact by establishing certain norms in the way in which we treat each other. It is all part of the civilising impact of the curriculum'. Curriculum planning remains a central concern.

Pastoral care

A phrase unused in any other system and unrecognised by government until the end of the eighties, 'pastoral care' is one of the strengths of our schools, and one of significance to all these heads.

This over-arching pastoral care is seen by each headteacher as very important. Valerie Bragg's description of the main mode of delivery is typical 'Each form tutor is responsible for a group of students and is the first line of contact with parents. Whoever the form tutor is, even in the case of very young staff, they carry this responsibility'.

Their vision for secondary schools is very wide, and its best definition is that the school should work to enable every pupil to grow as a person; Sue Benton speaks of this breadth 'I mean education in the broadest sense. We emphasise here very strongly that everybody has got skills and talents and that everybody can improve in personal terms'.

Governors and the local communities

James Callaghan re-focused educational discussion to include those outside the teaching profession in his 1976 Ruskin speech: 'It is almost as though some people would wish that the subject matter and purposes of education should not have public attention focused on it, nor that profane hands should be allowed to touch it'. Instead he proposed that a wide range of views, including parents, whom he listed first, should join together.

The Taylor report (DES, 1977) further stressed this, indeed redefined the role of governors in the country's schools 'There should be as much delegation of these powers by the local education authority to the governing body as is compatible with the local education authority's ultimate responsibility for the running of the school in its area, and as much discretion in turn granted to the head teacher by the governing body as is compatible with the latter's responsibility for the success of the school in all its activities'.

One of the mysteries of educational history is why the essence of the Taylor recommendations had to wait for nine years and another party in power before they were largely enacted in the *Education Act (No. 2) 1986*. The heads speaking in this collection seven years after that Act have all fully internalised Taylor and Callaghan: they demonstrably listen to, and are answerable to, the communities they serve, from Peter Downes touring Cambridgeshire villages to Elaine Forster in close touch with the school's area of Birmingham.

Peter Downes stresses in almost the same words as Michael Marland 'I undoubtedly front the work with parents, because I have made that a particular feature of my headship. Not all would say with Peter Downes that 'I accept all the invitations I get within the limits of human possibilities to all the local events', but all would agree that the profession of headship strongly involves community relationships. 'The head of the school is expected to be a local figure.' Furthermore, all would agree with the responsibility that imposes and the time it requires. Brian Sherratt sums it up 'Managing the interface with the local community, with the complainers in the local community, with the press, with the LEA and with the governors'.

Out of the culmination of Taylor in the Education Acts of 1986 and 1988 has come a new and immensely greater importance for the role of governors. All the heads acknowledge that the governing body is now one of the key concerns for a headteacher. Several stressed the need for mutual support and respect between the head, the governors in general and the chair of the governing body in particular. For each, working with governors is a major task in the new world of the school. It takes time, energy, skill, thought, and a strong personality. Indeed, with the governing body 'the node of power' in the British school system (Michael Marland's phrase), it could be argued that enabling the governors to work well is the prime task of the headteacher.

This can be seen in Peter Downes' remark 'I and the senior team spend quite a time preparing materials for governors' committees'. Although the phrase is used by only one speaker, Valerie Bragg, there is, it seems, little reason to doubt that a governing body is analogous to a board of directors, working within national and local laws, criteria and financial restraints, but otherwise independent.

> It is very much a working board of directors. I am accountable to them. I can assure you that when you have governors like Sheila Brown, you have to be. I have some high powered academic governors and industrialists who are on the Boards of companies like IMI and GKN. I have found them very challenging but also helpful. I think they see their function as advisory, supporting, facilitating, enabling industry to be brought much more closely into the life of the College.

Not that there is any hint of resentment in the seven voices: the governing body serves the school the better the head serves the governing body. There is a common need and mutual support. As Sue Benton finds it 'They have a confidence in the school, which springs from a trust in the competence and commitment of the staff and the senior management team. They are happy for us to get on with the day-to-day running of the school'.

Conclusion

The same structure of questions produced both striking similarities and some differences of balance. These differences are partly the serendipity of conversation, in which one aspect gains more ground than another on some occasions.

Some concerns did not feature extensively because we chose not to place them in the questions. For instance the work of a school for those pupils who have what we have come to call 'Special Needs' is only occasionally touched on. Sue Benton had had a period as a school's Special Needs Co-ordinator. All have to face the tension between the country's growing understanding of differentiation and special help (DFE, 1994) and the logistical and financial problems limiting that help. At the time of our interviews the revised *Code of Practice* had not been published, and we did not focus on that issue.

There is a very strong picture of schools really led, and of head-teachers who do not look to failures of national legislation or of LEA provision to excuse, but who are creative *users* of the current external constraints. Despite the few references to LEA changeover difficulties, these are heads for whom the revolution in school management of 1988 is thoroughly absorbed. It is difficult to believe that at the time of our interviews the heads were only three or four years into the new world: despite difficulties, these speakers used the voices of relish and activity as they spoke of the new legislative dispensation. 'Local Management' clearly means what it says for these speakers.

Perhaps the most powerful agreement in the seven voices is the range of responsibilities they see as carried by the contemporary head in aspect and degree of detail. A major role is accountability — knowing what is happening in the detailed texture as well as the main architecture of the pupils' experience, judging it against intentions, and addressing any mismatch.

The term 'headteacher' says a great deal. Internationally it is rare, so that the world-wide association is called 'The International Association of Secondary School Principals'. Yet these headteachers, even when admitting to appear to some to be remote from many pupils, are 'hands on' teachers, as likely to stop a boy with trainers at Great Barr as take a lesson at Hinchingbrooke, work in the classroom of other teachers at Handsworth, or visit homes at North Westminster.

Headteachers talk in a great deal of detail, with specific points about procedures and learning materials relating to broad principles about curriculum and attitude. Perhaps the most striking point about the voices of these seven is this range of their concerns. As Sue Benton puts it in a summary that speaks for all seven:

> I still find it all fascinating. I enjoy that sense of seeing other people develop and feeling that they came to you as little girls really and if they can leave as self-confident young women that is a source of great satisfaction and delight. I enjoy the management side of the job. I find structures, systems and processes fascinating. At the end of the day I enjoy being able to say these things happened and we coped. This child had a problem and we helped her. I enjoy my professional relationships with colleagues. I really do enjoy working in teams with other people and seeing members of staff develop in ways which parallel the development of the pupils.

Finally, though, coming through so many of the remarks in so many aspects is that intangible but powerful voice of pride in the work of others and for the school as a whole. The legal, political, financial and logistical aspects of current secondary school headship appear not to have eroded but perhaps even to have enhanced the role of a headteacher to be proud of her or his school, to convey that pride abroad, and to enable the staff to feel it. Brian Sherratt seems to speak for all seven when he emphasises that part of the head-teacher's task is enabling pride and, indeed, pleasure in the school: 'I think it's necessary to feel good about the school and to enable staff to feel good about the school'.

A coda

In this introduction to the text, we have set out to present our small cast to the reader. We have also sought to explain why headship is important and why a new direction to its study is necessary. A new direction founded upon the idea that existing methods need to be supplemented with research which takes a rather more holistic approach to the study of headship than has been common to date. An approach which reports upon real headteachers in real schools as they reflect upon their practice and go about their praxis. This kind of study, we have argued, can be made at three levels which, taken together, can be regarded as a whole but which can also be worth-while when undertaken separately.

This book reports on a first level study of headship. As such, it is made up of a series of chapters in each of which an individual head talks about his or her life and times. What each of them has to say is reported fully and it is possible for the reader to locate any particular claim which any one of them makes in the context of her or his wider views. So far so good. But it could be argued that in this chapter we have engaged in just the kind of decontextualisation in interrogating the view of our seven interviewees taken as a whole which we have ourselves been at some pains to criticise. The answer, quite simply, is that we have not wished to argue that such an approach has no value. Rather, we believe that what we propose has an added value. It will be for the reader to decide. We hope that you will suspend judgement until you have read the next seven chapters. The best is yet to come.

2 Sue Benton

with Peter Ribbins

PR: Can you tell me something about your early life?

SB: The key things which shaped me and led me to where I am? I
went to a girls' grammar school in Sheffield. Although I did not
realise it at the time, this experience was important to me in forming
the values and ideas I hold now. The most obvious influence was the
role models we were offered by some of the teachers. They showed
us that women could be clever and successful. They were quite up-
front about this. At the time we found it vaguely risible but in
retrospect they were right. I remember the headmistress saying to us
on the day that we left at the end of the sixth form 'You have all had
a good education. I do not expect any of you to get married before
you are thirty. You owe it to society to put back for what you have
been given'. At the time we found that rather funny but looking
back the message went home although we did not interpret it too
literally, I suppose we learnt the old idea of service. We also learnt
that girls could do everything. That was important in terms of where
I am now.

   The idea of education as something valuable in itself came quite
strongly from my grandfather and also from my mother and my
mother-in-law, whom I have known since I was very young. They
were both in the position of having passed the common entrance for
grammar school but having to leave because, during the depression,
their parents could not afford to keep them at school. So they both
felt a sense of frustration along with a strong conviction of the worth
of education and the wish to support me in something which they
had been unable to enjoy. They showed this by example too. My
mother exemplified the grit you need to achieve your educational
goals by going to night school and getting the 'O' Levels she had not
been able to get in her youth.

   My grandfather left school when he was fourteen and went to be
a miner. In the area of Yorkshire in which he lived that was all there

was. He then felt called to do the Lord's work and attended night school after he had done his shift. He got himself the qualifications which he needed, intending to train for the ministry. In the event, he did not enter the Church but went instead into the Church Army. But he too valued education and had that determination to achieve it, whatever the barriers. He also had a strong sense of service, becoming responsible for a number of hostels which the Army ran for deprived people. When I visited him as a child, it was nearly always in his quarters in one of these hostels. There was always a strong sense of helping people less fortunate than yourself and serving the community in which you lived. That has probably gone quite deep in me.

PR: Did he feel the education of girls was important. As important as that of boys?

SB: The notion of service was stronger and of education as being worthwhile in its own right. I suppose he was also very supportive of me because I was the first grandchild. He was very proud of me.

PR: Did you enjoy school?

SB: Yes I loved it. Although I always thought I was hopeless at Maths. I was in the second group of four in a very selective school. When I taught in a comprehensive school I realised that I was wrong, if I had gone to that school, I would have been in the top set. That changed my perspective and has influenced some of the ideas which I have tried to put into practice within this school.

PR: Was it always assumed that you would go to university?

SB: It was an unspoken assumption. Certainly a hope on my mother's part and an assumption on the school's part. It was that sort of school. One hesitates to say it, but the expectation was that the best went to university and those who did not achieve quite so highly went to teacher training college. We tended to accept that was the way things were at the time. I left the school having done all the usual things, such as being a prefect but not intending to go anywhere near a school ever again in my life after all that. I went off to do an English degree but by the time I had finished that I had decided that I did want to teach.

PR: How did that come about? There were no teachers in your family?

SB: No there weren't. There was a mixture of reasons. When I lived at home I had been a sunday-school teacher and rather enjoyed that. There was also the influence of my husband and his brother: I had known them since my childhood; they were both older than me and both went into teaching. I got interested in the kind of things which they were doing on their training courses and the experiences which they were talking about. I think that may have tipped the balance at that stage. In teaching, because women often have rather odd career profiles, I did all sorts of things from running a village playgroup to teaching in an FE college. This has been tremendously useful.

PR: Did you enjoy university? How did it compare with your school experience?

SB: There were particular teachers at school of whom I felt quite fond. My Latin teacher, for example, was a funny little Scottish lady who got very cross with people if they did not get their Latin right. But I did 'A' Level and was one of the people who could do it. In her brusque way she was quite fond of me. She and my French teacher gave me an image of scholarship in which an important part was that the subject was to be enjoyed. I can remember her giggling to herself as she read the Latin before she translated it to us. She was obviously getting enormous enjoyment out of it. As a teacher I have tried to share with my pupils that same enjoyment in the subject. You are unlikely to be much good in the classroom if you can't do that. There was also the obvious pleasure which such teachers took in our achievements. They were firm ladies who stood no nonsense but were very supportive and helpful and clearly cared a great deal about their pupils.

I went to Leeds University. That was quite an interesting experience in part because the course at that time included Anglo-Saxon. Being a 'girly swot' I enjoyed and was quite good at that, it had something akin to the Latin, a kind of logical structure to the language. It was a bit like doing a puzzle — getting all the pieces in the right place. I have always thoroughly enjoyed the literature side of things in English and in my languages. As I went more and more deeply into the subject, I got more and more from it. Because I was a reasonably able linguist, I took Italian as one of my subsidiaries. I thoroughly enjoyed this too. As something new and different, I also took up Art as a subsidiary. It was, in fact, an Art History course. That started off something which has become a life-long interest. I had dropped Art fairly early on at school because I was not very good at the practical side.

PR: Did you do a PGCE straight after your first degree?

SB: No I did not. In fact, I have not done a PGCE. I applied but there was some confusion over my papers; they got lost as they were passed from one university to another. By the time it was sorted out everybody had allocated their places. So instead of doing a Cert Ed I started teaching straight away as one could in those days. Once you have done this, you have less reason to go back thereafter. It was easier to do that at the time because the model of teaching in most schools was really very much as you had, yourself, been taught. Nowadays it is a very different matter and much more difficult to move from your degree straight into a school. I would certainly not recommend such a course to anyone now. I have been strongly involved with the development of the internship model of the PGCE with the heads' group working with Reading University. This is something I support strongly, despite my own lack of it.

I had decided to teach but there were the problems of a young woman with small children and, with the development of my husband's career, I had a whole series of part-time jobs. My first such job was in Manchester, in the private sector, I was teaching English as a Second Language. I found this quite interesting. And then I began to teach some private 'A' Level work. When we moved to Hertfordshire one of the local heads was desperately looking for someone to teach ESL and hearing that I had previous experience with TEFL he invited me to do this. Then another school heard and said as you are only doing part time on this please come and do some part-time work for us too. It all grew until it became, in effect, a full-time job.

PR: You did not take your head's advice and waited until 30 before you got married?

SB: No I did not. I had my children very young. This had some advantages. I really did not have a career pattern which was then interrupted. I was able, in effect, to start a normal career pattern, but later. And go for the top without time out.

Looking at my career as a whole, I started with a series of part-time jobs. But when I was working at Letchworth Grammar school, it became Fearnhill Comprehensive. We looked at what we were doing within the school, because we were anticipating a wider ability intake, and we set up a Humanities programme; I was one of the teachers closely involved in doing this. I found this very exciting. What we produced depended very much on what people were willing to do with a mixture of English and RE and History initially. Within the team we could see advantages in moving into other areas but this was not always viewed with equal enthusiasm by those already in such areas. I enjoyed the team teaching and curriculum development which this project involved. I enjoyed trying to bring in various areas of my interest into the programme. When we moved to Oxfordshire, in the first year I did a few bits of part-time jobs including some time in a primary school which was important later.

I then moved to Bicester School to the then Foundation Studies

Department. In terms of my career, that was a very important move. In the twelve or thirteen years I was there I joined at the bottom as a classroom teacher and moved up to be a head of department. I did a whole variety of things whilst I was there. The work we did in the department amounted to a unique piece of curriculum development. This is something which probably could not happen now because of the constraints of the National Curriculum. Our work covered the Humanities and Science and Art. You taught all of those in an integrated way to the groups in the junior years with which you worked. It also involved a good deal of involvement with the primary schools and this is one area in which my primary school experience was very useful. The approach we used has certainly been important in shaping my attitudes subsequently. We were teaching across the range of subjects. We had to work as a team in which everybody was dependent on everybody else for developing the teaching materials. We could not rely on existing schemes of work and textbooks, they were not available. We were developing everything ourselves. In this context people very quickly got used to preparing materials and putting them on the table for discussion and having other people pull them about and not feel offended. We also got used to working together and sharing ideas. It was a department where there was always somebody piloting something, where there was a strong educational philosophy which informed what we were doing: this held together all the many things which we were doing. This made it possible for us to include things which would not fit within separate subjects, an idea not so fashionable currently. We did work on things like listening and thinking skills.

PR: Who was the driving force behind all this? How much of this came from the head?

SB: The whole thing had a very interesting genesis. Its origins lay in the time that John Sharp was the head and Margaret Maden was the deputy. You need to understand it as part of the history of secondary schooling in the town. The school had been on two sites: originally the first two years were on the site on the other side of the town, and the middle and upper school were on the site I was working on. They decided that they would make the two schools separate, so the school was faced with taking first and second year pupils for the first time. This was seen as a great opportunity to start from scratch and really look at what they wanted to achieve with pupils of that age, what the ideal curriculum would look like with nobody around with a vested interest. So it could be a real innovation from the grass roots. I came in on the second year of that development to join the team as they moved into having to plan for the second year.

As a result of that experience I ended up with an ability to appreciate the importance of team work, of flexibility in approach to the classroom management of what constituted my subject. You did not have to have quite that identity of self with subject that you sometimes get. You had an identity with the department. It was important when I became head of department and we advertised for vacancies to be able to start from the precept that people's educational philosophy and approach were more important than their subject qualification. We were a very closely bonded team. Because of the way the department was physically organised we were always in and out of each other's classrooms. It was very exciting to be involved in. You really felt that you were involved in enabling the children to develop skills which would stand them in good stead. We were giving them the foundations. I have always been a believer in their being able to spell and punctuate correctly and being able to understand the grammar of the language they are writing. So it's not that we were trying to be trendies who did not believe in the need for structure. I don't think you do children any favours at all if you don't give them the opportunity to learn the basic tools of language. Particularly, I must say, in the case of working class children who do not always get the chance to get this from their home background.

PR: What part did the head and deputy play in all this?

SB: By the time I got there John Sharp had left and Margaret Maden had left the year before I had come. I only knew them from the influence which their thinking continued to have within the school. The person who was head of department when I came was also important. That whole experience was very important, not least because the children came from an interesting and wide variety of backgrounds: for some of them I realised the importance of school in providing support and stability. And because you had taught these children for up to half their total curriculum you could know them better than anybody else had got to know them in their school career. In a way it was a kind of primary school approach. Also because I was there a long time, I got to know the families especially when, as in some cases, you might be teaching the third and fourth member of the same family. But it did help you to build good links. It is good if schools have some people who can and are able to do that sort of thing.

I was head of the department for seven years. It did not feel as long as that. We were always doing different and interesting things. It really was an exciting place to work in both at the level of the department and of the school as a whole. The staffroom dialogue was very professional. When people talked at lunch time they would more often than not be talking about professional or intellectual issues. I remember at the time Richard Dawkin's ideas on evolution were the source of much discussion. We used to talk about it and swap books on it. There were endless arguments on the merits of biological determinism. We all enjoyed that aspect of the school and I think it was more generally valuable in creating the climate which was characteristic of the school.

PR: At what point did you start to think about headship?

SB: Once I had decided I was interested in becoming a head of department and became involved, through that, in much wider whole school issues and, more generally, in people's professional development I started to think about a more general management role. As this was happening I was also becoming more interested in the common ground of teaching. Partly because I was teaching such a wide range of subjects I could see that the things to do with classroom management and children's learning, which we as a group had to consider because we were developing our own ideas and had to produce our own material to support this, were of equal relevance to other subjects regardless of the matter and content of those subjects. Along with this I began to be increasingly involved with whole school development groups. I was elected as a teacher governor. I did a period as an acting head of year. I did a period as acting deputy. So I got a terrific range of experience.

I was also increasingly involved in a variety of professional development groups within the county. Oxfordshire was an excellent county to work for because it gave such support to its teachers and their professional development. It created many networks and I got involved in those and this enabled me to learn something about what was happening in other schools. For example, I was a member of the biology teachers' group as well as of NATE. As a member of the authority you felt that its ethos was set by a chief educational officer, Tim Brighouse, who had a genuine interest in children's learning and in supporting teachers. There was a sense of an authority-wide network of teachers sharing and exploring ideas together. Ever since I have felt that an involvement which goes beyond the confines of the school is important for me and for my colleagues. It gives you a wider perspective and helps to give you the confidence to put your head above the parapet to see what is going on elsewhere.

In my penultimate year at Bicester I had a year's secondment and went up to Oxford to do an MSc in Educational Management. By then I had decided I wanted to go for deputy headship and then headship and this seemed a good way of preparing. I was lucky as one of the last to get such a full year secondment. That year was enormously valuable. I took as my research theme looking at new heads and how they changed their schools. I was particularly interested in the management of change because this was something which I had a fair experience of but I could see that it was going to become more and more important in schools as the context in which they operated changed. Whatever I was going-on to I felt that understanding the processes of change and its management would be important. That was in 1985–86. I gained an enormous amount from interviewing the new heads I talked to. I was grateful to them for the time which they gave me. It was a very difficult time right at the height of the teacher action. Doing this study gave me all kinds of new perspectives. I found the whole idea of organisation theory immensely fascinating. I suppose this and the sociology of education made sense in terms of my previous interest in anthropology which had developed as a result of my work on the Foundation Studies course. It was also enormously valuable being part of a group of 14 of us on the course that year. We came from very different backgrounds and got on very well together. We had great fun, it was very stimulating and we worked tremendously hard. It was valuable to us and, I think, to our schools. I am very sad that the new funding arrangements have meant the virtual disappearance of such opportunities for full-time secondment.

PR: Who were the organisation theorists which you found most illuminating?

SB: All of the usual ones, people like Handy for example. I enjoyed the intellectual dimension of the theory. I found I could relate these as a head of department to what worked and what did not, at keeping people motivated and getting things done.

PR: Was it good preparation for deputy headship and even for headship?

SB: It was enormously good preparation. It was also valuable because it gave those involved in it, thinking time. The day-to-day pressure in schools is so great that it is very difficult to achieve this. It helped me to sharpen up some of my ideas. I am sure I have a better sense of direction as a head from having spent the time at Oxford.

PR: You have had an unusually wide range of experience and unlike many heads you had a formal period of training in preparation for senior management. Was it useful?

SB: I think both my experience and the course influenced, in particular, the priority which I have tried to give to the professional development of staff during my time as a head. The course also enabled me to develop specific skills which have been very useful once I was back in school. Some were simple things like how to organise an interview, to focus questions, to design a questionnaire which will enable you to produce information which you want to know and which enables you to actually do the things you want to do. Everybody thinks they can do all these things but none of them is as simple as they might at first seem. It helped me to understand how to carry out school-based research, how to set about a particular kind of change. Also from talking to different people and from visiting the different schools on the research and from the reading, I became very aware of the importance of the influence of context on what we can and can not do. At that stage I had had a long experience in one school and the course gave me the chance to look at things from a wider perspective. It made me a contingency theorist. In managing change, you should not readily adapt your aims and philosophy but you may need to adapt your strategies to the circumstances and context in which you find yourself and to the people with whom you are working.

After Oxford I returned to Bicester for a year as head of Foundations Studies and then I got a deputy headship. That was at an 11–16 school in south Oxfordshire. Again, here I had enormously valuable experience. I had quite a heavy teaching load for a deputy. I taught both English and Combined Science. That experience was helpful when I became head. As also were many of the other things, the gaps in the timetable, which I got slotted into as a normal part of deputy headship. I even ended up teaching junior maths. Given my earlier feelings about my abilities in maths that was an interesting experience. I was teaching SMP in a style which was very similar to my experience of teaching on the Foundation Studies course at Bicester. I have always been quite happy to be managing a situation in which six different groups are doing six different things in a classroom. I have also always been meticulous about paperwork, about keeping full and up-to-date records, which is essential if your teaching is to be effective in such contexts. I enjoyed it and learnt a lot from doing it. As always, I learnt a great deal from the children. I think it is very important that teachers do not think that they cannot learn from the children or from their colleagues.

PR: What sort of relationship did you develop with the headteacher?

SB: There was really a senior management team made up of the head and two deputies. We worked as a close team. We have very complementary skills and interests. One of my particular roles was that I was in charge of primary liaison, given my past experience this was an obvious thing for me to take on. Because of the way in which it was set up in that area, the head and I attended the primary cluster group meetings. In fact, the head chaired them. So there was a close involvement straight away with the people in the primary schools. I am strongly in favour of this. It was easy there because it was a rural area and so it was a fairly discrete group of schools. It is much more difficult here because we take pupils from 35 different primary schools and some of them come from cross-border. We set up a project which was similar to one I had been involved in at Bicester which meant having a room designated as a primary classroom. We worked with primary colleagues and set up a project in which we taught groups of partly our own first year pupils and partly top junior pupils. We paired primary and secondary teachers and encouraged them to engage in team teaching a joint group of children. This was valuable to both the primary and the secondary school and to both sets of teachers. It was also very valuable for the children because it helped to make the transition from primary to secondary school a more positive one than it sometimes is. It also helped to break down the barriers amongst pupils.

I was also the special needs co-ordinator so I was involved in all the external activities and agencies which that entailed. This was a new experience for me and provided a useful perspective when I became a head. In addition, I was in charge of staff development because it was known that was one of my main interests given my experience at Bicester. When I came back from my MSc I set up a Staff Development Group there. We worked on the inset programme. Through that I became involved in the Oxfordshire Professional Tutors' Group, of which I later became chair. The other external group which was important, and which I joined whilst I was head of department and stayed a member when I became a deputy, was SWOT (Senior Women Oxfordshire Teachers). I also came to chair this group. It was made up of a very lively group of ladies mostly deputies, heads of department and heads of year but with some others who held different kinds of role within their school. It was a self-generated group which set up training and inset for senior women across a whole range of issues. It was a very supportive group. We ran a training programme for younger women whom we had identified within our schools — mainly middle managers who were aspiring to deputy headship and deputies who were aspiring to headship. We got support from the county. All this confirmed me in my ideas about the need for such personal and professional support. It also gave me a perspective on the particular career needs and career paths of women and the problems which they face. It taught me the need to identify and value the experience which women could bring to senior management roles. I have talked to quite a lot of colleagues to try to persuade them not to undervalue the skills which they bring into teaching as a parent and as a home manager. If you can juggle a career and a family successfully then you are exhibiting skills which are of great relevance to the management of schools at all levels. I have pushed the idea that those years are not wasted years in a woman's career. I think the climate is now changing on this but at the time this had only just begun to happen. I am not a strident feminist but I think there are important issues there and they are relevant to my present situation as the head of an all-girls' schools with a largely female staff. I hope all this experience has fed into how I manage the school in, for example, how I look at the applications for posts which I receive. In terms, in particular, people's ages in relation to the levels of the posts which they are applying for. Women who have taken time out to have a family are sometimes several years behind where you might expect them otherwise to be in their careers.

PR: Are there two main themes in the issue of women into management. First, why are there so few senior women managers in education. Secondly, is there something distinctive about the way women manage?

SB: I think maybe there is. But I am not sure that those perspectives are not, in any case, beginning to move into more general management theory. The old macho image of headship, with the head at the top being all powerful, is changing anyway. The idea of people working co-operatively together in teams to develop things rather than being told from on high is now increasingly the norm.

PR: Some have suggested that democratised styles of management often masks a form of populist management in which, ultimately, the leader gains at the expense of middle managers. Do you think there is any validity in this view?

SB: Much depends on how the leader manages I suppose. Obviously, at the end of the day somebody has to make an ultimate decision. But I do think it is important for people to have had the opportunity to have their say. To contribute to that decision. I do not work on the basis that I have all the answers and they are set in tablets of stone which everybody else has to follow. I work on the basis that several heads are more likely to come up with a good answer to difficult problems than one head. I have always believed in the need to bounce ideas around with others rather than to try to act as the great leader who makes decisions and then turns around to find that nobody else is following. But I have also always believed, I don't know if this is regarded as a female perspective on management, in the importance of support from other people. I think the merits of such an approach are borne out in the management of change in the current climate. Motivation and morale are crucial issues at the moment. If you do not work in a way which enables colleagues to feel they are valued by you, in a situation in which they could be forgiven for thinking that they are not valued from outside, then you are not going to have a happy or an effective school.

PR: How long were you a deputy and what happened next?

SB: I was a deputy for three years. I then began to look at headships and put in applications. I thought it might take me several years to achieve this. But in fact I got one straight away. I was very fortunate that this school came up at a time when I was looking. It seemed a school at which I would be happy and I was right.

PR: Were you looking for a girls' school in particular?

SB: No. I was looking for a headship. There are so few girls' schools around that you could wait five or six years for one to come up. You have to be realistic in terms of what is available at the time you are looking. I had an application in both here and to a mixed comprehensive. At that point I would have been interested in either a girls' school or a mixed school. I would even have been interested in a boys' school. When I was applying for deputy headships I did apply to an all-boys' school. I have, in a previous job, worked in an all-boys' school. I had an open mind on all that. Now that I am here, with my past experience in mixed schools, it has convinced me that girls' schools are necessary. I feel committed to this and this is not just an attempt to justify where I am now. From what I have sometimes observed of girls in mixed schools I value what I see here.

PR: Some of the research is coming up with a worrying finding. Girls' schools may be better for girls, or at least some girls, boys' schools tend to be worse for boys.

SB: Girls' schools can be better for girls in all kinds of ways. I am not sure how you resolve the dilemma you have identified, but I am sure we should not sacrifice the girls to socialise the boys really. This seems unfair. On the other hand, I have two sons both of whom went to mixed schools. There was no realistic alternative, given where we were, but I doubt if I would have wanted to send them to a boys' school. We could have sent them to a private school but I cannot accept the idea that one should teach in a state comprehensive school and send one's children to an independent school. It would be ethically inconsistent.

PR: What was your initial experience of headship like?

SB: I was very thrilled at the prospect. I felt as well prepared as I could have been without actually experiencing it or having had a period as acting head. It felt like an enormous challenge and an enormous responsibility. At the same time it felt like something very exciting. I soon found out that it is totally different from being a deputy. I cannot imagine wanting to do anything else now. I love it for all kinds of reasons. Most of all I enjoy the pupils. That is the crucial thing and why those of us who are lucky enough to work in schools, should be in teaching in the first place.

PR: Some of the heads I have talked to, usually those who manage large schools, have told me that headship has made them rather detached from the pupils. They do their good work for pupils essentially through the staff.

SB: You are not involved with them in the same day-to-day way as when you were a classroom teacher. This is inevitable. Even as a deputy you are not involved with them in the same way as when you were a form teacher. But you can still play a part in enabling what they can do and take a joy in their achievements. You see pupils come in and grow in confidence and hear about girls whom you know would have sunk in a mixed school. I see them blossoming. That is a delight. If we can do that we are doing some good. I enjoy what I do. It is endlessly fascinating. I like the fact that every day throws up something different. You have things in your diary but you never know what is going to come up. You know if you have a gap, something, very probably a crisis, will come to fill it. I am almost at the end of my third year. There are ever new challenges, perhaps more than one would wish sometimes (laughs). As I have always done in whatever role I have taken on, I try to be professional about it. I like a job well done, whether it is my class having got the best exam results of which they are capable or helping people within the staff to do things well which six months ago they thought they could not cope with.

PR: How do you see your role as a headteacher?

SB: I see my role first and foremost to ensure that the kids get the best possible education which we can give them. By that I mean education in the broadest sense. We emphasise here very strongly that everybody has got skills and talents and that everybody can improve in personal terms if not, necessarily, in comparison with other pupils. Everybody can make progress of one sort or another. Everyone has something to offer and to contribute. If we can give them a sense of confidence, of valuing themselves, then we have done something worthwhile. Within the school my role is a bit like that of a parent within a family. It is a mixture of things. On the one hand you are a shaping force but on the other hand you are there to enable people to become independent, to become able to manage without you. There are always those two sides to the job. As the head you have to give the lead: you are the person with whom the buck stops; you are the person who has to make the ultimate decisions. In that sense you are a shaping force but you must also be concerned with empowering other people in the processes by which you achieve your purposes together.

PR: In doing all this you must work with a wide range of people. Presumably most closely with your most senior colleagues. What do you expect of them and what should they expect of you?

SB: I expect of them the same professional standards that I expect of myself. I expect them to help me as members of the team which carries the greatest responsibility for leading the school forward successfully. When we make important decisions, no matter who is responsible for the area in which the decision lies, we discuss it together and carry the responsibility for taking it forward together. We do not say this is my area, I will decide this. I trust them to get on with the jobs which they are responsible for but decisions are discussed together and are jointly made.

I have a weekly timetabled meeting with my deputies and we also have an after-school meeting, nominally every month but in practice almost every week with the wider senior team which includes the senior teachers. There are three senior teachers, two deputies and myself so this meeting involves six people. One senior teacher is the professional tutor. This encompasses everything from determining the programmes of students on their PGCE teaching practice through to the determination of the staff development programme and the management of the inset budget. A second is the Design and Technology co-ordinator. She also carries a broad responsibility for our interface with the world outside. She is our representative on the Parents' Society, looks after the general PR side of things and is our contact person with the local inspectorate. The third has a mixture of roles. She is the TVEI co-ordinator until the end of TVEI, and she is the school's systems manager. She works with the administrative staff as well as the teaching staff on developing the pupil data base and generating the information for Form 7 and things like that. She is also Special Needs co-ordinator.

One of the deputies is broadly responsible for the curriculum and also for finance. So she does the monthly liaison with the bursar and checking up on the print-outs we get from county. The other deputy is responsible for the sites and buildings aspect. She also does the timetable and carries a responsibility for day-to-day issues to do with the running of the school. The bursar is really more of an administrative assistant than a bursar in the fullest sense of the word. She is the head's secretary cum finance manager. As with many schools, since the advent of LMS, the head's secretary has gradually changed role. Also because I do a lot of my own typing and word processing there is less need for her to act in a secretarial role in the old sense of the word. She is much more concerned with the day-to-day management of the budget although, when necessary, she also does the personnel and confidential things for me. We have had a delegated budget since before I came. We were already into the first year of LMS.

We are about to appoint a new person to that role. My bursar is about to retire. We are keeping our options open because we have advertised for a school bursar of the old style but have said that this would be subject to a review in a couple of years' time when the contracts for cleaning, grounds maintenance and catering all come up for renegotiation. I can see that by that time there will not be the option for the county to manage those on our behalf. At the moment the governors have opted for buying into the county to manage those contracts and they do the specifications and tendering, and so on. We have opted for that package this time, but I would foresee that this will not be possible next time given the way things are being pushed by the government. We may therefore need to change the role of the bursar. We might need someone to take on those activities and also to take away the detailed financial responsibilities carried by one of the deputies who, after all, should have an educational function.

We have got to be aware, because of the new management functions we have had to take on, that senior staff do not lose sight of the fact that their main managerial functions should focus on the education of the pupils. One of the parent governors who was on the contracts committee said 'I want you (myself and my deputies) to be concerned with the teaching of my daughter and the pupils as a whole. I don't want you spending great amounts of your time chasing up cleaners and grass cutters'.

PR: Has there been some real risk that this might happen?

SB: It has certainly taken a lot more of our time to look at those kinds of issues. Particularly, it takes a lot of time in the first instance. If I think back, for example, to the start of LMS none of us was trained in managing budgets. None of us had come into teaching expecting that would be part of any role we would have to play as senior managers. Some of us were daunted at first to find that we had to exercise skills which our previous experience had not prepared us for. But like all these things, it takes longer in the beginning. You have to get your head down and come to terms with it and as you become more familiar with it you become more confident and more efficient. Once that has happened it takes rather less of your time. That is what has happened with LMS. Once you have set up and worked the systems they don't take as much time as they did initially. Of course it can also get more difficult as the budget seems to shrink and what you want to do with it expands. That is another issue. You have to be a fast learner to be any good at school management these days.

PR: Unlike most of the heads I am talking to, you must have known that these things would be expected of you when you agreed to be a head? On a related note, I know you have long been interested in curriculum development. Is this still possible given your other responsibilities? Two things might make this difficult. First, the site-based management issues we talked of earlier. Secondly, the imposition of a National Curriculum. Can heads and schools still exercise real powers in these areas? Should they try to? Should you be involved in curriculum development? What does this mean?

SB: It depends on how you define curriculum development. Your involvement as a head cannot be the same as that of a head of department nor should it be. It should not be about that nitty gritty examination of resources and detailed classroom management issues. If you tried to do these things you would be disempowering your heads of department. Part of the way they develop as individuals and as professionals is by taking that responsibility and leading their teams in doing so. If you take that from them then you are not doing your job professionally. At the same time you are still the person who is ultimately responsible to the governors for the curriculum of the school and so you have to have an interest in the curriculum and this needs to be wide ranging and detailed. Also you can't just give up something which has been so important in your professional life for so long. So I do not stop being interested in the teaching of English because I am no longer doing it in a classroom on a day-to-day basis. For example, this afternoon we have a poet coming to talk to the sixth form and I shall be there. I am interested and I think that it is important that I maintain and show that interest. My husband and I still write textbooks so I am involved with the curriculum through that. I think it would be a very dangerous thing if heads became very remote from the curriculum. How else do you know about what is going on in the most important aspect of the school? How do you know what is happening to the girls you are responsible for? You have to be interested in curriculum development but in a rather different way. So we have as one of our targets in the school development plan the need to consider differentiation. That is something I am interested in, particularly with reference to classroom management and resource material to support the teaching process. And so whilst it would be inappropriate for me to run it, I attend as many of the meetings of the development group as I can. I think it is important that it is seen to have my support and to demonstrate the importance I attach to this.

PR: It could be that you could be constrained in a different sort of way in that schools as a whole are constrained by the National Curriculum. Not all agree with this. Even some heads and teachers feel that the National Curriculum does not constrain schools to the extent which is often claimed. What are your feelings about the National Curriculum and the extent to which it constrains, desirably or undesirably, the ability of schools to shape their curriculums, according to national, local and individual needs?

SB: People in general, having got used to the idea, would now agree that from the point of view of ensuring consistency, continuity and coherence from the pupil's point of view, there should be a National Curriculum. Whether this should be *the* national curriculum as it stands in today's version is something which would need to be debated with respect to its particular aspects. At the same time, many of the most exciting curriculum developments which have occurred in schools have been the result of initiatives from particular departments, schools or local authorities. One thinks, for example, of Oxfordshire and the development of school self-evaluation. People like Tim Brighouse and the great Alec Clegg have been key figures in LEAs who have developed and taken important curriculum initiatives forward. Records of Achievement is another example. This has now been taken on as part of the national agenda but it began as a grass roots movement which evolved in different parts of the country. I was involved in the development of OCEA in Oxfordshire. It will be a pity if the introduction of a National Curriculum stifles that kind of grass roots initiative.

   At the same time I do not think it right that a pupil should have a very different experience depending on which part of the country and in which school they happen to go to. Of course there are all kinds of inequalities which one can never entirely eradicate. For example, it is hard to see how it is possible to fully compensate for every possible background. Even so it is in the interests of all pupils to have a broad agreement. But I also see it as one of the crucial roles of the head in supporting the morale of the staff, for them to feel that they still have some kind of control over the curriculum. That it is not just something which they must take. One of the most important things I can do for this school is to enable the staff to be proactive and not just reactive in how they respond to such things as the national agenda of reform. They need to be encouraged to be clear about what they see as important and how they fit external pressures for change into that conception of things.

PR: When I was an education officer I was shocked at how little the LEA knew about the curriculum which existed in its different secondary schools. It was equally shocking to find out how little a number of headteachers seemed to know about the curriculum which existed within their own schools. Whole-school curriculum planning seemed to exist in very few schools. How far have you achieved this here?

SB: It is an aspect of the responsibilities which the curriculum deputy carries. At this time we are undertaking a review of our pastoral curriculum as part of the curriculum as a whole and not as some kind of separate entity. We anticipate implementing the changes this will require as from next September. The three of us, the head and deputies, must have things like that as a priority particularly since we are in the process of working towards the introduction of a new timetable and structure for the day as from next September. This raises all kinds of questions concerning the balance between different subjects, how much time you put into, for example, what constitutes the English slot and does it include the Drama and the Library time? Somebody has got to have an overview in these things and that has got to be the senior management.

PR: How do you lead the work of staff as a whole? Is this a relevant question?

SB: Oh yes. First and foremost, you must lead by example. In the same way that as a classroom teacher you can't expect our children to get their homework in to you on time if it commonly takes you three weeks to get it back to them. Similarly, with the staff you have to lead by example in all kinds of ways including commitment to the job and to the girls, working hard, being professional, valuing people. This last is particularly important because I really feel that the health of any organisation depends on the quality of the relationship between its members. If you don't set the right lead on this, you should not be too surprised if it does not happen in a way that you want it to. You also need to have an influence in determining the framework of values and principles as a whole within which everything else happens and people can work.
     Of course, much depends on the context within which you work how you go about this. When I came here people, in general, had not had much in-service training nor had they been much involved in external groups. They had, perhaps a rather narrowly and institutionally defined perspective. Therefore, in leading the staff through all kinds of things which we need to do, you need to approach that in a different way from the way you might have approached it had you been in a school where lots of staff had taken

further qualifications and were deeply involved with a variety of external groups and projects. What is appropriate depends to a large extent on the characteristics of the situation in which you find yourself.

PR: You need to start from where people actually are?

SB: People can find change threatening: to suggest they change can be to devalue their perception of the things they have done before. You need to build trust, confidence and skills to manage change effectively. It is my job as a head to lead on doing this and to make sure that it happens.

PR: How do you relate with other groups who have an interest in the school. For example, with pupils, with parents and with the local community?

SB: I am involved with the parents in all the normal sorts of ways in formal situations such as parents' evenings and other kinds of public events and with regard to individual pupils. I am also on the parents' society committee which means that I am involved with some of the most active parents. Because we have an unusually large number of parents who are members of the governing body — some of our co-opted and LEA governors are, coincidentally, also parents — so that gives me a great deal of contact with parents through that forum. Otherwise it is just the incidental contact which one has with parents around the place.

PR: Are you conscious of a greater exercise of power by parents along the lines predicated by a number of the government's reforms?

SB: I think people in general are more aware of educational issues than they used to be. They could hardly fail to be, given the high profile education has had in the media and elsewhere over the last few years. Interestingly people will now use some of the jargon which was once restricted to the professionals. I hear people talking about SATs whereas in the recent past you might have expected such terms to be restricted to discussions within the educational world. There is a wider awareness of the relevant issues. They are aware that things are changing rapidly and almost every time you do a presentation for parents you have to begin by explaining how things have changed from the last time you spoke to them. They are also more aware of the market implications of recent legislation and its implications for schools. One or two might be rather more critical than they would have been in the past. By and large, however, as with most schools our parents are very happy with the education which their daughters are receiving here. In fact the governors' external relations committee has sent out a questionnaire to the parents of Year 7 pupils. The response has been most encouraging in terms of customer satisfaction, if that is what we are looking at (laughs).

PR: I can see the importance of this. My colleague Hywel Thomas argues that under the present system pupils are effectively vouchers. Are you a school which has no problems, recruiting pupils?

SB: I do not like to look at them in that way or as age-weighted pupil units. We are oversubscribed. We attract pupils from a wide catchment area and from across the county boundary.

PR: How do you work with your governors?

SB: I am very fortunate in the governors I have. They are very supportive of the school. There are not political factions amongst them, in the way I have encountered in my past experience. A lot of them have long contact with the school and are very much doing a PR job for the school amongst the community and stressing how good a job the school is doing. Many are parents. As such they are involved in a grass roots way by their daughters right the way through the spectrum from Year 7 to the sixth form. They have a confidence in the school which springs from a trust in the competence and commitment of the staff and the senior management team. They are happy for us to get on with the day-to-day running of the school. They do not come in, as some governors do, and demand to check the budget every month. They get auditors' reports, they know we have sound systems in place which are efficient in day-to-day monitoring.

In terms of staffing, we talk to the curriculum and staffing committee of the governors about the needs of the school and the different subjects as these vary from year to year and what that means for the staffing profile. And obviously, governors are involved in interviews. They are not generally involved when it is just an internal appointment where somebody is taking on, for example, the work of somebody who is going on maternity leave or if we are promoting somebody internally to a head of year post. But for external posts, even Scale 1 posts, they are involved.

With the new governing body the new subcommittee structure seems to be working quite well. There are four subcommittees — finance, sites and buildings, external relations and curriculum and staffing. The governors were happy to agree that the subcommittees should have staff in attendance as participant observers, if not as voting members. This has meant greater contact between staff and governors and a greater staff input. I think this is very helpful.

PR: How do you think they see your role? Do they see you as their chief executive?

SB: I am not sure that I can answer on their behalf how they see my role. I think they do see me in a chief executive role but they also see me as the school's principal educational leader. Some of them have industrial experience and, as such, may be sympathetic to the chief executive model but even they, since they tend to have daughters in the school, still emphasise the importance of my educational role.

PR: What of your relationship with your chairman of governors?

SB: I think that is very important. I am fortunate in that I have a chair of governors with whom I get on very well. We have a high level of respect for each other personally. She has a high-powered job in a computer firm. So we understand each other's perspectives. I can talk to her about things within the school and she will immediately be on the right wavelength because she is also in a position in which she has to manage teams of people or projects within the company. She understands about things like appraisal, which has been such an issue in some schools. She understands about development plans and target setting and all the kinds of things we are now concerned about in managing a school today. She is very busy so we don't have a regular meeting but we do ring each other up at home quite a lot at the weekends and in the evenings. So we keep in close touch. We discuss how we are going to approach things which have come up or which might come up and this is very helpful.

PR: How would you describe your relationship with the LEA?

SB: Coming from Oxfordshire where there was a very strong culture of partnership between the schools and the LEA I will regret the passing of the LEAs, should that happen. Since I have come here I have an LEA liaison officer who is very valuable and I would regret the loss of someone who is in that role and who can come in from outside and look at the school as a kind of critical friend, who can look at things from the critical perspective of knowing what is happening in lots of other schools and who can give one all kinds of professional advice and support. It will be a sad day when we lose that kind of support. The loss of LEAs may mean possibly the creation of a situation in which a large number of schools are isolated from each other. A situation in which each runs the risk of losing that sense of collective responsibility which was so much a strength of the previous system. My primary responsibility is to the girls of this school but as a head I also feel that I should have a responsibility for the education of the wider community. That can take various forms. Such as, for example, working with other heads in a variety of ways and purposes.

PR: We are going through a period of multiple change which makes it very difficult to keep up with developments as they come on stream. How do you keep up? I know how difficult this is from my conversations with large numbers of heads. I also know from them how impossible they feel the job is becoming.

SB: In a sense it is an impossible job, but as I said before I would not want to do anything else. You keep up by trying to find time to read professional journals and books. You have to be very selective and prioritise carefully because, it seems, that there are ever more books which claim to have the ultimate answers to all school problems. I also find it helpful to be involved in professional organisations through things like SHA and the Berkshire Heads Association. Such discourse is immensely valuable. I have found my contacts with higher education helpful. My husband works in a University Education department so I have a vested interest in this too (laughs).

PR: What do you enjoy most and least of headship? What interests you most and least?

SB: I don't think anything interests me least. I still find it all fascinating. I enjoy that sense of seeing other people develop and feeling that they came to you as little girls really and if they can leave as self-confident young women that is a source of great satisfaction and delight. I also enjoy the management side of the job. I still find structures, systems and processes fascinating. At the end of the day I enjoy being able to say these things happened and we coped, this child had a problem and we helped her. I enjoy my professional relationships with colleagues. I really do enjoy working in teams with other people and seeing members of staff develop in ways which parallel the development of the pupils.

PR: How do you cope with the stresses and pressures of headship? How do you cope when things go wrong?

SB: We could all do with 48 hours in the day but these are not available so we have to do the best with the 24 that we can! I suppose I cope with stress in a mixture of ways. I try to delegate appropriately which is partly to make it possible for me to manage but also partly to enable the development of other people. I have tried to make some space for myself. This is a job which could easily become your life. It takes up such a lot of your time and energy. In one sense it has to be your life but you are not being fair to yourself or your family if this happens. I suspect you are not really being fair to the school either. You can become a very one-sided person. In terms of your efficiency on the job you must maintain a sense of perspective. You have to have other interests. I do try to make parts of every weekend times which have nothing to do with the school. I try to set aside Saturdays although, of course, this does not always work because sometimes there are school functions or conferences then, but if you try you might be able to achieve it some of the time.

One of my coping strategies is to try and keep reasonably fit because I know I can cope with things better if I am reasonably physically fit. There is a danger that the time you set aside for such physical exercise gets cut into by the demands of school. There is always more that you could do. You have to try to keep a reasonable balance. In achieving this, good forward planning is important and I try to do this. So I can phase things properly I write myself little rough reminders in my diary. I write myself lists of things I must do. You always end up by adding more things to the bottom than taking things off the top but this is unavoidable. One of the crucial things is keeping a sense of perspective. It is very easy for teachers in general and heads in particular to become institutionalised and to lose their sense of proportion. You must also retain your sense of humour. I do not think you could cope without your sense of humour.

An important factor in my ability to cope has been my family, both in terms of helping me retain my sense of proportion and of the support they give me. My sons may tease me about being 'Miss' but they're also quite proud of me and very helpful. My husband had always been very encouraging and supportive, right through the children growing up, and especially now. In fact, I suppose we're mutually supportive; since we both work in education, we tend to talk things through together.

PR: If you were asked to, what would you advise Sir Ron Dearing in terms of the changes you see as desirable in the curriculum and on assessment in so far as secondary schools are concerned?

SB: The crucial issue with this review is the necessity for somebody to look at the curriculum as a whole. There has been talk of slimming down individual subjects but this will not do. The problem, everybody now recognises, is that each subject was developed separately. We should not be surprised that those involved tried to grab as much of human knowledge as possible and tried to fit it into their subject. If you go about things in that way this was inevitable. But when they all started recommending what percentage should be devoted to their subjects the total came to something like 130 per cent of the time available. This is a nonsense. Somebody has to take an overview. We need some common sense. In terms of the programmes of study there really has got to be a different kind of balance. They should provide a framework within which there is flexibility. The needs of pupils in different schools in different areas are different. If you wanted a motivated, and therefore an effective, teaching force they have got to feel that their professional expertise is respected. If you try to prescribe everything down to the last detail they will not feel valued. If you want effective schools you have got to get teachers to feel that their professionalism is respected.

In terms of assessment they really have got to make up their minds what they want the assessment for. You cannot expect a single one-and-a-half hour test to serve a number of quite different purposes. We know, because we have been doing it for years, that we can set tests for our pupils which are diagnostic and informative, which we can use to discuss with individual pupils in a formative way what progress they have made and where they need to go next. That the results of these same tests can be used to inform parents about their children's progress. But those tests cannot, at the same time, be used as the yardstick by which the performance of individual teachers or schools can be measured and compared with other teachers or schools. To do this you need other things. In fact when the OFSTED model of inspection is in place we will have a national system for monitoring the effectiveness of schools.

Also, of course, there are only certain things which can be measured using a formal test. There is a great danger of a distortion if we become wholly or exclusively reliant on such a method of examining performance. It has got to be used in combination with other methods if we are to have a full picture. There is a danger that in its simplest form a pencil and paper test will be seen as the be all and end all of things. This will lead to severe distortions of the curriculum and therefore of the experience of pupils. If we are going to be judged by the tests which our pupils have taken and the league tables in which these are presented then inevitably this is what teachers will be forced to teach to. That may well not be in the best educational interests of the children. We must recognise the limitations of that kind of test.

PR: The government claims its reforms are justified by the fact that the standards of performance of our pupils have in important respects been inferior to those achieved elsewhere. They also claim the reforms they have implemented are already beginning to improve standards. Do you agree?

SB: It depends on what you are measuring. I think it is really rather soon to be able to say with any confidence. I doubt if we know much, for example, of what effect the introduction of the National Curriculum has had on standards. After all it will not be until well into the next century before the first cohort has been right through the

system. I would hesitate to think we will be able to make anything
like a definitive judgement until we get to that point.

In my view to date the introduction of GCSE and of course work
has had a more obvious effect for good than the National Curriculum
as such. This has been a great motivator of pupils right across the
ability range. I think there has undoubtedly been an improvement in
standards in some areas like English which are course-work led. This
makes the views of the current Secretary of State all the more sad. I
am sure that most educationalists, most heads, most teachers would
agree that there is a place for both course work and for more formal
styles of examination and testing. What we should be looking for is
the most appropriate balance in particular subjects, levels and contexts.

PR: Finally do you see the school as 'your' school?

SB: I suspect that there is a touch of the Jean Brody in all of us. In
one sense it is my school but it also has to be our school. It is my
school to the extent that I have to give the lead and am the public
face of the school in many ways. But it is also our school because
people's view of the school depends upon the experience of the
children every day in the classroom. So however charismatic I might
be in public forums if I did not have a staff who were able, caring,
supportive and who worked tremendously hard and who taught well
and got good academic results then I would be wasting my time. It
must be a joint effort best described in the old term of *primus inter
apres*. The ultimate test is not that it is my school or the staff's school
but that it is the girls' school. I hope that most of them enjoy being
here. I think they feel they get a lot out of it. As I go around they do
seem fully involved. Just today I got a letter from the parents of a girl
who is just about to go on study leave in preparation for her GCSEs,
thanking us for the way in which their daughter, who is not one of
the academic high flyers, has blossomed whilst she has been here. To
that extent it is also the parents' school.

3 Valerie Bragg

with Peter Ribbins

PR: What do you remember of your early life and education?

VB: I did not like school very much. I did not enjoy it, I was not motivated and I was not switched on. I was one of those children who wasted their time and was going to leave school at sixteen. I did my GCE and got both a job and a place at a college to do secretarial work — one of those rapid training courses. I told my father I was determined to do one or other of these things. He told me 'Sorry you are not going to do either of those things. You are going back into the sixth form'. I rebelled of course but was marched back into the sixth. I did not enjoy the lower sixth, mainly because I felt I had been forced to go back against my will but continued and then suddenly, for no reason I can remember, I came home and said to my parents 'Right I am going off to university'. In the middle of the upper sixth I started to work hard. I was going to do Geography and got a place at Southampton University. But I did not really feel fixed on any subject and increasingly felt that I did not really want to do Geography, and said to myself 'I will do Zoology instead'. Eventually, I ended up in Leicester University reading Zoology. I am still not sure if this was the right choice for me but I quite enjoyed it.

I applied to get a job at the Ministry of Agriculture and Fisheries because at that point I wanted to do some research into getting more food out of the sea. That seemed an interesting sort of job. However, when I discovered I could not get to sea as I was a woman, I abandoned that idea. I can remember my professor of Zoology spending the whole day trying to persuade me to teach. Teaching was the last thing in the world that I want to do. In the end I tried teaching and to my surprise I found it absolutely fantastic. I really enjoyed it and decided almost immediately that I was going to be a head. I also think it was about that time that I first started to enjoy learning, because I began to see how exciting and interesting it was. I have a very good memory but had never really used my brain properly. With teaching I found that I had to because you had to explain things to people. You had to think carefully about what you were doing. I believe I matured and was far better from that moment because I suddenly realised what was involved.

PR: You began your account with your life at school. What about your life at home?

VB: I was born in Cheshire but I did not live there. There is no history of teaching at all in the family. My father was a director at Pilkingtons. My mother is a potter but at that time she was a housewife. In thinking about how my parents influenced my education I need to stress that I did not much like school. I was very lazy. Rarely did I relate to a teacher but when I did I worked hard. When I think about the subjects I did well in and enjoyed, it was almost always in situations where I had a good personal relationship with the teacher, or I thought they were good or I liked them. I remember when I was at secondary school I liked the Chemistry teacher very much and therefore that became my favourite subject. My parents moved, they moved quite often, and so I had to move school and I did not like the Chemistry teacher at the new school. Therefore I went off Chemistry and became more interested in Geography. Only one or two teachers really sparked me off. Most of the time I tended to feel things were boring and uninteresting.

My parents tell me they can pin-point when my attitude began to change. They believe this came from conversations I had with our next door neighbour, who encouraged me to go to university. They say I changed almost overnight and said 'Right, I am going to university'. From that point on I started to really apply myself and worked hard in the upper sixth. In applying for university I began by applying for Geography, because that was taught by the teacher I had liked. I was offered places in Geography but, and this shows how confused I was, I decided that I did not really want to do Geography and would rather do Zoology. My Zoology teacher had been very boring and had a droning and monotonous voice. I remember that when we looked at our 'A' Level exam papers we discovered that we had not done most of the things which we found there. It was a real shock at first but then I said to myself 'I will show that wretched woman'. I can remember being furious in the exam. I needed a good result and she had not taught me the relevant work. I think that was the first time that I had to wrack my brains to answer the questions rather than rely on my memory. That was probably one reason why I did well. I had been forced to think hard.

PR: Did your parents explain why they wanted you to go into the sixth form rather than get a job?

VB: I think they knew I was a bit mixed up at the time and not in the best frame of mind to make such a decision. I suppose they were typical middle-class parents who felt their daughter ought to go on into the sixth form. I also think my father wanted to make sure I did what he had not been able to do. He had wanted to go to university but never had for various reasons including the war.

When I finished my degree I was still very young and naïve. I think I was one of those people who would have gained a good deal from having a year off and working before going on to university. I might have been a bit more mature when the time came to leave university and go out into the world. But this was never a likely option. When I went up to university I was thinking that I would have to be there for three years before I could really get on with things. That seemed, then, far too long. In fact I had even considered doing medicine, but five years or six years of training was simply more than I could contemplate at the time. I was very anxious to finish and to get out into the real world as soon as possible.

PR: Does this explain why you did not do the PGCE before going into teaching?

VB: I felt I had had enough education and training and the sooner I could get started the better. I also wondered what is the point of doing it anyway. I thought I would try teaching and see if I liked it. If I had completed a year on the PGCE and then discovered I did not want to teach that would have been a total waste of time. With the advantage of hindsight I have rather come to believe that you can either teach or not. In many ways it might be better for everybody to start teaching to see if they like it, and if they do, perhaps after two or three years, then they might really benefit from training. You do learn a great deal at the beginning and if you have this experience you have something to build on when you do your PGCE. If you go straight from doing your degree, the PGCE can seem like a bit of an anti-climax and you can waste time.

PR: You loved teaching straight away?

VB: The job was at a girls' public school. It was a fairly privileged environment for the students who were there. I was also lucky in that the other Biology teacher, who had been there a long time, did not want to teach the advanced work. I started teaching 'A' Level Zoology, Botany and Biology to girls who were going off to university. I really got on well with them. I enjoyed it. I had to work incredibly hard because I had done very little Botany. I think it switched me on. That was when I started to enjoy working. I had to think very hard about how to put things over and how to explain concepts. It all just clicked.

I was there for only a year. I then looked for promotion. I could not wait any longer could I? It was also partly because my husband had to move after one year. He started teaching in a grammar school not far away from where I was teaching. He did not like the school and went into further education, so I moved to be near him. I applied to two schools. One was in Southend and the other in Hornchurch. The former was for a head of department but despite my lack of a PGCE and only one year's experience, I was offered the post of head of Biology. This was a bit far from where his new job was so when the job at Hornchurch Grammar School came up and I was called for interview, I telephoned the head and said 'I have been offered a head of department post, is there any chance of having an allowance with you?' He said 'Come over for interview'. I did, and was offered an allowance, so I went there. I stayed there for about seven years and was promoted to head of department. I really liked the school which was co-educational. In fact, I still keep in touch with some of the students even though they are in their forties now. Several came to my wedding. I was one of a few new teachers starting at the same time although there were also a lot of very traditional teachers at the school. I learnt a lot. It was a good school and had a good reputation. There were many highly supportive parents and a lot of creative and high flying students. I started by teaching Nuffield science which was then being piloted. I enjoyed that a great deal as it allowed one to be creative and flexible and encouraged the students to be imaginative.

It was a good time. It was a time when I got married and started a family. Mark was born in December and I think I had three weeks away in all. When I had Julie, she was born in August, a month early, and so I worked until the end of July. I think I took one day off in all. I was totally committed to teaching and to my work. I just could not stand being in the house with nothing to do. Not using my mind. So I would take them to nursery and drop them off. My mother was horrified and would say 'How can you? How terrible'. I said to everybody 'We will try it and see how it works: If it does not then I will give up'. But I had no intention of giving up. In that sense I was a bit selfish.

Up to that point I had only worked in grammar schools and knew nothing else. Then my husband got a promotion to Worcester. So I had to look for another job. I suppose this shows the strength of my ambition because even then I applied for deputy headships. I applied for a deputy post at Waisley Hill High School in Rubery. I did not get the deputy post, but the head asked me to stay behind after the interviews and offered me a job as head of sixth form. I leapt at the chance as it meant starting it off from scratch. That was great since it meant creating something new and different and was a real challenge. Incidentally, it was only when I went to Waisley Hills that I began to become aware of just how privileged I had been in both my own education and in my teaching up to that time. It was only then that I began to realise what the rest of the world was like. Which again shows my naïvety. My own children went to a comprehensive school and I am sure they have had a much broader education as a result of this. I can remember the first lessons I took at comprehensive school and thinking that the children were playing me up because I had not realised how limited they might be in ability and aptitude. I was only there about one and a half years before I got a deputy headship. I was anxious to get on. This was at Pershore High, another co-educational comprehensive.

PR: You worked for four heads. What were they like? What did you learn from them?

VB: They were all very different. My first head was a typical female public school head, near to retirement. I did not see much of her. I was far too busy with my teaching. I got to know my second head well. He had some lovely little quirks. He was the sort of head who was forever sending memos. The staff would regularly have memos galore in their pigeon holes. We would look for our pink slips. I recall one lovely one he wrote which said 'Please come and see me at break' and underneath 'On second thoughts do not bother'. He was near to retirement so we had a change of head whilst I was there. The new one was young and enthusiastic and wanted a lot of change. This motivated me further. He had been brought in because the school was changing status to comprehensive. The head at Waseley Hills was also near to retirement. He did not want change and wanted life to be easy. I would go to him and suggest this or that and he would initially say no. But I would keep going back until he would tell me to get on with it. I learnt a great deal from my last head. He had previously been a lawyer which was useful for learning aspects of headship. It certainly made me more careful. He was a good mentor but sadly is now dead. He had been looking forward to retirement and retired at 57 but died a couple of months later from a heart attack.

PR: What did you learn from them which was relevant to you as a head?

VB: My last head was not very good at talking to parents. He would try to avoid them. I felt that was a bad mistake. When I started my first headship, when a parent wanted to see me I did all I could to be available. One does tend to learn what not to do rather than what to do. I learnt just how frustrating it can be to work for some heads, which was partly why I wanted to move on. I hope I give space and freedom.

PR: When did you realise you wanted to be a head? Did you plan your way to it?

VB I suspect I knew from the beginning — almost as soon as I started teaching. I took a very traditional route. I obtained an early promotion to head of department, went on to be head of sixth form which gave me plenty of pastoral contact, then on to a deputy headship and then to a headship. I attended carefully selected courses on time-tabling, pastoral care, curriculum development and the like. I suppose the whole thing looks carefully planned but I did not have a conscious checklist. But I knew I wanted to be a head.

I was seven years at Pershore High before getting a headship. I did get frustrated towards the end of my time there. After four years there I started applying for headships but kept coming up against the same problem. I would be told at the end of interviews that I was the best candidate but had a young family and they did not want to take the risk of appointing me. That was when I started off my antique shop, which provided me with another outlet. When I got my first headship I had, in fact, decided not to apply for it. It was a large comprehensive high school (13–18). I suppose I thought that they would not give that to a woman. But my last head called me in and suggested that I apply for it. He said that the other two deputies were applying and that I ought to as well. So I did.

PR: What do you think the role of the deputy should be?

VB: First, you sometimes stand in for the head. Secondly, you are learning to be a head so you need to have the opportunity to try a variety of tasks and gain the necessary experience. Thirdly, the role of the deputy is also a dogsbody's job. It is part of the learning process. You are picking problems up, filling in the jigsaw, noticing what has not been done and doing it.

PR: What was your feeling about the school when you took up your first headship?

VB: I am apprehensive about this because I do not want to be misunderstood. During the interview process I walked around the school and was struck by its tatty, worn-out appearance. It did not look terribly inviting. The furniture was in a dreadful state, the students did not wear a uniform and some of them looked awful. My first impression was of a run-down school which had seen better times. It had a head who was retiring and who had been there for a long time. All this meant there were things to do. But this is only part of the picture. In many ways it was a good school with many good staff. Some of whom were rather demoralised, as the reputation of the school in the area was not good, so parents were taking their children away. From that point of view it was not a school in which one's first impressions were very positive. On the other hand it had tremendous potential. So that suited me. We were shown around by the deputy who badly wanted the job and did not get it. It was not the easiest of headships to take over, but I did feel quite well prepared, although I doubt if anything in my previous experience had prepared me for working with somebody who resented not having the job. At a personal level we got on well but I'm not sure that I got the best out of him.

PR: Why do you think they appointed you? Was it a strong field?

VB: It was a strong field and included the other two deputies from Pershore High. We had an initial interview with members of the local authority where you moved from person to person. I felt this part went well and I would have been very disappointed if I had not got through to the afternoon interview. I was surprised they appointed me as a woman, and this was twelve years ago. There were few women heads of large comprehensive schools at the time. I think perhaps I just clicked with the interview panel, who could have been looking for a breath of fresh air. I think they were worried about the school's reputation and I was very clear that I would want to change things. I said I would have a uniform, build up the sixth form and enhance the appearance of the school. With hindsight, I had a very big agenda of change in mind. I am still in contact with some of the staff, in fact some joined Kingshurst. The first thing I did was to tackle uniform, which may sound like a small thing but was not. I constructed a questionnaire which was sent to all parents and staff. The vast majority of parents wanted a uniform but most staff did not. They saw it as a potential hassle. If it existed they would have to check up on it. I just lumped the findings as a whole together, which meant there was a majority for a uniform. Once the students wore uniform it had the most dramatic effect. I had people 'phoning up from the town saying how much better behaved the students were. It was wonderful. The other thing I wanted to do was to change what the school looked like. I decided to start with the toilets which were in a disgusting state. So I told the LEA I was inviting the Department of Health who would condemn them as unfit. The Chairman of Education visited and nearly fell over a manhole. After his visit they were refurbished immediately. We went on from there. I was always on the 'phone to the local authority asking for this, that or the other. The local authority were very helpful, for example, they carpeted much of the school. We also did a lot of self-help. I used to say to the LEA 'I have an army of parents ready and willing to help, will you pay for the paint?' Then I used a different approach in which I would offer to do one part of a job if they would do the other. I had vast areas of the school refurbished and renovated. Once this started, the staff and students developed a different attitude. The school was looking better, it made them feel better. The school was getting better comments from the town, and so on.

PR: You feel very strongly about the environment of the school? You have perhaps the nicest head's room in the state sector that I know of. Did you have much more money available to you for refurbishing Kingshurst than would have been available to other schools? You have taken a traditional fifties-style three-storey block and made it look very attractive. How?

VB: Yes, I do feel strongly about the environment of the school, but it does not have to be very expensive. It costs no more to paint a wall pink than white. It is about giving care and attention to these things. To think about things from an interior designer's point of view. My room was not expensive. If you look around, the table might look expensive but it was made on site from a piece of wood stained black. A bit of flair and creativity can make a huge difference. I would like to be an interior designer and really enjoyed planning all this. I did much the same at Stourport as well. I remember walking along corridors and saying this blue and that yellow. They had never had anything like that before.

At Stourport, as well as changing the environment, I decided to concentrate on academic achievements. The school was very good in arts. We entered some students in the Dr Barnardo's competitions and we won three years on the trot. The students received their prizes from people like the Princess of Wales, which became national news and helped the school to start to believe it had a lot to offer. The sixth increased in size. The number going to university increased sharply and we had students go on to Oxford and Cambridge. Everything worked. There was some concern amongst some staff but because things were going well this was not serious. I was sorry to go.

PR: You seem to have been successful in turning the school around. Why move?

VB: I think the idea of turning the school around puts it rather too strongly. I would like to emphasise that the school had good points to build on when I arrived. All I really did was to market it properly and improve it cosmetically. It might have looked like a grotty school when I went in but it was not.

After four years, I did not feel that I had finished the job and I was not really looking to move. But I remember Kenneth Baker making his announcement about CTCs. I remember thinking to myself that they seemed like the schools of the future. In time, I saw the advert for a principal of the first CTC but I really did not know whether to apply or not. One of my staff who was leaving for promotion came to see me on the last day of term to say goodbye and handed me the advert. He said 'This is just the job for you. Why not apply?' That re-awoke my interest but I still did not apply. It happened to be August. I rarely read the newspapers because I just do not have the time but I was away on holiday and read an article which said of the CTC that 'The *headmaster's* first job would be to appoint the staff and *he* would be planning the curriculum, etc.' I said to myself 'Right, this is it. I am going to apply!' I told my husband and he said 'You do not stand a cat in hell's chance. They will never give the first one to a woman. They might give the fourth or fifth'. I posted my application. I was called for interview. There were two interviews. One was on site, although we were not allowed to look round the building! I might have changed my mind! Then the shortlisted candidates had a second interview in London at Hansons. That was a very long interview where the interviewers seemed to spend most of the time telling me it was going to be a very high profile job. The panel consisted of a director from Hanson, a director from Lucas, an HMI, the project director, a retired local education officer and a DFE representative. I enjoyed the interview.

PR: What did you think you were letting yourself in for?

VB: I knew it was going to be very high profile with a great deal of media interest. But I was still pretty naïve. I thought the thing would be a five-day wonder and then die down. I really did not think it would be the kind of political football that it has been. I saw it as a real educational opportunity and a chance to put into practice many of the ideas I had built up over the years. I thought, with this in mind, how wonderful to start from a blank sheet of paper.

PR What was the first year like?

VB: From the moment I was appointed, life was hectic. It was a very fast-track development. We had less than a year to sort out the buildings, appoint the staff, recruit the students, obtain the furniture, equipment and fittings, the lot. I had to work at weekends at Kingshurst whilst still doing my job at Stourport. The press, radio and television phoned Stourport constantly. The secretary seemed to enjoy it. She phoned me up one day to say 'You have *Woman's Own* on the phone'. All that was amazing. The first two years were more or less a constant bombardment from the media. The day after I was appointed I had to go down to London to meet Kenneth Baker. He was sitting on the settee with the television people all around him.

He said 'Come and sit by me' and we were straight into a television interview. Then I came back here the next day for a press interview. Imagine what it was like for a head who had just come from the state sector, leading the perfectly ordinary life one can expect there, to be face-to-face, in a huge room, with a hundred people from the press and three or four television companies. They were all firing questions. That was my baptism. The only question which they seemed to be really interested in was how were we going to be different? I learnt that I had to make the place different. I felt I had to make it unlike a school. I decided we would not have wooden furniture, nor rows of chairs. Every room would look different. It could have a different colour, shape or style, there could be different desks, tables, chairs, etc. I started with the idea of creating a different kind of environment, for example, we tried to make the entrance more like the reception of a hotel. I felt it would have an impact on the learning.

PR: It has been said that it took a lot of money to make all this possible?

VB: It cost £10m to build the school and this had to pay for the site, the buildings, the furniture, all the equipment, the lot. We have 1300 students. That works out very reasonably and is cheaper than an ordinary school within the state sector. We had to pay 20 per cent to the government. So the actual cost to the government was £8m. The amount we received is the same as any school in the state sector. The press might have conveyed the idea that we were generously funded but this was not the case. We were well within the DFE limits on amount of space and cost per square metre. When we developed phase 2, we did that cheaply, as we did not have architects. We were able to build a sports hall which was not originally planned as a result.

PR: In trying to describe how the school would be different, you began by describing the environment rather than its distinctiveness educationally?

VB: It may sound strange but I strongly believe that the quality of the environment does affect the quality and style of your educational provision. If you have a room which is laid out differently and does not have rows of desks and chairs, you are forcing a change upon the teacher which has pedagogic consequences. I set up a very different organisational structure, with no heads of department, no heads of year, no deputies, nothing like that.

In environmental and educational terms I had a vision of what I wanted to create. I wanted to create corridors with a quiet ambience. I had been in schools when the corridors were noisy and somehow seemed to encourage students to hustle and push along them. I wanted to create social areas in which the students could sit, relax and read and work quietly. I wanted work areas which were totally unsupervised. I had in my mind what I wanted to create.

PR: What kind of management structure did you want to set up?

VB: I decided to go for a flat hierarchy. To an extent this can be explained in terms of the frustrations which I had experienced earlier in my career, when I had not been able to do things I would have liked to do. Of working with heads of department who kept most of what was considered the best for themselves and gave as little as possible to anybody else. I wanted to give everybody significant responsibilities and opportunities so they could take initiatives in areas in which they had the expertise. Much of what I have set up has had that purpose in mind. All the probationers and young teachers at the college have the freedom, if they are interested, to be a co-ordinator, or to manage projects, chair meetings or talk to the whole staff during staff development work. I believe if you give the responsibility, staff enjoy it and it also provides opportunities for them to develop things they are interested in. This motivates them, which, in turn, is then communicated to the students. Everything we did was aimed at making the place fun, stimulating, exciting and motivating. These were the things which I had not had much of in my own schooling.

PR: Did you have difficulty in recruiting staff?

VB: There were hundreds and hundreds of applications. But I have to say it was hard to find the kind of staff I wanted. There was a far greater variety in terms of background and experience than I had encountered in my previous headship. They came from industry, business and commerce and from universities and higher education. A number had not taught before. But there were also many from traditional teaching backgrounds. The spread was remarkable.

In thinking about the staff I wanted to recruit, I wanted to get away from the idea that you had the teaching staff on one side and technicians, secretaries, and the like on the other side. In too many schools I have heard comments like 'They are only the secretaries'. I think the secretaries have a very important role. So also does the caretaker. I wanted to involve everybody in doing things. Therefore, the secretary or the caretaker can teach if they want. In fact, they did. We have an enrichment programme which I deliberately put in because I thought it would be a motivator for the staff. We have a longer day and so we can provide extra enrichments. I asked the staff 'Which four things would you really like to do?' Each was then translated into a course with aims, objectives, progression and so on built in. These courses are the enrichments that we offer to the students, who can choose from a range of over 100 enrichments. They choose them each term and can spend time at something they are really interested in or something they enjoy. In my experience if someone is excited and enthusiastic about a topic, it switches on students' enthusiasm. I thought this would help to make both students and staff well motivated.

Another aim was to provide a different system to the one where heads and deputy heads of department did the interesting things, and most other members of staff were left feeling that they could not take a lead until they, in their turn, became heads and deputy heads of departments. We also have a very different salary structure, with no allowances, so staff do not say all the allowances have been used so people who warrant an allowance must wait until one becomes available. I did not have heads of year because I believe everybody should have the opportunity to exercise pastoral leadership in the same way they have the chance to exercise academic leadership. In my experience, the existence of posts such as heads of year tends to encourage staff to pass pupil problems on to them rather than trying to deal with them themselves. What I did instead was to make each member of staff a form tutor with a responsibility for being the point of contact with parents. They each have about twenty-four students and are totally responsible for that form. They can phone up parents regularly for good or bad reasons. They can invite them in, write letters to them. They do everything. They get support from the manager if they need it, but they are the point of contact. They follow the students through their years at the college, and get to know them and their families and to develop relationships. The form tutor is therefore the most important person in the college for pastoral contact.

PR: Who are the managers?

VB: I started with four managers, it grew to six and now I have ten. They have very different roles. In most schools you have the head, deputies, senior teachers, heads of year, heads of department and so on. I rolled all that together and created area managers. I gave them administrative tasks as though they were deputies, curriculum tasks similar to those of a head of department and a pastoral responsibility. I tried to set up a system which embraced all these managerial tasks without curtailing time in the classroom. Too often, under the traditional system, when you wanted to be a deputy you had to leave the academic side behind. Here, they retain contact with an academic subject and also hold other kinds of responsibilities. As the college grew, so too did the managerial structures. I now have ten

managers, their responsibilities can best be represented diagramma-
tically (see Figure 3.1):

As you can see, they are not all curriculum managers now
although all have a supportive role and a delegating role. They make
things happen but in doing so allow others to contribute. In that
context they are expected to monitor, evaluate and act as mentors. It
has taken a long time to get the roles understood, as changing a
culture is hard. Changing traditional expectations on school management structures and salary structures is also very hard. People come
with a certain amount of knowledge and attachment to what they
have experienced previously. I now have about 120 staff, over half of
whom have never worked anywhere else. It is also a very young staff,
although this has been beneficial. At least they have not come with
fixed and preconceived ideas about what school structures should
look like. That also has disadvantages because they come to believe
that this is the norm. To some extent it can make some staff com-
placent as their expectations about what is the norm are raised.

PR: What kind of a manager are you?

VB: I am not sure, perhaps you ought to ask my staff. I suspect
some would describe me as a benevolent dictator. To an extent,
when you are setting something up, you have to be autocratic. You
have to be clear in your mind where you are going or things do not
move. If they do, it often happens in an uneven and fragmented way.
I am trying to create a situation where others can take a major lead in
the way in which we develop. As this is a team effort, there has to be
a leader who ensures developments take place with the right aims
and objectives, and according to a development plan. Our development plan was produced in a bottom-up way with everybody
involved and hopefully there is a feeling of 'ownership' and responsibility by all.

PR: You said your aim was to make Kingshurst different. How is it
different?

VB: The college has had many and varied visitors lately. They all
comment on the ability of the students to communicate with them.
The fact that they look them straight in the eye and talk in a very
clear and lucid way. They say that, when they walk around, the
students look as though they are involved and happy. The catchment
area of the college is a social priority area, with many wards having a
high level of deprivation. A visitor last week said she thought we had
created here an environment and culture, so that students seemed
the same as those who went to Eton. That to me is a fine compli-
ment.

When I started at the college in 1987 I spent some time with an

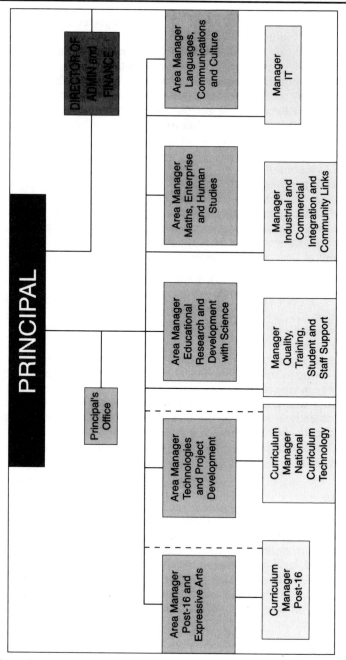

Figure 3.1

architect deciding how the building was to be refurbished. His ideas were very traditional, with English groups together and the Sciences together, etc. It was like any other school. We had to deliver the whole curriculum in a tall four-storey block that consisted of many small, dark rooms and lots of narrow corridors. We created an environment which put a premium on lots of light and space, and knocked down every possible wall, just leaving the load-carrying ones. I produced corridors with uplighters to create a quiet restful atmosphere, large social areas and individual work areas, built another building to link in and also refurbished more buildings. We have kept to the concept of the spread of clusters of rooms. I have always felt that one of the problems in many schools is that staff do not talk to each other across curriculum areas. For example, all your scientists go and have their coffee in their prep rooms but they do not really mix with other staff. By mixing rooms around you are creating circumstances for staff to meet together and talk to each other, which facilitates the development of real cross-curricular links and enables ideas to be shared across subjects. Some things which you might be doing in Maths could be very beneficial in other lessons. The college is designed with the idea of enabling the development of cross-curricular links. Such an approach has possible disadvantages as well as advantages, as it means that subject teachers are spread all over the place, which has its problems in developing co-operative work.

PR: You did not create such things as Humanities or English suites of rooms?

VB: That was a conscious decision. It was also to some extent forced on us because initially we had to deliver the whole curriculum in a four-storey block. We were doing more than just making a virtue of necessity, as the choice was a deliberate one.

PR: Creating an appropriate environment within the school is very important to you?

VB: Getting the environment right was crucial but not the only thing. I also wanted proper recognition of teachers. Teaching is a profession which has experienced a great deal of 'knocking' in recent times. There are some excellent teachers, and as a profession it is full of committed people. However, too many people go into teaching as a last resort. I did myself. Perhaps some see it as a nice nine-to-four job. We have not always attracted into teaching creative and innovative people. I wanted to try to raise the status of teachers so that people realised how hard-working they are. In too many schools problems were created because of the structure of the salary scales, as they were then, with a hierarchical structure and a spread of allowances. Once you have given out the available allowances anybody else, however good or dedicated, was stuck. If you want to promote somebody you had to wait for somebody to leave. This is very demotivating and stifling. We drew up our own salary structures, which involved no normal allowances, nor heads of department, heads of year and deputies. I had always felt that if you were a head of department you would enjoy the academic contact and the classroom contact, but if you then decided to be a deputy you had to leave the classroom behind. That is sad. Also, when schools changed status to become comprehensive, they created the head of year type role simply as a means of giving people allowances. I do not think you can or should try to separate the academic and the pastoral. Everybody should be a pastoral teacher in the same way that everybody should be an academic teacher. So I did not want heads of year. Furthermore, deputies too often are rather low level administrators, which seems a great waste of talent.

Staff found the system difficult to understand at first, but when we produced clear and full job descriptions, it was better. Staff became more comfortable with the system as a whole and their work within it. People had not experienced the flexibility it offered elsewhere. They did panic a bit about status and what was expected of them. We produced the job descriptions on the computer and used a template so there was some uniformity and compatibility. Depending upon their role, they picked up 'bits' from the template. This enabled us to build up a general set of responsibilities which all shared, then add to this specific responsibilities for particular individuals. As soon as we did this, staff knew where they and others were going and what was happening.

If that was one fundamental step, another was the idea of the form tutor as the most important person in the life of students. The idea is to try to develop a relationship with the parents and in doing so to gain experience of working with them. It was a way of ensuring form tutors got to know their students and their parents. They deal with all contacts, but if necessary, the area manager can assist. It is a high risk strategy but it has brought great benefits to the students and to staff development.

PR: All that is very different from what exists in much of the rest of the educational system. Did you have difficulties in getting it accepted?

VB: Yes. People have felt uneasy. In the state sector they know where they are and what salary they are getting. There has been some concern and I am still not sure we have entirely got over this. The new salary structure which the state sector now has, shows similarities, so it will help the problem. We have had yearly reviews, operate an appraisal system and have an element of performance-related pay. The sponsors have very generously made some money available each year.

PR: How do you see yourself as a headteacher?

VB: Gosh, what a question. I have had two quite different head-ships, my headship at Stourport was completely different from this one. It was far less stressful, much less in the public eye with less to do. However, I am sure that staff at Stourport would say I worked incredibly hard. If it is possible, I work twice as hard here. The stresses and strains are very different. Being the first head of a new type of school has its own difficulties, but it has been very exciting and has had all sorts of rewards and benefits. I have visited the United States to look at American schools and spoken at conferences all round the world. It has been a bit like living in a dream world. However, the fundamental in both establishments is the students. They are what it is all about and if you are doing a good job for them, then the rest of it matters very little. Headship here is dealing with so many more people than is usual, such as the DFE, our sponsors, the industrialists and politicians. Here I am the chief executive, at Stour-port, although the school was a big one with over 1200 pupils, the job never seemed as big.

PR: Are the conventional categories into which educationalists are sometimes classified — such as conservative or progressive — rel-evant to you? Also how do you see yourself as a manager — are you a democrat or an autocrat or whatever?

VB: I am a progressive. In both my headships I have had to be fairly autocratic as I had to bring about change. It was necessary to have a very clear vision of where we were going. In order to get there you sometimes had to be a benevolent autocrat. Now it is more about being a leader of a team of capable and dedicated people who con-tribute in various ways. I think that managing change in an organis-ation forces you to go through a series of stages. At the beginning you need a clear vision, you need to know where you are going and to have a clear sense of direction. Only when you have this can you have an input from other people in achieving that change. Your leadership then needs to change to cope with this situation. So, for example, as my area managers become more used to their roles and more confident in undertaking their responsibilities, it becomes possible to delegate more and more responsibility to them, and, in turn, to delegate to other staff. As staff become more and more confident, they can delegate so the whole organisation gradually gets used to working in this way.

PR: So in your view a headteacher needs to be fairly autocratic in the early stages of the management of change if they want to succeed?

VB: I think so. You have to be totally convinced about what you want to do. In public you must have no doubts that what you want to do is right and that it can be done. Your attitude should be very positive and confident.

PR: How do you lead the staff as a whole? Have you got a central management team? Do you have anything like a conventional deputy?

VB: My deputy is in fact the Director of Administration and Finance. I felt that schools are often narrow, so this was an ideal opportunity to bring in somebody with a different background and experience to the management of the college. One of the criticisms about educationalists is that too many of them went to school, went to university and then went back to school. I wanted to get away from that. So my director of administration and finance, who used to be a director for one of Hanson's companies, is my deputy. He comes to management meetings and brings a totally different viewpoint. This helps him sometimes to challenge our fixed assumptions and to put in ideas very different from the rest of us, which can be beneficial. The area managers have a rota each month, when they carry the responsibility when both my deputy and I are away from the college.

PR: His background is not in education?

VB: He is an industrialist, who worked on the shop floor initially and progressed to MD at Ever Ready. He took early retirement but was phoned up by one of Lord Hanson's colleagues and asked if he would like to help with setting up the CTC at Kingshurst. He came here as the project executive. As such he was involved in my appointment. I came to believe that he brought a very different dimension to the management of the college and so I persuaded him to give up his consultancy and to become director of administration and finance.

PR: How are staff supported if they have problems here? To what extent is your deputy involved in this and how?

VB: The form tutor is at the front line. Then the appropriate manager supports the form tutor. If more help is needed they ask one of the managers who carry the overall responsibility for the pastoral system. We have been fortunate. Although many of our students come from working-class backgrounds they have adapted to the freedom and trust the flexibility of the environment we have tried to create. We leave large amounts of equipment around all over the place. No doors are locked. The pupils can go anywhere. They are trusted. They have responded as mature adults.

PR: Do the social areas apply to the students as well? Are they like 'houses' within traditional pastoral care systems?

VB: No they are not like houses. There are just little social areas all around the college. If you walk around the college you will find students sitting around working or talking. They work in teams. Whatever we do is team based. For example, form tutors meet as year tutors. For example, all year seven tutors meet together. Different members chair the meeting and take the minutes to vary the experience. We have many co-ordinators, e.g. BTEC or IB. Staff are in different teams and have different roles in these teams. Students work in teams too. It could well be you will find groups of students working in one or other of the social areas. They might be working with the computer, or on the floor doing some drawings or building up a project. Students understand the value of support and co-operation and sharing skills — sometimes better than the staff.

PR: That presumably means almost every member of staff carries responsibility for leading a team? The criteria for selecting team leaders has less to do with their position in the school's formal hierarchy and more to do with their expertise and experience in the particular case? In some cases this could be a young or new member of staff.

VB: That is right. Why not?

PR: One of the criticisms sometimes made of the kind of anti-bureaucratic approach you describe is that it only works if it is driven by populistic yet autocratic leadership from the top. Those who take this view tend to argue that, whatever its limitations, a bureaucratic system has the merit of ensuring that power within an organisation is shared at a number of levels. You have the leader but you also have others who exercise power and authority within a system of checks and balances. Without this there is a tremendous emphasis on the leader and upon his or her power.

VB: I had not thought of that. I just felt that I had been frustrated in some of my jobs because I have never been able to do some of the things which I thought were important and which I had wanted to do. This is why I feel that one of the ways of motivating people is to give them the opportunity to do what they want to do, and then hold them responsible for it. I believe our system is working well now, and many staff have benefited from the experience, with some obtaining promotion as a result. There has been a great deal of discussion about the approach. The concept of the form tutor being so important works very well.

PR: The system seems highly organic, requiring strong leadership to work, particularly in its early stages. Do you see yourself as a charismatic leader?

VB: That is not for me to say. I have always been confident, doing what I believe and the development at Kingshurst comes into that category. I am quite happy though, to say I have made mistakes. Not everything necessarily works, it may need modifying. But what is important is that we learn from mistakes.

PR: What would you describe as the biggest mistake you have made?

VB: Did you have that question on the list you sent me? (laughs).

PR: No.

VB: My biggest mistake was in assuming that everybody is like me, and feels comfortable with change and a flexible system. I like change and freedom but I rather over-estimated the extent to which others would as well. Some staff needed more structure. Having altered all the traditional ideas of organising a school, I expected staff to adapt. I did not realise the significance of the security of providing staff with what they are familiar with — English suites and Science suites being what people tend to be used to. We went for clusters of rooms for subjects which has disadvantages but there are also disadvantages in having suites. If you have the subject all together, curriculum isolation can develop. A few staff do not like or cannot cope with our system. I recall one who stayed for a very short time. That is fine. Everybody is not going to like the same kind of thing. Just as everybody should have a choice of school so too should staff. Ours is very different from a traditional environment.

   The college has changed and grown since its origins. We now have our own day nursery, offer evening classes, are linked with the local TEC piloting GNVQs pre-16 and have a unique post-16 curriculum. Also we have visitors constantly, plus visits from industry, business and commerce. It is very different.

PR: How do you relate to pupils, to parents and to the local community?

VB: When we started off we had 180 students and of course I knew them all. It is nice to know them and stop in the corridor to talk to them. In any case the students are very friendly here. They are responsive, which is great. When we grew it became harder and harder to get to know them all but I think it is very important to try to achieve this. I put a lot of time and effort into developing and implementing ways of doing so. For example, I have lunch-time meetings with all of the post-16 students in their subject groups. I get an opportunity to chat and they can feed back information about their course, how it might be improved, things which could be changed in the college or whatever. I see students regularly when they are given effort grades for good work. I ask the form tutor to send six students they would like me to see for various reasons. I would see them after their report. I have been seeing students all day today, for example. It is only for a couple of minutes, but you can learn a lot. Also you begin to get to know the students and they have a chance to get to know you. I always find that I seem to generate an agenda after I have seen students in this way. You identify things which you need to do or talk to someone about. Students show me work regularly. I have some stickers (little badges) which we stick on and laugh together about whether it is an octopus or a funny animal but they seem to enjoy that. I think as a profession, we do not praise people enough. I try to walk around as much as possible. I stop and talk to students and notice things which I might otherwise not have noticed. We have many visitors so I am often taking visitors around, and I see what is happening in lessons. I have, in the absence of certain staff, acted as an area manager for spells which has meant I have seen staff regularly in meetings at 'grass roots'. I look at students' workbooks and planners. I also find assemblies useful and important. I think you can give many 'messages' in assembly. I like staff to go to assembly because some are aimed as much at the staff as the students. I do try to get to know all the students, to talk to them, to be available. Many students do just come to my door and say they have a problem which they would like to talk to me about. I value that. I hope I know, despite the fact that we are a big school, most of our students.

With regard to parents we have a support group but it is not yet big enough. As form tutors are the first point of call for parents, I have less contact with parents then I used to in my last headship. There I was always seeing or talking to parents. But my priorities are different here. I am available if parents wish to see me. For example, we have a new format to our reports and a parent did not like it as much as the last format so I saw her at the parents' evening. With our admission policy we interview all students who apply and that includes parents. We do not really need to advertise but we put an advert saying we are recruiting for 11-year-olds. We have applications from between 800 or 900. Members of my management team interview every single one of those applicants. There are about 12 of us interviewing over 800 students and they come with their parents, so at that point the parent is seen by either one of my senior managers or myself. We then have to allocate places according to ability. The parents then come in again to look around the college and to a parents' evening. Our key aim is to enable form tutors to get to know the small group of parents with which they will work in the future. They only have to know about 24 sets of parents. They become familiar with background and family problems.

We have tried to make good links with the local community but this has not been easy to achieve. It has been difficult because some of the animosity generated when we were set up remains. Also I am aware that, because we cannot take anything like the number of students who want to come to us, we inevitably upset people. If we have open days we are saying to the community look what we have got but we are sorry that most of you cannot benefit from it. We participate in musical or other events in the local shopping centre, local library or old people's homes. We have regular lunches where the elderly come to the college and the students look after them. We have an art group for some disabled people who come to the college.

PR: Has the level of hostility which you encounter diminished? Particularly with regard to professional colleagues within the area?

VB: Yes to a degree. I never really believed it would happen. When I applied, it seemed this represented a genuine educational opportunity from which we might all learn. I knew it was going to be political. I was going to do what I thought was right for my students. But it has been very sad to find that so many people would not communicate with me or who have walked away when I have been to meetings. Or said things which are grossly untrue. There are times when it has been upsetting, or stressful and difficult for me and for the staff to cope with. Sometimes when staff have been on a course they have felt that they have been more or less attacked by people who have implied that they have sold their educational soul by accepting an appointment at the college. I have had a number of staff who I would have liked to have appointed here, and who would have liked to have come, but felt that they could not because of their political beliefs or because of how they felt they might be treated by other colleagues outside the college. That has all been incredibly difficult and there is little sign of any real change. I thought things would change but even in our latest round of interviews we have heard from people who told us that 'I told my head of department that I was applying here and I could not believe the way in which I was attacked for doing so'. It does seem, curiously, that the animosity which we encounter is far greater even than that which is experienced by grant-maintained schools.

PR: What is your relationship with your governing body?

VB: I am very much chief executive with a board of directors. I have a director from Hanson and a director from Lucas. They have been there from the beginning. They were on my appointment panel. I get on well with them. As they appointed me I feel they have confidence in me. We have built up the sort of body most likely to benefit the college. I have a group of industrialists, in effect selected these from amongst the firms which gave us the most money. In addition, I have some academics who can assist very much with the curriculum and the running of the college. Finally, I have various others such as an accountant and other similar professionals who can help. We do not have any parents or any teachers either because of the charity status of the college. Or, at least, this is written into our articles and memorandum of association. It is very much a working board of directors. I am accountable to them. I can assure you that when you have governors like Sheila Brown you have to be. I have some high-powered academic governors and industrialists who are on the boards of companies like IMI and GKN. I have found them very challenging but also helpful. I think they see their function as advisory, supporting, facilitating, enabling industry to be brought much more closely into the life of the college. My chairman is an industrialist who was deputy chairman of Turner & Newall, but also has a list of directorships. He has been interested in education for a long time and is involved with ASE, SATIS and Nuffield.

PR: How do you keep up with the pace of change in education?

VB: I am fortunate as I read very quickly and effectively. I was invited to speak in Canada which meant I had to develop a really good understanding of the National Curriculum. The industrialists on my governing body have helped with their own news cuttings services. They probably have better access to information than most of us. I have built us some useful networks including the Principals' Association of CTCs. We are trying to develop TQM in the college and are working very closely with Land Rover. Sponsors give us all kinds of help, support and guidance. But really it is a team effort with staff disseminating information too.

PR: What do you feel about the idea of the National Curriculum?

VB: The idea was a good one. I felt at first that it was a bit overprescriptive and lacked a little, for example, on Religious Education. Now it is unrecognisable. I think that the current 'slimming down' will help.

PR: Can you be a curriculum manager in the sense you could be a decade ago?

VB: It depends on what you mean by a curriculum manager. As a head you still have an overview and an understanding of the whole of your curriculum. It is not possible, though, to know all the strands of every particular subject. Nor should you try to. I try to meet regularly with the staff, rather like I do with the students, so that one gets to know what they are doing, what their curriculum contains and how it is going forward. You can still make suggestions and motivate. We are fortunate because we have a longer day than most schools, so we can do the National Curriculum and lots of other things as well. I feel the National Curriculum is a framework and as such has helped staff. Also, although the recent tests were not ideal, some good came out of them.

PR: What is your function in the management of the curriculum?

VB: I believe passionately that students should have a curriculum which has breadth and balance. I have seen schools where subject empires have been built up and acquired more money and status than others. I see my key task as ensuring a level of fairness across the college as a whole. You might think that as a CTC this should not be so but I believe every subject has its place and its importance. Subjects like Humanities are important because it is part of the whole curriculum which students need so they can become fully rounded people. My role is to protect the interests of the whole against those who are effective in arranging things in their own interest.

PR: What do you see as the function of assessment and its relationship to the National Curriculum? Where do you stand on the disputes currently taking place?

VB: Much of what has been happening is very good. In the past far too much was left to individual teachers or schools. Some people have carried this responsibility very well, others adequately and still others very badly. The levels from 1–10 have helped students set a real goal to aim for. They can feel that they have achieved, and then aim higher. To me, much of what has been attempted in assessment is potentially beneficial.

PR: Reflecting back on eleven years of experience of headship, what aspects do you most enjoy and what, if anything, do you hate?

VB: I have great difficulty with that question. Especially in terms of what I hate. I think I enjoy everything. I love innovating as I am not a maintenance manager. I have been fortunate in the schools I have been working at, because I have been able to innovate. Although I think that in part you make your own good fortune. Much change has been necessary and I have had the opportunity of trying things out. I have really enjoyed both of my headships and would find it difficult to identify things which I have not enjoyed. Having said that, the thing I least enjoy is having to fight for money and plan before the 'goal posts' are in place. My biggest problem is money. When we started Lord Hanson paid the first million into the fund, although I did not see any of that, as it paid for the site. Later, we used another £1.2m we had raised to pay for the bricks and mortar and for equipment such as tables and chairs. We had nothing left to buy the kinds of extras which might make the college distinctive. As you know, we have been in a recession over the last three years so it has been very difficult to raise money. I have to spend hours trying to raise money. I enjoy walking around talking to the students who are wonderful. They are my best ambassadors. Most come from working-class backgrounds but they talk eloquently and confidently to all.

PR: How do you cope with stress?

VB: There has been much stress but I cope well. I am able to sleep and switch off. I have always been interested in antiques and used to go to auctions in my spare time. I built up loads and loads of antiques and many years ago decided to set up a shop. I enjoy going to car-boot sales looking for bargains. When I came here I kept the shop for the first few years but did not have any time to buy new things. So I closed it. But I still have many antiques, and hope to start it again soon. I do have two children so they have taken some of my time but I regret I have not been able to give them as much time as I would have wished. This is a most stressful job but I seem to thrive on it.

PR: How important a driving force in your career has been the assumption that headship is for men and not really for women?

VB: I thought that until I got my headship. I always felt that I was the best person for the job, but that they might not give it to me because I was a woman. I have been lucky. I enjoy interviews and obtained more or less every job I applied for until I started applying for headships. I was young. I had a young family. I was actually told at one interview that I was the best person, but that I had far too many interests and couldn't give enough time to being a head. This upset me for a while. It was at that point that the head at Pershore encouraged me to apply for the post which I eventually got. It was a big school and I did not think I would get it because I am a woman. Since obtaining this headship, I now think being a woman is an advantage. It can also be a disadvantage. People consider me as a rather strong and dominant person — in a man this is perceived as being a good quality, but in a woman . . . !

PR: Do you think women manage headship differently than men?

VB: I am not sure whether one ought to say this but I think women are generally more caring and more compassionate than men. I also think women are better than men at coping with a large number of things at the same time. We are used to having to cope simultaneously with problems of the family, the house, food, etc. I find 'juggling lots of balls' at the same time very stimulating. However, women are their own worst enemies. If only they would push themselves forward a little more. I try to appoint women managers and give women responsibility. The girl students need to be prepared and encouraged to become good leaders. I think an appropriate role model or models is very important. It is interesting to note that the number of women reaching headship and other high positions has increased dramatically.

PR: Where do you go to next?

VB: I wanted to be a head and therefore have achieved my main career aim, but I have always taken the view that something else exciting might come along and I need to be ready for it. That I should find what I am doing exciting is important to me. Since I have been here, I have tried to be involved in things both inside and outside the college. This has helped me to be a better head. I am a non-executive director on Solihull health authority, which has brought me in contact with hospitals, the community at large, the sick and the elderly. This has facilitated work experience for students, helped me to identify potential speakers, and find 'real' projects for students to complete. Being a governor at the University of Central England for five years has helped me to develop links with higher education. I chair their audit committee so I have become familiar with financial matters. I have many contacts with industry and business, have attended Ashridge management courses, lectured abroad and have 'suffered' a plethora of media interest. Other things that are beneficial to the college include my being trained as an OFSTED inspector. In thinking about what I might do next, I do have a strong social conscience and I think there is a lot of wastage of talent in this country. I could have been one of them if things had been different. I was lucky in my upbringing but there are many children who are not so lucky. We are an all-ability college with the average IQ below 100. If our pupils, from all walks of life, can achieve more than they ever dreamt possible then I will feel this has been a worthwhile contribution. As you get older and a bit more philosophical you become increasingly interested in putting things back.

PR: Has the school been researched?

VB: When we developed the post-16 curriculum, we had a book published on its uniqueness. I talked to sponsors, parents and students. It appeared the following skills were necessary — communications, numeracy, business understanding, science, modern foreign language, information technology and leadership. These became our core and everybody does them all. 'A' Levels did not fit this, as they are narrow and arbitrary, so we discarded them and went for the International Baccalaureat instead. That fitted in ideally with our notion of the core. We decided to go for the vocational BTEC courses, so we offered a whole spread of courses including the performing arts and business and finance. Last year we piloted GNVQs in all five areas. This year we are offering science GNVQ post-16 and also all our 14-year-old students are studying one intermediate GNVQ. We are the only school in the country to offer GNVQ in all five areas in addition to the National Curriculum. All that is tremendously exciting. There is no doubt that being innovative and a pioneer is difficult. The staff need much support and have found it very stressful. Not only have we been engaged in all this change but we are in a goldfish bowl. Not everybody would be sad to see us stumble. I have learnt how to cope with that but even I get a bit depressed that some people continue to be so anti-CTCs, as we are providing a very good education. I would like to spend a term away writing up what we have done, perhaps I will. In our second year Aston University, Geoffrey Walford, did research here and wrote a book.

PR: Are you disappointed that there are not more CTCs?

VB: Well, there will be fifteen in September. The one in Bristol may be the last. I hope they can be of benefit to the whole of the education system. I am not unhappy about being one of the few but I am unhappy about the views people have us. Often when people come here they say 'I did not realise you were like that' or 'I did not think you were doing this kind of liberal education'. That is sad.

PR: Do you feel the school is your school?

VB: Having been involved from its inception, of course I feel like that. However, in saying that, none of it could have been achieved if it had not been for my excellent team of staff, and also the support of governors, sponsors, parents and others.

4 Peter Downes

with Michael Marland

MM: What brought you into teaching?

PD: I have always wanted to be a teacher. As far back as I can remember I never wanted to be anything else. My parents told me that I played at being a teacher very early on in my life. When other children were playing cops and robbers or mummies and daddies, I was playing schools. My father (who was a primary school teacher in the second half of his career) actually kept an essay that I wrote when at the age of eight I saw myself as a headteacher at the age of forty. Given that I have always wanted to be a teacher, at secondary school it was only a question of which subject I wanted to teach. I have been interested in teaching *method* as long as I can remember. I have always been very interested in teachers and in the way they taught. I have been very responsive to teachers, both negatively and positively, and I would often, so I was told by my parents, go home and talk about why Mr so-and-so was a good teacher and why Mr so-and-so was not a good teacher. By the time I was in the sixth form at school and was a senior prefect, I was already being used by the teachers as a kind of student teacher when the regular teacher was away. At university I was temporarily interested in the Christian ministry, but deep down I always wanted to be a teacher.

MM: That suggests that you came from a church family.

PD: Yes, we were fairly keen middle-of-the-road Anglicans with a strong Christian service ethic in the family. My parents were anxious that I should have the best possible education because they had both been frustrated in their education; they were both quite bright but lived in Salford at the time of the Great Depression and therefore both had not been able to fulfil their educational potential. Therefore they wanted me to achieve everything I possibly could. I got a scholarship to Manchester Grammar School and later a scholarship to Christ's College, Cambridge and so on, and they fully supported me in wanting to make the best of my education. But alongside that there was a very strong public service concept, which could be paraphrased as: God has given you great gifts and you have got to use them to serve other people and the way you can serve is through education.

MM: That's what brought you into teaching and it also moves to what brought you into headteaching because that was implicit in being a teacher.

PD: I enjoy the process of teaching in the classroom, I am fascinated by the actual performance and the capacity of one person to inspire and instruct others, that is something that I continue to find intriguing. But I have also always been interested in the ethos of the community and it seems to me that the way you organise a community, the principles on which it is based can also be very influential. I do actually believe that a school as a community can make a difference to performance. I sense that instinctively and I think it has been very well proven by research. Quite early on in my teaching career I began to be aware of what we would now call 'management issues', the way people were handled, the way the school related to the pupils and to the parents, and I almost naturally evolved towards a leadership role. I don't think I set out consciously to plan a career for headship. In fact my career is very odd in that my first twelve years were back in the school where I'd been a pupil myself. Nowadays it would be very unusual to advocate that someone went back to their old school, and similarly to spend twelve years in your first post is unusual. I was head of department by the time I was twenty-seven and perhaps Manchester Grammar School was an exceptional setting in the sense that it was seen as an outstanding place to be at. I found myself at about thirty-two having been in just one institution apart from Cambridge and a year in Paris and, therefore, I deliberately took the sideways step into a comprehensive school and that's where I feel I really began to be much more interested in school leadership. I was with Harry Judge at Banbury School for a few years, and then went straight from head of department to headship, missing out on being a deputy head. So I think I began to feel in my mid to late twenties the way schools were organised could significantly affect children's lives both in terms of their academic performance and in terms of their general development.

MM: So during your period at Banbury you must have decided that headship was the next step.

PD: Yes. To work for Harry Judge is always an inspiration. I think I have learnt from all the heads I have worked with. One tends to admire their strengths and perhaps think that in some ways one would do other things differently. As a person I react very strongly to other people. I am very quick at picking up ideas from others and learning from them. I will also pass on good ideas like a transmitter. I think there is a particular type of person who has a special gift for being ready to take up other people's ideas but also passes them onto others effectively and persuasively.

MM: That's very interesting. The next point that interests us was illustrated rather well by your, shall we call it, 'unusual' preparation, which is how did you at all manage to prepare for that first headship? And what was it like being head for the first time?

PD: I think my preparation was skimpy. I went on one preparation for headship course run by the College of Preceptors and, although there were one or two useful parts to the course, I was very frustrated by it. I think it was because I had been at Banbury School where I felt that we were doing so many experimental things at that particular time that were almost ahead of the game in terms of being aware of the issues. My specific preparation for headship was minimal other than, especially after I had gone comprehensive, trying to read as widely as possible, going on lots and lots of day conferences and being aware of the issues. But in terms of specific training — nothing.

MM: Which is fairly common. But what you were looking at in these conferences was not specifically headship: it was those matters which are common to everyone else.

PD: Issues of behaviour, or ability grouping. For example, I was involved at Banbury in this great mixed-ability/streaming research project which happened exactly at the time I was there. I got very caught up in all that and its implications. The outcome of that project in terms of the way schools are managed and organised is directly germane to headship. Now you can rightly say I have not been specifically trained for headship, but the fact of being involved in a major educational research project was a very good preparation for headship.

MM: That's very interesting. That leads one to the experience of your first headship at Henry Box in Witney. Was it as you expected it to be? Or were things coming at you that you didn't expect?

PD: What surprised me most of all was the expectation of the staff that you had some instant wisdom to pass on and this great sense of the 'office' giving you authority. Now I had not been used to that in that my attitude towards the heads that I had worked with was obviously to respect their ultimate authority but to have a robust relationship and give-and-take and to challenge and to discuss.

When people came and said things like 'what is your policy on this, we will do it' that took me by surprise. My inclination was to say, 'hold on, what is *our* policy; what do you think it should be; let's talk about it'. I think I was rather less authoritarian than they had been used to. The previous head, who had died suddenly in office in his late fifties, had been twenty-five years as head and it had been a small grammar school run with a family atmosphere. He had lived on the premises, and had become very much the focal point, the father figure, and people did what he said. This expectation of *ex-officio* omniscience was the main surprise for me.

The other surprise was the way one found it difficult to make slightly facetious, casual or humorous remarks without people either taking them seriously or misinterpreting them and passing them on, so that sometimes staff got entirely the wrong end of the stick as the result of a quite casual throw-away remark. The position made me become more serious and more cautious than instinctively I felt I was.

MM: If we move to your views as a head in your present school, could we think about those who work with you in managing the school. What do you see as the role of your senior managers?

PD: In a school the size of mine, nearly 1800 pupils, the senior managers are virtually my equal in the sense of the shared responsibility that we have for the school. Each of my deputy heads has a sectional responsibility for a part of the school which in terms of pupils is bigger than most of the schools in the country. My head of middle school (Years, 9, 10, 11) is responsible for 800 pupils which is equivalent to a very substantial secondary school. Lower school covers Years 7 and 8, and then after the middle school 9, 10 and 11 there is another deputy in charge of the sixth form. Each deputy has a number of whole-school roles as well, one co-ordinating curriculum, one co-ordinating appraisal, another on staffing, and so on. But they each have a versatile role as mini-head of a school within the larger school. Therefore, in that section they lead a team of heads of house and tutors, they are responsible for discipline, the attendance, the behaviour and the extra-curricular life just as if it were a mini-school. They have a great deal of individual responsibility but it is crucial that we meet as a team very regularly; we co-ordinate what we are doing and we try to get the interpretation of policies consistent across the whole school.

MM: Do you find a conflict between their age-focus role, head of lower school, and their school-focus policy role?

PD: No, we haven't found that. We move people around from section to section and it is our policy now, with changes in personnel, that people will rotate. So it is already planned that the present head of lower school will become deputy head in charge of middle school next year and new people will come in. We have two recent changes of deputy headship and that has enabled us to institute this scheme.

MM: Within their whole-school roles who, for instance, co-ordinates the curriculum?

PD: We have a deputy head who co-ordinates the curriculum, who is one of the three, but he has a director of studies who is a senior teacher, a scale-E post, who assists in that and he also has a senior timetabler, another scale-E post, so that the deputy head, though he co-ordinates the work of a team, is not lumbered with a lot of the practicalities, thanks to having a specialist director of studies and a senior timetabler.

MM: If we leave those particular people, we are interested in the relationship between the head and all the staff. How can you in a school your size feel that you are leading all these teachers? Or do you consider that an old-fashioned concept anyway?

PD: I think it is a slightly old-fashioned concept in one sense but I think the teachers still want to feel that they can relate to the head and they still feel the head has a titular role. Although I try to get over to my colleagues that if they speak to myself or *any* of the deputies it is like speaking to me, they still feel in certain cases that they want me personally to be aware of their concerns. They still have this inherited view that it is the head in the end who makes the decisions, although in my own school I feel that I make hardly any decisions personally. We arrive at a decision by a process of consultation which is long and tortuous and sometimes the outcome of that is that I am implementing decisions that would not be the decisions I would have made if I had been running matters on my own. The decision has arisen out of staff consultation. Clearly the staff still feel they want to have this direct relationship to the head and senior staff. What we have done in order to go some way to achieve that is we have 'attached' deputies and the head to three academic departments each, so we are each now very much closer to the delivery of the curriculum and therefore well placed in terms of quality appraisal and preparation for OFSTED because we have got our finger more directly on the pulse of the school's curriculum life than we used to have.

MM: Therefore of the twenty new teachers that have just been appointed they will fall into different departments, therefore a head or a deputy will be responsible for their welfare as well as the leadership of that department.

PD: Not quite. The leadership of the department is obviously the direct responsibility of the head of the department. Our role is to monitor and to support but also to have pastoral oversight through the head of the department for the teachers who happen to be in that department. So a teacher who wants, for example, to have a career discussion or an in-service discussion, outside the appraisal process, just the sort of professional contact one would hope to have, would have access to a deputy head or the head who would know the work of that department fairly well. In individual cases, we might share out the discussion, sometimes personality is more appropriate, sometimes a person wants to speak to a man or a woman, and we sometimes agree among ourselves to take on particular cases. I see us as a *team* of four. Clearly I have got a co-ordinating role, I have got the responsibility, I have got certain clearly defined tasks in relation to the governors, in relation to the parents, in relation to the press and the media and so on, which I take on. But, for the running of the school, we are very much a team.

MM: I was going to move to parents next. What do you see as your role apropos of parents? Is it more significant? Or do you divide that amongst the others too?

PD: I undoubtedly front the work with parents, because I have made this a particular feature of my headship. I have always felt from very early on in my teaching that we under-use and under-involve parents. In my first post after only six years of teaching, I was responsible at Manchester Grammar School for setting up a parents' association which they hadn't had. It was quite unusual in 1966 to be setting up parents' associations. In every school that I have worked in I have been very much involved with the parents. I had a very good parents' association in Henry Box at Witney and similarly here we have got an outstandingly good parents' association. My main principle is to try to involve as many people as possible for a small amount, rather than expect a great deal of a clique and I have worked at that policy systematically over ten years now. It has involved an enormous amount of my time and it has been worth it because, although parents recognise that day-to-day tasks are delegated within the school, they still like the human touch of seeing the head personally involved. They still have their own picture of schools as they were in their day when the head was something of a figurehead. I explain to them, that we have a management *team* and that somebody else will deal with this or answer that for you, but they still like the fact that they know the head and the head knows them. I set a pattern in 1982 of regularly consulting the parents, going round to the villages holding a series of meetings in the autumn term where we talk very frankly and very openly about the examination results, about any problems the school has got, and I ask for *their* views. This year we have had a consultation on the Dearing Review. In my meetings with parents, I have explained to them what Dearing has said so far and asked them what they would now like us to say to Dearing particularly about the flexibility of Key Stage 4.

MM: What about their youngsters, their pupils? How do you see the head's role in a school your size with the pupils?

PD: I don't ever make a pretence that I can personally know all the pupils but since we have had our new buildings and we are all on one site I now believe that most of the pupils know who I am. I appear at or take assemblies very regularly. We have a cycle of assemblies where I am on duty with a deputy one week and the heads of house take assemblies the alternate week. So I am seen in that titular role and I hope I have a cohesive function, I symbolise 'the school'. That is what people expect and I think you have got to play that role. But I recognise and the pupils have to recognise that day-to-day they are dealing with their teachers, form tutors, their heads of house and their deputy heads. I try to make myself accessible in the sense that I don't walk around ignoring people but I try to get involved with them. I play in the orchestra whenever I can. I take part in the sporting activities; I referee football matches. It is what I call the dipstick approach. I dip in intensively at certain points in the school's life, but I don't make any pretence to know all the pupils and all the activities.

MM: Do certain pupils get referred to you for whatever reason, because another deputy head has done his or her best but wants another opinion?

PD: Yes. There is a chain of referral. There will come a point where I might be brought in because the children concerned had gone through all the stages of treatment and I will generally be brought in when things are getting pretty serious and exclusion looms. Then there are a few children who sidetrack the system altogether, whose parents will ring me direct with a problem and will expect me to do something about it. I often will then go back down the line to find out what has actually happened. That is all part of this head–parent relationship. If a parent does approach me, I never brush them off and say 'that's not my job, you must refer to someone else'. I say to them 'you understand that in a school of this size I do not know personally the details of your case, but I will look into it for you and I will come back to you as soon as possible'.

MM: What would you say to the criticism then that that is favouring a particular kind of parent who has the sort of nous or the sort of push to get to the head?

PD: Yes, that is a fair criticism. But the converse would be that I would alienate far more parents if I wasn't seen to be accessible. I am quite open and straightforward with them on this. That if they have a problem, the best person to approach will normally be those at the right level, but because it is a big school, parents can't always know the intricacies of the internal management of our secondary school and their instinct will be to go to the head. So if they go to the head, I as head will say 'I am very pleased to hear from you, I am sorry you have got a problem, I will look into it and will come back and we will then talk it over'. It may very well be that when they come in to see me I will say, 'Pleased to see you, I understand this is the problem, now I would like you to discuss it with the . . .'

MM: Let's move to the parents of the children. You mentioned you go to the villages, which is going into the communities but what about other community contacts? Does the head have any responsibility to the community in other representations?

PD: Yes. I accept all the invitations I get within the limits of human possibilities to all the local events, so I attend all the district council receptions, the town council receptions, I am a member of Rotary, largely because of all the contacts that there are between the school and Rotary. I haven't really got time to be a proper Rotarian, but I think it is important to be involved. I sit on the community education panels, I attend virtually every meeting I am invited to. I can't actually physically go to them all but I either go, or make sure that somebody represents me there. In a small town like this you have got a very strong relationship between the school and the community. This is particularly true in the case of Hinchingbrooke which is still in the eyes of the local population the old grammar school really; it is the grammar school gone comprehensive. Boys and girls are still wearing the same uniform that they did. We have still got the same house system that not only their parents went through, but also their grandparents. So there is a very strong community sense and the head of the school is expected to be a local figure.

MM: Can we look at one other external group, which is the governors, who are both internal and external, since the big changes of '86 and '88 legislation. What do you see nowadays as the role of the governors and of the head?

PD: The big change now is that the governors are very much more knowledgeable about the detail of the school but it is not they who 'run' the school. We have a clear understanding that it is the head and the staff who run the school — but the governors know a great deal more about it. The structure we have developed is a substantial committee structure and every governor is on at least one committee. I and the senior team spend quite a time preparing materials for governors' committees where we look at things in considerable detail. In addition every governor is attached to a department and every governor is attached to a section of the school so they have a number of contact points. They now come to meetings knowing a great deal about the school in detail but they have to take the overview when they come to the governing body and try to evaluate the advice that is given. I now put to them alternative strategies and they sometimes choose to do things that I would not myself have chosen, particularly in the financial area. Two or three years ago we had a little money in hand, about £30,000; we appeared to be able to cover the school costs and I put to them the alternatives of what we could do with the extra money, and they chose expenditure headings which would not have been my priority. Now we are in the opposite position of having to cut costs; we had to cut out £100,000 last year and we are going to have to cut out another £100,000 this year. And I am having to put to them the various alternatives and ask them what they would do. Sometimes they dig their heels in on points of detail. This year, for example, they insisted that we should keep in the ALIS survey (Advanced Level Information System), whereas I would have made that a small saving. Broadly speaking they are fully involved, they know what's going on, but they don't interfere in the day-to-day nitty-gritty. They work hard; they have an extensive programme of meetings. I calculated that I attend twenty-nine governors' meetings a year, including two full meetings a term and committee meetings. This is slightly larger than normal because, in addition to being school, we also have a foundation, therefore there is a foundation management committee. In a sense you ought to subtract four or five meetings for that, but it is still a hefty programme. It virtually writes out every Monday evening for some form of governors' committee meeting.

MM: You have seen this school through from being a LEA controlled school to being locally managed. What do you see as the new role of the LEA?

PD: With local financial management in 1982 the LEA started to put itself at arm's length and the length of the arm has been increasing as time has gone on. You must remember that Hinchingbrooke was a pilot school for LFM as it then was, so the year I came here, it was with the understanding that schools were going to become more autonomous and that we would detach ourselves more and more from the LEA. In practice we have always had extremely good relations with the LEA. I'm a strong believer in the need for an LEA or some locally accountable body. I haven't supported LMS because I have any grudge against the LEA. I think an LEA should be there to support and to plan. Certain support services could be more cost-effectively provided by an LEA than by independent agencies. There are certain things which are best done collectively. The other most important thing is the planning and the numbers strategy development, which I feel would become very difficult if we were to have administration by a Funding Agency instead of or as well as the LEA.

MM: Do they do anything or demand anything from you that you resent?

PD: At the moment I am rather irritated by the bureaucracy of their financial management systems. I am having something of a dialogue with them about the extent to which they monitor and vet our work. Not because I have anything to fear in terms of audit but they are cross-checking our budget planning in a detail which I think is a waste of time. But in general our relations with the LEA have been good. We value their input.

MM: Could we then move back to teaching. How are you finding it possible to reconcile the external demands for change with focusing on the quality of teaching? Is there a conflict here or is it possible to see these two things separately?

PD: I find the external pressures for change very irritating because I feel the anomaly of the last few years is that while there has been greater so-called *local* management there has been less flexibility in terms of developing a specific curriculum for your school. In terms of the quality of teaching, what we have tried to do is obviously to respect the National Curriculum and so on, but also to get the senior managers of the school into the departments more regularly; that is the way in which we are trying to provide quality assurance. We also do a very rigorous scrutiny of our examination results. I have a statistics officer, who is a mathematics teacher, to whom I pay an allowance of a point, specifically to analyse the examination results. We do a great deal of work on that. We test all our pupils on entry by NFER standardised tests, and then we do our own value-added analysis. We do it subject by subject and by gender so we do a great deal of detailed research on our academic outputs.

MM: One of the interesting things you said in there was that the senior management team are getting into the departments more than perhaps was traditionally the case. Do you have any resentment from the departments of this?

PD: I think it would vary from department to department. On the whole I would say no. I think they recognise that it is necessary. I think people are now having to come to terms with being seen in their classroom, usually as part of their appraisal. For some it is uncomfortable, but I think it is broadly recognised as a job we have got to do. Heads are now being asked why our results are what they are and if we haven't got a clue what's going on in the department, how can we answer that. One of the good things that has developed over the last few years — in spite of all the negative effects of the government's policy — is a generally more positive attitude towards accountability. We needed to become more accountable and we have done so. That accountability has got to be detailed and practical and one of the ways is for the senior managers to be there working within the teaching departments.

MM: If there was the financial leeway, if you were able to say we can show that this particular kind of group of pupils, be it those who come in with low standards, or those who come with high standards, or whatever, are not performing as well as they might, then you could alter your regime to put in extra support.

PD: That's right. But you see we are now so tight financially that we are just simply struggling to survive. It is a question of how the cuts for each successive year can do the least damage.

MM: We have been talking about the school for some time as a whole. If we now come back to where we started which was with you as a head, speaking quite personally, what do you enjoy most about the job? And then in a moment I will ask you what you would like to ditch if you could?

PD: I think that the moments that I enjoy the most are seeing the school working together in extra-curricular productions. That is one of the most personally satisfying aspects of the job. When I see a school play, or a school concert, and I see children's talents being developed and I see parents' responding and I see staff involved — that gives me an enormous amount of personal pleasure. I still get a great deal of pleasure from teaching.

MM: Can you justify the expense of you teaching?

PD: No. I can't on any rational grounds. But I can justify it on the grounds of the morale and the sanity of the head. If a head enjoys his subject, and has something of an academic commitment to his subject, and has, for the sake of argument, been a reasonably good teacher in the past, I think to deprive him or her of the chance still to exercise their basic craft is an impoverishment.

MM: What proportion do you teach?

PD: I am teaching notionally ten out of twenty-five on the time-table, but because of my responsibilities with SHA I 'buy in' some periods and I am actually this year teaching five out of twenty-five, but that's an 'A' Level set and a GCSE set. With examinations to prepare for, it's work I take very seriously. I regard my performance in those lessons as a major part of my work and I don't allow myself to be interrupted. I make a point of being sure that everything is properly prepared and properly marked, even though I am very busy. Hence my interest in your talk this evening on the 'Craft of the Classroom'. So, I get a great deal of pleasure out of teaching, I get a great deal of pleasure out of the extra-curricular life. I get a great deal of pleasure out of my contact with the parents. I don't do that out of a sense of obligation, I do it out of a sense of real enjoyment. Last year we had a summer fete which raised £4000 of which £2000 we gave to the SHA project to build a school in Namibia; well, getting everybody to work together for that, to get the parents, and the pupils and the staff preparing for the day itself was challenging and rewarding. You might regard it as the icing on the cake, but I regard it as more than that, I think it is a community event where we are genuinely working together.

MM: And you run a series of musical concerts?

PD: Yes, that's all part of the promotion of our unusual buildings. The particular circumstances of Hinchingbrooke are such that we can put on all kinds of events and activities in the school buildings. I enjoy the entrepreneurial opportunities of being in a school with a stately home, a country park and a performing arts centre. It is extremely demanding, but very fulfilling.

MM: Let's look at the other side. If you could wipe something off your responsibility list, what do you enjoy least?

PD: At the day-to-day level I enjoy least the errors and the prob-lems that are caused by the way the LEA oversees our finances. One of the few attractions for me of the school becoming grant main-tained is that we could become more genuinely autonomous in the administration of the school.

MM: In terms of the legal requirements concerned it sounds as if the LEA is going further than it needs to in that respect.

PD: I think they have become very pernickety. I think they may have sensed that in some schools things weren't as they should be, and I think they are being over-legalistic in their requirements. I would like to be freer. I am in a real dilemma in relation to GMS. I oppose the concept as such. The idea of free-standing, market-driven schools is anathema to me. But I can see some management simplification in it, which I would welcome. That is the bit that I would like to have and, of course, I would welcome the flexibility of better funding. I also resent the excessive inflexibility of the National Curriculum. I think we are being over-regulated from London. I would like to get back to greater freedom at institutional level, but with clear national guidelines and rigorous scrutiny by OFSTED.

MM: If you were to look at this mixture of the challenges and the pressures, in the peak of your years as a head, what has helped you most as a personal influence on organising and developing the job?

PD: I have drawn a great deal of strength from being a member of the Secondary Heads Association. I value enormously what I learn from colleagues. This is my professional support mechanism. I regularly attend branch meetings and area meetings. I came onto Council quite late on in my career really as I have only been on it for four years. I have worked on several committees and I have tried to contribute through LMS to the better management of schools. I hope that I have been *giving* something but I have also drawn enormous strength from other people. As I said earlier in the conversation, I am the sort of person who is quick to pick up ideas and also quick to transmit and pass them on. I am a great believer in spreading good practice. I don't accept the ethic that if you have a good idea you hold onto it for yourself. I believe that we are all part of a public education service and that good ideas should be disseminated. I see SHA as being the way in which I can fulfil that and that is what has guided me and I have found a great deal of support from working with colleagues locally and nationally. I have enjoyed being very much involved with the LEA in their planning. The Cambridgeshire LEA have encouraged heads to be involved in planning groups. I had two years as a seconded one-day-a-week inspector for the LEA. All this has kept me stimulated and professionally alive.

MM: It wouldn't have been possible to have been entirely locked up within the school. You have got to have that external intellectual and practical input.

PD: Obviously Hinchingbrooke could have taken up my professional life fully because it is such a huge, complex and unusual job. But I valued the external opportunities, and I think the school has benefited from that.

MM: When it comes to the inevitable stresses which could be any aspect of the work that makes your job as head painful sometimes, how do you keep sane?

PD: I have to confess that I probably work too hard. I think I probably work about 75–80 hours a week. Some of that is self-inflicted. As well as my school I have got my SHA work, my external lecturing, my writing and so on, so you might say that I have chosen to make the pressure greater than it needed to be. The difficulty in working such long hours is that I find myself having to make certain decisions without having given the matter enough thought or without having read widely enough. I get anxious about the speed with which I have to react to situations and move from one topic to another. The jumping about from topic to topic is a source of stress. One of the reasons that I enjoy my teaching is that I can do one thing for sixty minutes without any interruption. On the positive side I value my holiday time. I try to get a clear break in the summer and that is when I go back to my French roots. During term I try to have one-night-a-week off, playing in a local orchestra.

MM: You mentioned earlier that central government's curriculum requirements had become too precise and too onerous. To what extent has this meant that you are unable to shape the school curriculum in the way that you wish?

PD: It has meant that I feel I am now less able to cater for the children at the extremes of the ability range. My main worry is that the National Curriculum probably provides an appropriate experience for the majority of children, but the most able and the least able are not well catered for. The most able are not stretched fully. We used to put on a more demanding programme for the most able. It was possible for them to do three separate sciences and two foreign languages, for example, which is extremely difficult now under the new arrangements. And at the other end, we were able to put on some quite imaginative courses for those children who found the full academic curriculum rather daunting. I regret that. That's why I want to press Sir Ron Dearing to try to reduce the compulsory core to about 60 per cent of the total curriculum in Key Stage 4.

MM: Yours would have been a school in which there would not have been any large gaps, like for instance there were some schools in which languages hardly flourished, but you had a pretty broad curriculum.

PD: Yes, three years ago we had, in my view, the ideal curriculum: languages, for example, for all up to fourteen, and guided choice beyond. Practically everybody would do technology, practically

everybody would do at least one Science and one Humanities subject. I think we need guidance into these broad areas but I think to
insist specifically that everybody must do a highly prescribed curriculum is unhelpful.

MM: Finally, to what extent do you see yourself as chief executive
of an organisation or to what extent do you feel this is, in a sense,
'your' school? How personal do you feel about the school?

PD: I feel very personally involved in the school. I feel personally
upset when people speak badly of the school. I feel almost a sense of
guilt when a member of the public, as inevitably happens with 1800
pupils, rings or writes in and says that somebody has done something of which they disapprove. I still feel sufficiently paternalistic to
feel that I have failed. If I see an ex-pupil of mine smoking, for
example, I still feel a sense of failure that somehow they've gone
through my school for seven years and come out and they're still
smoking. On the other side, I feel great pride in the things ex-pupils
achieve. I feel a great concern when ex-pupils let themselves down,
let me down. I must have a strong paternalistic streak, so, yes, I do
feel that it is 'my' school. I feel that the school is based upon features
I attach great importance to: the involvement of parents, the involvement of pupils, the *interactive* nature of the school. I don't feel that I
am here to turn out government calibrated sausages. I feel that the
'sausages' must be *active* sausages, they must be involved in the
evolution of themselves, into many varieties of sausage! I don't have
any particular hang-up on my own 'status'. I don't hold onto any
perks or privileges at all. I don't have any special parking place or
any special loo. I buy my own tickets to go to all school events. I
don't see myself on a pedestal though I recognise that there are times
when the public expectation is that you will fulfil a titular role and I
have to go along with that as expected.

MM: It sounds as if the style and feel and atmosphere of the school
is partly of your creative efforts.

PD: Yes, I think it is, but the creativity needs the support of staff,
parents and pupils if it is to work. I think it takes a while to achieve
progress. One of the things that strikes me is that the larger the
school, the longer it takes to make any significant change and the
more difficult it is because you have got to carry so many people with
you. And I think that inevitably my period as head was marked by
the teacher action of '85 and '87 and that is something which is
almost indelible. That did, as you know, unsettle teachers and shook
a lot of people and shattered some of the principles on which we had
previously worked. I think we are slowly on the way to recovering
from that, but I don't think we will ever fully recover. That was a

great sorrow to me that that happened, just as I was coming into my own in the school. I was fortunate here in that I inherited a school which was very good indeed. I know sometimes people want to become heads in schools that are badly run in order to show how well they can make them work and turn them round. I inherited an extremely well-run school from a previous head who had very high standards and was a meticulous administrator, but I think I have been able to bring something distinctive in terms of a wider range of activities and a greater level of participation. I have also been able to develop the role of the school in the community and particularly this entrepreneurial side of the school, which is both good for the community and good for the school. By entrepreneurial side, I mean the cultural, the artistic and the commercial sides of the school. For example, we now expect to raise £100–150,000 a year from lettings at Hinchingbrooke. That's got a strongly commercial aspect to it, but also it means that the buildings of the school are in use and they are being used almost night after night for conferences, for in-service training, and at weekends for wedding receptions, for banquets, for trade fairs, for annual general meetings. All kinds of things are going on. Now I recognise that there is a financial overtone to all that, but it also means that the school is into the community and the community is in here too.

MM: There's a very real sense in which whilst you are having to do that which a school requires by a range of standards, you are putting your own enthusiasms and your own personality and character at the service of the school, thus it is the expression of your highest ideals and interests.

PD: I believe that we must give *all* children the maximum range of opportunities. Hence my interest in everything that is cultural, musical, dramatic, sporting, and so on. I believe that very strongly. I believe it is our job to extend the abilities of all children and I have no hang-ups at all about doing very well by the most able but here we have also invested just as much in children of low ability. I am quite committed to the idea that children themselves should have an active role in the education they are getting. I would like to go further than current conventions allow in getting student feedback and I would be very pleased to see more systematic student feedback on the quality of the teaching they are receiving. I have already spoken about the extent to which parents are involved. I obviously value and respect the input of the staff that we have and I consider the training of staff, the training and development of my teachers for future responsibilities as an important part of my role. I don't have the view that I have got to hold on to my teachers. I believe that my job is to make this school as good as it possibly can be, but that I am part of a state education system and when the appropriate moment comes for teachers in my school to move onto something else, I don't stand in their way, I won't use salary 'retention points' to hold them with me. I will encourage them, I will give them all possible opportunities so that they will go on to be an excellent head of department, or a deputy head, or head somewhere else. A very important part of the role of headship is to identify and train future leaders of schools and I hope secretly that some of the ideas and the practices and the principles that they have shared at Hinchingbrooke will be spread elsewhere.

MM: I think that that is a lovely place to end. Thank you very much.

5 Elaine Foster

with Michael Marland

MM: What brought you into teaching in the first place?

EF: I suppose teaching was a second favourite of mine. I came here in 1967 to join my parents. I was said to be a bright teenager — I had after all taken the 11+ examinations back in Jamaica and had gone to Manchester High School, and had hoped while I was there to go into medicine. But when I came here, I joined Shireland Girls' School which is a secondary modern school, and the only Science subject I did then was Biology, so that wasn't going to set me up for a career in medicine. So, my second choice was to go into teaching, and this was against the advice of my careers teacher who actually said that I should go into nursery nursing. I suppose he thought it was less strenuous, and that I would probably be better able to cope with nursery nursing rather than teaching.

MM: What took you to that secondary modern school then, given that it didn't have the whole range?

EF: I don't think my parents were aware of the range of schools that were available. They chose the school that was nearest to home.

MM: What examination level could that school go on to?

EF: CSEs. I did CSEs and then I went on and did some GCEs and 'A' Levels at a sixth-form college, and then went on from there. I decided that I would do Religious Education and English because at that time Religious Education was said to be a shortage subject, so I suppose I did have a little bit of forethought, and decided that if I was going to get a job then I really ought to go for something that wasn't so popular.
 So teaching was a second choice. On reflection I can say that I really do enjoy working with children and young people. I think I enjoy the challenges of education. I love being in the classroom. I thrive on that sort of thing. I am not really certain that a black

youngster of sixteen, seventeen, eighteen, in 1967, 1970, could actually have thought that in England it was possible to be a teacher. Had I stayed in the Caribbean, in Jamaica, the range of opportunity would have been different and I think the expectations of people, my family and my friends would have been very different. I think people would have been surprised. Why go into teaching when you could do something else? Because there was that sort of thinking in my family that if you can, then you should at least try. On reflection I can't say that I said, right I am going to be a teacher because I am going to be good in the classroom, or I enjoy working with children. I think it was after going through college and then taking up my first teaching appointment that I felt this is what I really enjoy — being in a classroom and working in the ways in which I have done.

MM: Well, that's very interesting. Then one wants to know — how soon did you think about headship as a possibility?

EF: I don't think I started out thinking that I wanted to be a head. And I think it was quite a while, in fact it was probably only about five years ago that I thought, this is what I would like to do, at which point I had just come to the end of three and a half years of deputy headship and had started to work with Her Majesty's Inspectors. It was probably while I was with HMI that I realised the challenges and opportunities of headship and thought that if I was reading legislation and educational thinking at the political level right, then headship was the place I needed to be. I also realised that a head can actually be very influential in trying to determine the lives and careers of children. I think perhaps that is why I decided that I would like to go into headship.

MM: And you got that understanding more clearly in your HMI years.

EF: Yes, when I had the opportunity to be an observer of headteachers in practice.

MM: Can you remind me, were you seconded from the deputy headship?

EF: That's right. I was seconded from the local authority out of the deputy headship.

MM: And that position was yours to go back to.

EF: Well, yes, I suppose technically I could have done, but because it was likely that I was going to be away for three years, they couldn't have held the position open for me. I think perhaps there were one or two people whose ideas I felt were really interesting. I have known you, Michael, for quite a long time and I was very interested in what made you tick as a head. I'm interested in how some of the theories that you talked about could actually be put into practice. And I did spend quite a number of days before joining HMI looking at some headteachers at work and that I think gave me the opportunity to see a range of practice.

MM: You were able to do that from your deputy head position. Take a day here and a day there. I would have thought that was fairly unusual and must have been particularly helpful to you. You made a study of half a dozen people if I remember rightly?

EF: It might be seen as unusual, but I think if you are preparing for any job, or even if you are not preparing for any particular job, if you are questioning ways forward, and thinking 'where do I go from here', I think it's only wise to look at what is available and gain as much insight from practitioners as is possible. Since I have been in this school, which is about three years, I have probably had two or three people who have been recommended to come and talk with me as a black woman secondary school headship about ways into management. And I do think it is a big issue for women, and a big issue for black women, and black people in general because I don't think there are enough of us and I don't think the channels and the opportunities are there for black people, and let me say black women in particular, to map out the path they wish to take. Not in the same way as I think white women and white people have those opportunities, because more times than not my white colleagues will probably have friends who are deputies or heads and very few of my black colleagues probably socialise with white deputies or heads or local authority advisers.

MM: So, during your deputy years when you were doing these exploratory visits, were you sharply conscious that being a black woman would make the route different?

EF: Yes, I was aware that it was different for black people. I think my involvement in setting up the African/Caribbean Teaching Unit and the Afro-Caribbean Teachers' Association taught me quite a lot. There were just not enough black role models, deputies and heads, who were able, willing or available to give support and guidance to the younger teachers. I felt that this was a gap in the system.

MM: Your HMI secondment of three years must have again been unusual preparation because there weren't many such secondments into HMI. You mostly either went in or you didn't go in. No doubt a secondary function was in fact a preparation and training for headship?

EF: Yes, I think if you are planning a career, then where you are at any one moment in time should be seen as a stepping stone or preparation for something else. So yes, being with HMI gave me those opportunities. I saw at first hand, as I said earlier, head-teachers, deputies, all sorts of teachers working in a number of schools across the country and I was able to analyse some of the practice and to pick up some of what I thought were good practices from various heads from various schools, and I think I have gone some way in implementing some of those things in the school.

MM: Well that brings me on to the question of how did you find being a head when you got to it. Were there aspects of your initial time here that were different from what you expected despite all that preparation?

EF: The school is a very interesting school. I had been at the boys' school which is just across the playing field for three and a half years. I think there was a perception that the girls' school was an easy school, that everything just sort of ran smoothly and there were no 'militants' on the staff and the kids were really compliant. When I came to the school I think there were some people who had very interesting, perhaps even negative, responses to my appointment and I remember thinking that there were two ways of dealing with this; you can either say nothing about the rumours you have heard, or you can confront the rumours, and deal with them that way. So on my first day here, having prepared a talk which was really about the achieving school — an achieving school having good leadership and people working together for this, that and the other — at the end of my forty-minute talk to the staff I said: 'There are one or two things I would like you to know. I intend to lead from the front, but that does not mean I am not going to consult with staff. I will consult; that's one. Secondly, I understand that every school has its inner cabinet and the main job of that inner cabinet is to subvert head-teachers and the management teams. I don't want to know who is in that inner cabinet. I just want you to know that I know that you are here. And thirdly, I don't believe in rumours, but rumour has it that there are some people who didn't want me to be the head of this school'. And I think I shocked people by actually saying what I did. There was about a minute where people looked and thought now did I hear that, did she actually say that? And then somebody laughed, and that broke the ice. So the first day here saw me setting the pace, and saying these are some of the things that I would like us to be involved with and this is the way things are going to be run.

The first term of my appointment I spent listening. I listened to all sorts of people, every member of staff I could talk with, I spoke with and listened to and felt by the end of the first term, perhaps the end of the first two terms, that I had a good grasp of the views and understandings of a range of teachers in the school. I then went on to looking at some of the sort of developmental issues around educational initiatives and found that there were gaps and that a lot of people had not done anything since 1987/88, and that we needed to do quite a lot of work. Now that took some doing because there were things around helping teachers to feel valued and that they would be supported while at the same time, making heavy demands on them, because there were people who were being paid well to do jobs that they weren't actually doing. I think a head walks a very fine line between supporting and demanding and I found that I have had to do that to a good many teachers and for a long time, and to the extent that some of them thought that I was just 'that bloody woman'. I think that was the way in which I was described — 'that woman again'. But I think a lot of it has paid off.

MM: So although you were deputy of the school on the same campus previously, the school you took over was not as you had perceived it.

EF: I don't think I came to this school with any fixed perception about the school, because when I was at the boys' school, we were very formal in our communications and I am not the sort of person who listens to rumour or gets involved with gossip. There were more people who knew many more things than I did about what was happening in the girls' school. So, as far as I was concerned, I approached the school with a clean slate and spent the first two terms really learning about what the school was about, what made it work, and what its chinks were.

MM: How do you feel you lead the school as a whole? What are the methods? You have given one, which was in your initial phase, listening to as many different people as possible. Now that you have been in office for some time, and you can't be doing quite as you did in the initial listening stages, how would you say you influence most broadly across the school?

EF: One of the things that I am keen to do in the school is to improve pupils' attainment and their achievement, and I realised that I could not do it on my own, and that I actually needed systems and structures in place to do that. So out of several discussions with heads of departments and individual members of staff, I have this system where once a year I actually have about an hour and a half with each member of staff, where I talk about a range of things some of them to do with raising achievement, classroom practice, and so on. We decided that we would structure the school into faculties with each member of the senior management team having a monitoring role for each of the faculties and therefore of each member of staff in that faculty. Basically we wanted to talk with staff about what they considered to be effective teaching. If we could agree on a list of things then we could then go on actually doing them in the classroom. So each member of the senior management team — there are four of us, two deputies, a senior teacher and myself — decided to go into classrooms and to monitor teaching and learning.

MM: So each of the four takes a couple of faculties.

EF: Each of three. I don't actually have a monitoring responsibility in that sense. I monitor the learning support teachers. So it has been very interesting because going into classrooms and looking at what is happening was not the 'done' thing. To start with I think people were afraid.

MM: And was there a sense in which the forthcoming legislative requirement for appraisal as it were muddied the waters of being observed?

EF: No, we managed to keep the two things separate, because they are separate.

MM: They should be separate, but I have found that pushing, monitoring or observing has been made slightly harder by the fear of appraisal. But you have managed to keep the two things quite separate.

EF: We started doing our monitoring before appraisal came into being in the way in which it has. The monitoring of classroom practice actually raised the level of educational thinking and talking from about minus one to somewhere in the plus. Because a lot of teachers were not used to talking about their practice and putting that practice in a theoretical context and moving away from the subjective and the anecdotal to actually saying 'what are the educational things that we are doing here?', 'How do pupils learn?', 'Is my teaching effective?', 'What makes my teaching effective?', 'Why am I teaching this rather than that?' and I think just having someone independent in the classroom to share ideas with made a big difference. I am not a scientist, but I am a teacher. I don't necessarily know the content, but I do have some questions that I can ask that are generic questions that anyone can ask of any teacher in any subject area about why they are doing this, what they hope to achieve, how they are going to assess this, have they realised that this child does not understand what a three-dimensional thing looks like, or this child does not understand the language. There are two things we do when we go to a classroom: we talk with children about what they are learning and we talk with teachers about what they are teaching and we observe what both are doing; and that has been a good thing in the school, and in a sense what has happened is that more and more people are beginning to take charge of what is happening in their classroom.

MM: Do you sometimes find that the objective disinterested helps the teacher see things about her or his lesson, good things sometimes, which she hasn't seen or known about before?

EF: Absolutely. I can see the delight on some teacher's face when I've said 'that was really good' and they reply 'I didn't think of it in that way'. I went into an English lesson once where they were doing some poetry and the children were struggling with the idea of what makes a poem a poem. I said to the teacher 'these kids don't actually know why this is a poem, and not a story', and the kids were fantastic because they were saying things like, there aren't any full stops, the sentences are short. And he said, 'I didn't think about that'. But the next time I went into his classroom he had developed a whole range of things around what makes a poem a poem and he had got the children involved, the planning was superb and the teaching was superb and I like that. I like to see 'enlightenment' following the discussion. So OK, involving teachers in the classroom and at the middle management levels has been important in managing the school, but I think when all is said and done you have actually got to do a lot of it by example. I have got to be seen to be a good teacher and a good leader.

MM: How much teaching do you do yourself?

EF: I don't do a lot of teaching. I do three out of twenty-four periods. But I do some team teaching. I had hoped to have done a lot more; going into the classroom and working alongside teachers has been very interesting.

MM: Presumably your HMI experience helps you with this part of your role because you will have observed more teachers than most of us heads have.

EF: Yes, but when I am team teaching it is very much we are colleagues, working together, and I am there to learn from you, as much as you might be able to learn from me.

MM: Are there any other aspects of your role where you feel you are actually giving an example even if it is not such a direct example. That's a one-to-one example, teaching to teaching. Are there any other aspects of things you do that you think have a knock-on effect.

EF: There are a number of things that people have pointed out to me. Some of them have appeared in the first instance to be negative. I think I have a rigour. If I am going to do anything, then I want the best. I have pushed and pushed individuals; I have pushed heads of departments. If I take, for example, documentation, it's got to be good. And though I might not know the extent of the content, I know that there are certain things that must be there and I have been able to ask questions and suggested ideas 'Have you included this?', 'What about this?', 'What about that?' and not to accept from anyone, not from myself, not from staff, second best. Of course, there are times when you have got to accept second best. Especially when there aren't enough hours in the day. But I think it is important to help teachers approach their work as professionally as they possibly can, and I mean the whole range of their work, whether it is teaching, writing, or putting together some documentation or even having a parents' evening; I really do, through example, go for the best.

MM: You have mentioned one important role of your senior management team which is to take a couple of faculties for general leadership and monitoring. How else do you divide the roles of those three people?

EF: There are certain things that I see as developmental. There are certain things that are mundane and administrative, and those things have to be done. The developmental things would be things like staff development, curriculum development at a Key Stage and the development of pupils so that they do have a pastoral responsibility as well. My two deputies have responsibility for two faculties each. One has responsibility to Key Stage 3 and transition (6–7) and the other has responsibility for Key Stage 4 and sixth form, or post-16 work. Now in all of that they have both the academic curriculum and the pastoral curriculum, even though one of the two takes the lead on the pastoral and the other takes the lead on the curriculum. Then the range of administrative things like the building, and supervision of pupils, completing and returning documentation and forms, examination work, and so on, those sorts of things are shared between the two deputies. The financial management on the whole I do, with a very able finance officer, and my two deputies do not have responsibilities for finance.

My senior teacher has responsibility for two faculties and she does the careers education and co-ordinates the PSE programme across the school. They do a lot of developmental work, they are the ones who advise me, or we talk together about issues to do with marginal practitioners, people who need support and help, departments that need particular advisory work, as well as about pupil behaviour, pupil achievement, the building, resources and so on.

MM: Now that is a clear picture of the internal relationships. Could we look now outside the school, and start with the governing body. How do you work with the governing body?

EF: The governing body that I inherited when I came here was a very interesting group. They were divided almost to a person along political lines and they were very fractious. They wanted the best for the school but their bi-lateral approach hampered the development of their work. We have now got a new and mainly inexperienced set of governors. They are keen and they are supportive, but I still think that we have a long way to go in terms of sorting out what are the executive and non-executive roles and responsibilities of the governing body and moving away perhaps from being supportive to actually being much more hands-on. I have toyed with all sorts of ideas around governing bodies and what makes a governing body an effective governing body. I would like to see them much more involved in the running of the school. At the moment I feel that I carry the governing body a great deal, that I am actually having to do quite a lot of the work that perhaps a good and efficient clerk should do, or could do.

MM: That must make it difficult for you to play your headship role?

EF: It does make it a little bit difficult. We have got a clerk, but my understanding of the role and the responsibility of the clerk is that here is someone who understands legislation, can give advice, can support governors, can actually say, well governors you should be doing this and not that and I find that I am sort of training my clerk.

MM: Is the clerk a member of the school staff?

EF: She is at present, administrative staff. That is an area of difficulty for many schools.

MM: I suspect that possibly you and I have inherited a different understanding of a clerk because in the days when a clerk was the LEA officer and was interpreting the LEA's regulations the clerk told the governors what they were allowed to decide. I have now come to think that the head, as chief officer, has the prime task of enabling the governors to work, and that this means setting out the options, and then putting in recommendations.

EF: Yes, a head has to set out the options and put in recommendations but a head needs to be enabled. An efficient clerk who could do the first bit of the work which is setting out what legislation is about would be a 'Godsend'. I have to know what the legislation is about and I have got to be able to say this is my understanding, or this is what is being recommended, but I still feel that to have to do all three of those things in the sort of depth that you need to do it, is very very difficult. It is also very time consuming. If I had a clerk who was working with me and I could say, look could you just read up on that bit of legislation and let's just go through it or could you give me a briefing paper on. ... That's the sort of person I would like to have working with me. Somebody who could say right I have read this, I have read that, here is the briefing paper, this is what you need to know. I often end up doing briefing notes for my chair of governors and am therefore researching, interpreting legislation and making recommendations; but I find that to be time-consuming because I am having to do things from scratch.

MM: In the old days when the LEA was a significant body, then what you had to do was read the LEA circular. Now one has to read the original legislation. I find it takes a considerable brain and considerable experience to be able to do that, in particular to see what legislation is really saying, rather than what the newspapers say it is saying, and a clerk to do that would have to be a pretty good person. I wonder whether they would still be a clerk?

EF: I think it is possible for us to get very able people who have both the time and the intelligence to do that sort of work.

MM: That is one aspect of the work of the governors; how about what one might call personal relationships: How possible is it for you as a head to know them?

EF: I happen to know my governors fairly well. Basically, because they are all people from within or around the Handsworth area and they are parents, they are people who have a track record of working in local community or in local politics, or in local business. They are all right as individuals and as people they are fine; they are very supportive of the school and they are very supportive of me and the work that I am trying to do in the school. But sometimes I just feel that support is not enough. To actually say, well you are doing a good job is good, but to actually have someone in who will say right I am going to take charge of such and such, or I will help with this or that would be good.

MM: We are also interested in a new relationship, post the '86 and '88 legislation of the school and governing body and the LEA in each case which will have changed during the period that you have been a head.

EF: There are key departments and key officers in the local education authority who I could not have done without over the past three years. In my first year I had to take disciplinary action against two members of the teaching staff and one member of the auxiliary staff. Now as a new, inexperienced head, I needed the advice, the support of the people in personnel.

MM: That is an interesting example because that is a clear example of where there is a proper responsibility because in law the LEA are the ultimate employers. And any tribunal to which these people appeal would be the authority having to defend.

EF: I am also talking about the type of advice. Because there are lots of people to give you advice, but they wouldn't necessarily give you the best — and I feel that the local authority, especially in the personnel department has a very good team of people working for them. So the advice and support that I got from them was absolutely crucial. I think more recently the advice and support that I have received from the school's adviser and the advisory teachers has been exceptionally good and this is in terms of support for staff, support for curriculum development, support for pupils and pupils' needs. If schools, governors and the local authority decided that they were not going to keep the advisers and advisory teams I would be disappointed. It is very difficult to find the time to interview all these consultants, many of whom you have never seen or worked with, you don't know their track record and do not feel particularly convinced about what they are offering. For me, knowing the advisory teachers and the advisers is important especially in an era of OFSTED inspections. Both their pre-inspection and post-inspection work has been invaluable.

MM: Some authorities have found it difficult to give up some functions which they no longer need to carry out. Are there any attempts by the authority to do things which you feel are not their business any more?

EF: No. There is nothing that I can think of where I think the authority is overstepping the mark, or trying to hold on to things that are no longer really required.

MM: I suspect that older authorities, like Birmingham, saw the '88 legislation for what it actually was, whereas the new London authorities saw it primarily as setting up a new authority and tried to do so in imitation of the old authority, instead of changing it. So it sounds as if you see the LEA as having, shall we say, a backstage role, but nevertheless an important role.

EF: I don't know whether you have read *Aiming High*, the Birmingham LEA, Education Commission, report which highlighted some of the difficulties, mainly in the past, with the local education authority, officers within the authority, and headteachers in schools? In the main the report highlighted the sort of 'politicking', which has gone on, people confusing the role of perhaps officer with that of councillor. To a great extent this is no longer the case. The roles are being more clearly defined.

MM: It could be argued, indeed I don't know in your HMI days whether you would agree with me here, I argue, looking back at the 1944 legislation that until the '86 legislation the great problem in this country was actually nobody knew where power was supposed to lie.

EF: I think you are right, and there was great confusion.

MM: After all the 1944 Act actually says that the LEA 'shall control the secular curriculum' which it singularly didn't do; but when it did start trying to do a bit, heads didn't like it.

EF: I think the way in which the local authority is operating now is in line with, and in the spirit of, the '88 Act and subsequent acts. I mean they are advising and supporting, rather than seeking to control. I think with some good leadership — for example, Tim Brighouse has been with us since September and he is like a new broom — is the key to a successful LEA. There is a sense in which here in Birmingham there is a common purpose emerging. People are feeling that we are really into this business for the children, we are here to improve standards for the pupils, and so on. The one area which everyone is talking about is City Council's priorities, there are a number of people who are sceptical — they are uncertain about the city's commitment to education. For me, one difficulty is capital expenditure on additional places for this school. I have the pupils on waiting lists, but not the space. The physical capacity for this school is just over 600 children, I have over 750 on roll.

MM: So your standard number on accommodation would have been 200 less, which is a quarter less.

EF: The class sizes range between twenty-six and twenty-eight. What happened was that five years ago the governors decided to go from a 120 intake to a 135. Now what they didn't realise was that once you did it for one year group, you did it for the whole school. It works its way up.

MM: And you did this largely by increasing class size. Many people would say that 26 to 28 is still on the modest size.

EF: We went from 120 — four forms of entry — to five forms. So we managed to keep most class sizes between 26 and 28, though there will be one or two of 30 pupils. But we have very small classrooms and we really cannot accommodate children at lunch times, running over half-an-hour into the afternoon sessions. We have got a problem.

MM: That's one could call the improvement side of capital works. What about the maintenance side? Are they honouring their responsibilities to their share of the maintenance?

EF: By and large they do. Things are still a little bit slow, I think, just from that initial phone call, or from that initial pink slip, it does appear to take a bit more time than other things do. If a pane of glass is broken we just ring up the contractors and they come out and do it. That is our responsibility. Things do get done faster where the school controls the budgets.

MM: That is very interesting on governors and the LEA. You mentioned parents in two or three different contexts. What is your approach as head to parents, the great unloved of the British education system?

EF: I have often said that without parents we wouldn't have schools. So, respect is due! I think one of the things that I have been acutely aware of is the fact that many parents in districts like Handsworth, although they would have been through the education system as pupils they still haven't got a good grasp of what it is about, what the school is trying to do and I have set about trying to empower parents by actually saying these are some of the questions you should be asking us. Don't take at face value what is written on your child's report: come and ask us these questions. If you are dissatisfied then you must go to (a), (b), (c) or (d), not just within the school but within the local authority. I have a leaflet called *The Effective School*, which is based on the talk I gave to my staff when I took up my appointment and I always give this leaflet to parents when we have parents' evenings, intake days and so on, and I do talk to parents. I say, you have got to ask the most difficult questions and here are some ways of asking questions and if you are not satisfied with the answer you get then you must know that the school is an institution and that there are people within the school who are responsible for (a), (b), (c) and (d), and you need to go and knock on the right door in order to get the answers you need.

MM: And how often do they knock on *your* door?

EF: Often enough. But I think what I've tried to do is to get parents knowing who the right people are and getting the right people to take up the responsibilities, so an issue around a child not wearing uniform is not necessarily my responsibility. It's the form teacher's or the year head's responsibility. And parents need to know that they go to this person for this reason. And that it is probably only after they have exhausted those channels that they actually need to come to me as a sort of last resort.

MM: Now you've built a new reception there since the last time I was in the school, does that relate to this relationship, or . . . ?

EF: No. It came out of the siege we had in July. It's for security more than it is for welcome. But it is more welcoming. We have got a Section-11 home–school link worker who is doing some interesting work. One of the things that I found when I was with HMI was that parents didn't know who to contact when they went into schools and they often didn't know why they needed to attend school apart from when they are told that their child has been naughty. Or it's a parents' evening. And I have tried to develop what I call a covenanting system where we say to parents look you can give us an hour of your time, and you could be involved in this or that or that or that. So it is a more sharply focused involvement that we are seeking to have with parents.

MM: Have you found it difficult to put this across to the staff as a whole? Some schools in some parts of the country still would rather parents were seen and not heard.

EF: Well, one of the questions that I ask each member of staff is how they view involving parents in the work in their classroom around the school. The heads of departments have to answer that question and every member of staff has to answer that question, so it is very much on the agenda. And some departments are rising to the challenges and they are actually doing their best.

MM: You have mentioned the area a number of times. Do I take it that the huge bulk of the parents live within walking distance?

EF: Yes. The other thing that I was going to talk about with the work with the link worker and parents is that we are trying to be a little bit more pro-active in informing parents about what the curriculum is about, what their child should be learning, and what their child should be doing in school. So one of the things that we are hoping to develop in the near future is a set of packages that you can actually take up when you go to visit parents. It should say this is what is happening in Maths. This is what we expect your child to have done by the end of the Key Stage. This is how you can support your child. Here are the books we are using in the Maths department. As well as the sort of general information that the DFE sends out about the National Curriculum. We are also trying to move away from sending letters home which are all very negative, complaining about what a child has done — to sending out praise letters. Your child has done such and such, and isn't it wonderful and we would like you to know. So when my link worker goes out she has both negative and positive letters that she can hand out to different parents for all sorts of reasons.

MM: Now you said that her position is funded from the Home Officer Section-11 grant, does that means she is working only with children of minority backgrounds?

EF: No, she works with all pupils in the school, because all children in my school are from minority backgrounds (even the 4 per cent — English, Scottish, Welsh and Irish).

MM: I was going to ask a last question about parents. You said at the very beginning that being a black woman coming into headship was an issue. Now, in a girls' school for parents it wouldn't be an issue being a woman headteacher, but have you felt that parents have in any way made your ethnicity an issue, or seen it as an issue?

EF: No, they haven't. What I think is important isn't necessarily your ethnicity. It's whether you share the values that parents have and I have found that I have probably got more in common with a lot of parents out there from whichever ethnic background, than my appearance would suggest. Shaved head, and young looking — those things don't really matter. I think what matters to parents is that the values and those things that they see as important are actually things that you are promoting. They also value hard work, self-discipline; they want their young women to be people of worth.

MM: And they want a head who is listening, and not taking a high and mighty point of view.

EF: And I do a lot of listening. I hope I do a lot of listening and a lot of affirming, because I think there is a sense in which parents have felt that the values and customs and traditions of their homes are undervalued by the school as an institution and that if I can say yes, I understand and I agree with that, and this is what the school is about, and what I am saying is very similar to what they are saying or what they hear me saying is very similar to what they are saying or understanding, then I think it makes for a better relationship.

MM: If they have spotted something that is not as good as you would have liked it to have been, do you feel able to admit that you have made a mistake?

EF: Yes. I'm quite an open person in that sense, in that I will say yes, I agree, or I am sorry about that. I don't see anything wrong at all with apologising or admitting that what we did was wrong or improper. I did send out a letter to children and I did use a four-letter word which some people find difficult to accept and I didn't actually have any parents come to me and complain. I am not sorry I used the word: it was appropriate in the context.

MM: But you used it, because you needed to because you were speaking about the use of that word.

EF: That's right. Some people who were not parents found it difficult to handle. None of the parents that I know of actually came in or wrote a letter complaining.

MM: You said that during your HMI time you were reading legislation at a high level, and you had that three years when studying changes was part of your actual task. But now that you are head how do you find it possible to keep up intellectually and in terms of reading with that which you think you should?

EF: With difficulty. Number one: my days are very long and it's the only way that a head who is conscientious can actually keep on top of what's going on. I start early in the mornings, around about 7.0 a.m.–7.30 a.m. here. And sometimes I am still here at 8.0 or 9.0 o'clock depending on what I have to do. I have tried to divide my day into two or three bits. Time when I am in a classroom or around the school looking at what's going on, just present. That does matter. You have got to walk the plant, you have got to know what's going on. And your kids have to see you and you have got to be able to talk with them. And teachers must see that you are around and you are available. So there's that. And then there is time for some of the administrative things that you have got to do like opening the mail and reading things that are quickly digested and responded to. And then there is a little bit of time, more in-depth reading and work, and that time is normally after 4.00 p.m. or after 5.00 p.m., since some people have got wise to the fact that I am here late in the evenings, so it's normally that bit of time between 5.0 o'clock and 7.0 p.m. or 8.0 p.m. or 9.0 p.m. when I can actually settle down to the work which requires a bit more concentration. So I often say to people, don't expect a meeting with me during 9.0 a.m. to 3.30 p.m. because that is really school time. It's the only time that I have to see the pupils and teachers in action.

MM: Which aspect of your job do you like least?

EF: I find the reading of legislation irritating. I need to know how a lot of that impinges on the education of children in the classroom. Take the examples of truancy, attendance — I would much prefer to see somebody say something about the educational activities that people should be engaged in which would mean that youngsters actually attended school and they felt motivated or wanted to learn, rather than actually going through twenty or thirty pages of legislation which said, how you should calculate different types of absences. And I think the second most irritating thing is the regularity with which legislation changes. I just find it hopeless.

MM: That started about the time that you took over headship and you have had the peak of it. That's something you would like to get rid of. Or have done for you in summary form. I take it you don't find something like Croner's summaries useful?

EF: I find Croner's to be very good. It's my bible. Those summaries are very good, very useful. And it's the sort of thing that is easy to access and not only access because I think there is a sense in which Croner has tried to remind you that the child is still at the centre of what's going on.

Let me tell you about the two things that I have found exhausting. One is disciplinary procedures, and the other is incidental things — well there are two levels of incidental things. I don't like informal meetings in the corridors because they are time-consuming, and there is an expectation on the part of those people who are speaking to you that you are going to make decisions on the hoof, and I think it is really bad management because somebody will say, oh but you did say, and you are thinking, well when did I say that, did I, could I have? You did say that we could do so and so, and I am thinking, well I didn't. But, we had the conversation in the corridor. I have said to people, if you want to talk to me about any issue you must make an appointment with me, while the meeting might only be five minutes, it might only be two minutes, but there is an order to it. It means that at the end of that meeting I can write a memo or I can write a list of things that must be done. But these incidental meetings, they are time-consuming and they can mess up the management of the school because the message will always go from one person to the next person, 'the head said', and you are thinking when the hell did I say that? Only because it was said between trying to organise a group of kids who are wandering around the corridor and trying to get in touch with the caretaker, or whatever. So I avoid those like the plague and the other thing is the big incidental things like when you have mischief-making people who leak things to the press and then you have to respond to that, that is very time-consuming and you can't please anybody at all, so you end up doing what you feel is right. And I say *feel*.

MM: You mentioned the pain of disciplinary proceedings and you had to go through I think you said three. Without giving details or being indiscreet, did these lie in the improper behaviour end or the inadequate behaviour end?

EF: Improper.

MM: In some ways that is perhaps easier because whilst still painful, the judgement is easier than if you're actually judging on inade-
quacy.

EF: I think there was a combination of the two in one of the cases
that I had to deal with. The processes of researching and writing a
report doesn't bother me — I think it's more the time when you see
people in a position where they feel very pained and there is a lot of
anguish. It's very difficult then to stand back from that and to
probably face the fact that somebody's mortgage might not be paid
at the end of the month. Those sorts of interpersonal things are quite
worrying.

MM: Now one of the things you have spoken strongly about could
come under the word 'curriculum'. You obviously care about that
which is selected for the teaching of the pupils. Do you find in a
school of this size (it's quite large, there is quite an age range)
difficulty as a head getting a feeling of control of the curriculum or
have you managed by your delegation into the faculties . . . ?

EF: I am beginning to feel that I understand a lot more than I
probably did when I first came into the school. Apart from having an
interest in a range of subjects, it is easy now to raise questions with
the senior management team, or the advisory teachers who come in
to support teachers in the classroom, and I do have a feel of where
the curriculum as it is taught in the school is going. The sort of issues
that are emerging I feel able to deal with and to comprehend.

MM: During the period of your headship of course there has been
the debate resulting from the curriculum legislation of '88. Looking
back to your days first when you were deputy head, and indeed
before that, in many schools in the early '80s the curriculum was
divided into teams and the baron in charge of that department didn't
really expect anybody else, including the head to have any interest.
Have you found that legislative requirements have created curriculum debate even if it hasn't always been happy debate and therefore
paradoxically made the head's penetration of the curriculum easier?

EF: Yes, I think the National Curriculum documents do give
heads, or anybody for that matter, an entry into curricular areas that
are not necessarily your field of work. And I think that perhaps the
wisest of heads will not necessarily want to be fully informed about
the content, but must be able to raise issues around the teaching of
that subject or a group of subjects. I don't think it is necessary to
know every little bit of detail. I am not really interested in detail in
that way, because I wouldn't be able to take everything on board.
But what I am interested in doing is knowing the right sort of

questions to ask so that we can focus on the right sort of teaching and educational issues because a lot of the content is outlined for me. I am not certain that I want to know all the scientific and technological and historical terminology but what I can ask is 'Are these children getting what they ought to be getting at this Key Stage, or at this point in the curriculum?' and leave it to the advisory teachers (from the authority) and heads of department who are better at it than I am.

MM: You explained earlier your division of responsibilities in the school. I realise that I didn't quite ask one question there, which is you said one of your two deputies, whilst they share things between them, has a prime concern for the pastoral aspect and one a prime concern for the curriculum. Do the heads of faculties have a special relationship with the one who has a prime concern for curriculum planning?

EF: They do at certain levels, in particular post-sixteen curriculum, but the zeal with which members of the senior management team have taken on their responsibilities in terms of monitoring curriculum and so on has meant that that role of leading on curriculum issues is distributed across the SMT.

MM: Now you could say that in the past in schools curriculum planning really meant only one thing which was how many periods in which option this subject went. Obviously, to you curriculum is much more detailed than that even though you have spelt out that you don't want to be fully involved in the tiny detail. But somebody still has to decide which combination of options for Key Stage 4. How much time is given. Who does that?

EF: That's a shared responsibility. It's done through consultation.

MM: Who does the actual timetabling?

EF: One of the deputies, the one who is primarily curriculum. A lot of that is done through consultation both at governing body level and at staff level, with departmental heads leading on the discussions.

MM: I have two more questions which in some ways are perhaps a bit more personal. For every head there are times in which something isn't going well, something is going wrong. How do you cope to avoid too much actual worry, too much actual distress, too much depression?

EF: You have got to be able to laugh. I think I am one of those people who tends to nip things in the bud. If I think things are not going right, rather than putting it off I will say, I have noted that (a) or (b) or (c) isn't going right, do you think you could come and tell me why not, or how, or what have you. So, I think as soon as the warning signals are out, that's the time to deal with things, rather than leave things to sort of fester or grow.

MM: How about when the thing that's going wrong is a mistake or an error of judgement that you feel that you have made?

EF: I can go in there, and I say, I'm sorry, I think I've done this wrong. And I think that's probably one of the things that people have found a little bit difficult, because I am not superhuman, and I am allowed therefore to make mistakes and I think it's perhaps a humbling thing to actually say, I was wrong or I didn't have the right bits of information together, and I made a judgement on insufficient or inadequate information. I don't find that a problem, I don't see why it should be. I am learning all the time, I am growing all the time and therefore it is not difficult. It would become a difficulty if I in any way suggested to staff or to pupils that I was infallible. As I have said before I don't want to be an angel — I would prefer to be a goddess.

MM: If you were a goddess and could use godly powers, what do you think that a head — and I don't now mean in your own knowledge and skill — what magic wand waving could make you better placed to carry out your job that at the moment is beyond your scope for whatever reason, financial or . . . ?

EF: I think there are several things. If I had some more money, I think that I could do with another five or so members of staff at various levels in the school. I do think that at senior management team level we need at least another one, perhaps even two people to lead and co-ordinate things at the level at which I think they ought to be led and co-ordinated. I think the other thing that I would like to do is to stop any more legislation coming into being for the next year or two years so that we could just get to grips with the ones that we have got now, we could really get to the bottom of them, put them into practice, monitor them and evaluate their effectiveness. And I think just supporting teachers. I think they have a had a hard time, they have had a raw deal and if at the end of the day we are going to have children who are well educated, who are attainers and achievers then we actually need good teachers.

MM: Thank you very much indeed.

6 Michael Marland

with Peter Ribbins

PR: Can you say something about your background, early life and education?

MM: My father and mother left school at twelve. My mother lived in a Manchester slum. She was one of twelve children born, only six of whom survived. My father came from a Lancashire mill town where his father kept a pub and was an amateur pianist. He made his way in the world by becoming a very successful dance band pianist and composer. He was Henry Hall's pianist and arranger. My mother sought respectability and worked in a stationery shop. Later she came to London to work in Whiteley's Department Store and for her, selling sheets there was a major step up.

I was born in 1934 and when the war started my father went in the Navy as an Able Seaman. He clearly was not an 'able seaman' and when they discovered he could play the piano they put him in the Royal Marine Band. My mother was determined I would be well educated. She did not know what all that meant but knew it was important. She knew, for instance, that you had to speak properly. We were evacuated during the blitz from the centre of London to a hotel in Bournemouth where we met a family which had two boys she thought were well behaved. She established they were at Christ's Hospital school. Until then I had been at various Catholic convent schools. Christ's Hospital has a negative income bar, unlike a comprehensive school where you can get in however well heeled you are. As my father was in the Navy at the time his income was low enough to count for this. You could either get in as a clever London boy on a scholarship or you could get in on a governor's nomination. This required tenacity from the parents and so my mother kept pestering until I got a place. I was nine when I first went and stayed as a boarder.

It was a very unusual place. It was tough and harsh. You were expected to be good at fighting and at catching and kicking balls. I was not good at these things. But it did have something I try and replicate in the day state school and this is that the teachers and their families are devoted to the good of the school. They lived there. They gave well beyond the bare minimum of time. For example, in our housemaster's study, from fifteen onwards, we used to have a play reading every Sunday after supper with his wife and daughter. Whilst this was happening he would be drinking elsewhere but he used to come in at the end to lead a discussion on why whoever we had been reading was important. All this meant that if you were interested in something you would almost always be able to find somebody who would support you. I was interested in the theatre and was able to produce plays at a very early age.

PR: Were any teachers particularly influential on you?

MM: I don't think the standard of teaching in general was very good. I can remember some awful ill-discipline and some improper goings-on. One teacher was after one of my friends. He asked him to come to the darkroom to pose in his bathing costume and told him not to bring his friend Marland. But he had the wisdom to take me as protection. But there were also some very good teachers. I recall a History teacher called David Roberts who was an intellectually charismatic teacher. Similarly, Music was very strong. I suspect that because 1000 boys had to be got into lunch together there was a military band to march them in. I used to play the clarinet. The visual arts were good and there was an excellent library. There was also very vivid English teaching.

PR: What do you remember of the head?

MM: He was known as 'Oily' because he once said to some senior boys, and it was the senior boys who ran the school, that 'You are the machine and I am merely the oil that helps it to work'. I had little to do with him. He did see all the boys at something around their lower-sixth year and when he saw me he read from my notes that I wanted to be an actor. He said 'You don't act well enough to convince us that you are working'. He had an influence on pupils but it was mainly indirect, just as mine has to be here. The way in which it can be direct is by example. For example, I remember one London headteacher I used to know who whenever he got to a door would stop and wait for someone to open it. I knew another who would happily put his hand in his pocket and find change for a pupil who did not have enough. In my school you never really saw the head with a pupil.

PR: Were you successful academically?

MM: I was not very successful. I had a very chequered early education, with a number of moves from one Catholic school to another. Remember I got in not through the competitive route and I was not all that successful at school. We all did Greek and I could never remember very much of it. When I got into the sixth form it was into the 'modern sixth' which was a euphemism for 'not so good' — we did things like History, Geography and English and not the Classics. It was only at this time, thanks to a few inspiring teachers, that I started to enjoy writing essays. It prepared me quite well for Cambridge in that it was prepared to trust its judgement and not just rely on examination results. I don't remember how I did at matric but I do remember that I did not pass English Literature although subsequently I read English at Cambridge.

All this influenced me in that I still do not think our profession understands the purpose of testing and the government is not helping us to do so. People are tending to use tests as if they were an overall judgement instead of a surrogate indicator which helps you to identify the right questions to ask about a pupil's progress rather than giving you the whole answer. I suspect I got my Cambridge place at least as much because of the work I had done in the theatre as for my 'A' Levels.

In my holidays at the end of my fifth year I decided to produce Shakespeare's *Twelfth Night*. I got a whole group of boys willing to do it. I got a boy who would design the scenery, another to write the songs. I thought I would hire fourteen church halls in Kent and Surrey to put them on. The head heard about this — I had intended to call us the Christ's Hospital Players but he said that this would not do. We renamed ourselves the Elizabethan Players and he said we could do it only if a teacher went with us. Two wonderful teachers agreed to do this. They played no part other than keeping an eye on us. In the following Easter I took over a bombed site in St Anne's in Soho where I planned to do medieval miracle plays. I went to see the vicar to get his agreement to use this very beautiful site. He said 'Christopher Fry did try and use it in the Festival of Britain and did not succeed but I am sure you will'. We did this twice-a-day for two weeks and it got much good publicity. Those kind of things helped me at the interview at Cambridge.

I had a year off before going to Cambridge. In those days of National Service you booked your university place two years ahead. But when I had my medical they did not like the look of my nose so I was judged unfit. It was not possible for me to bring my place back for the next autumn. This left me a year to fill. I was stage struck. So I had this great idea. I thought I would take the theatre to theatreless towns and raised money from old boys of the school to do this. I quickly discovered these were theatreless towns because they did not want theatres. I hired professional actors and a lorry and the rest but

after about nine weeks it all collapsed. I then worked as an assistant
stage manager in a touring company. I had a lot of interesting
experiences. For example, when once the stage hands went on strike
and went off to a local pub. I was sent to get them back and was
singularly unsuccessful. As well as being stage manager I had a
number of tiny parts. That was how I filled that year.

PR: Then you went to Cambridge. What do you remember of that?

MM: I had an unusual time there. I really went there to produce
plays. I wanted to be a director and, in practice, I spent a great deal
of my time doing just that. But I met my first wife, who has been
dead since 1968, in a Charing Cross Road theatre and music book
shop. It was during the Easter holidays when I was putting on those
medieval plays in Shaftesbury Avenue and during the Spring Term
of my first year I kissed her and she said 'So we are getting married?'
I did not know what else to say other than yes. I then said 'We can't
possibly get married straight away because we have nowhere to live'.
She answered 'No problem, we will just find a house we like'. This
seemed a silly thing to say. But we were walking down the centre of
Cambridge, a really nice street, and a man came onto a little flight of
steps and she said 'He looks a really nice man, let us see if we can live
there'. I said 'You can't do things like this'. But she went up to him
and told him 'We are about to get married and we are looking for
somewhere to live. We would like to live in your house'. He said
'Well we are about to convert a flat. Come and look at it'. When we
were married and returned some time later the place was not quite
ready so we lived with him for free. He turned out to be Francis
Crick and it was the year in which he published his findings on
DNA.
      Living there with him was the first time I had experienced intelli-
gent artistic dinner-party conversation. I went to see my tutor and
told him of my plans to get married and he said 'You can't do that'.
In the end he came to the service. I think I can say, and this
influenced my thinking about education subsequently, that I got
very good pastoral care from Sidney Sussex College. When in due
course we had the twins, the college gave us £50 from the contingency fund and the college gardener crossed their little palms with
silver. Basically I had a happy time at both school and college.
Although school was tough in many ways, and as a young boy I cried
every night and hated the cold baths and the PE without shirts and
all that, nevertheless the devotion of the teachers both there and at
the university was something terrific.
      Christ's Hospital was one of those places who regarded adol-
escence as something rather regrettable. At Christ's I was not happy

until I was about fifteen. I would never send my own children to a boarding school.

Perhaps all this relates to my own experience. I was an only child. My father was away a great deal. In the navy and then on tour. We tended to see him about once every five weeks. I had no social life as a boy at home and in a sense I had no social life at university either since I was married and having children. I did a lot of theatre. I was president of the amateur dramatic club. This was quite an achievement. My predecessors included Peter Hall, Peter Woodthorpe, John Barton. Some people were only there to get their careers started. I had had no social life at home. Nobody ever visited the family. I was quite shocked when people came to dinner at the Crick household. But I was brought up gently. I have developed a phrase from the research I have read — 'fixed by four'. I reckon adolescent behaviour is fixed by four. The study by Martin Bax and Kingsley Whitmore done in the late 1970s which suggested that from the tests which they undertook at four they could identify the children who would be causing their children trouble at nine. There is a similar study in a current issue of *Child Psychology and Psychiatry* conducted in Birmingham on Pakistani and white problem toddlers which suggested that there is a positive correlation between the degree of problem and the degree of smacking. One of my ambitions for the school is to create a physical and interpersonal environment which is gentle and relishes beauty. We have just had an exhibition in the school of the work of Govier, an East Anglian artist, which includes a set of etchings of the naked female form. Most schools would not dare to put that up. We put it up as we have others and have never had any damage. Sometimes in an assembly I ask the pupils to consider the beauty of a piece of art or of music. In my view, in our society we create tough boys. We 'masculinise' them — we need to find a way of gentling men. I try and run a regime which makes that possible.

PR: I am struck that in describing your school and university career you stress the kinds of places they were rather than the contribution they made to your academic or intellectual development.

MM: I do remember what they did for my intellectual development. The first lesson I can remember was an English lesson when I was about thirteen and a History teacher, in a Welsh accent read some Welsh poetry. And he said, 'Is that not a beautiful language?' I am not a natural linguist but since then I have become very interested, analytically, in the English language. I remember making a deep linguistic remark at the time. I asked 'Please sir how can it be that those sounds are more beautiful than English sounds — is it not that they sound more beautiful to us because they are different?' At school, I mainly remember Geography, especially Physical Geography, taught with great clarity. I still remain interested in Physical geography. In History, when I took 'A' Level we were taught by a teacher who would go very carefully through your essays with you. I also remember for the first time having to write longish essays and saying to my friend, Young, how much I liked these. I remember his mode of teaching. We used to call him 'Mr Yes But'. He was a real intellect, a high-level academic. Not all our teachers are high-level academics. He would take you carefully, in your essays, through the relationship between their grammar and their logic.

I did English Part I and History Part II. I wanted to do English straight away but my tutor, a distinguished medieval historian, took the view that English had no discipline and so I started on History. I had the privilege of being tutored by people like David Thompson. Really to go to him in his room and to read my trivial essay on nineteenth-century towns and for him to take this seriously and try and push me further has been a great influence on my views on teaching. There were also a number of well-known teachers of English there including Leavis. I was not taught by him but went to a number of his lectures. I remember Smail, my History tutor, telling me I should go and hear Pevsner lecture. Doing so profoundly shaped the way I look at buildings and has had its influence on what I have tried to achieve in the curriculum at North Westminster. A child should be able to look at a house and say, why is it as it is and how could it be otherwise?

I did not do as much study at Cambridge as I should — what with producing plays, being married and having twins. Also I did not do a PGCE. In those days you did a PGCE if you wanted another year at Cambridge to do sports or whatever. At that time I had not made up my mind to teach. I wanted to direct plays.

PR: How did you get into teaching?

MM: I worked all the vacations after my marriage either at the switchboard at the Arts Theatre, or, significantly, Cambridge was full of foreign students, and I taught in a language school in the evenings, weekends and holidays. Teaching English to well-educated and keen students from Italy and Spain taught me a very great deal about my own language. When I corrected them they would ask for a reason. I had not been taught this at school — we practised what might be called the assumptive approach in which you were expected to pick things up as you went along. I found thinking about these things intellectually deeply fascinating. I find youngsters are generally similarly interested. In getting a job, we both felt a need to get out of England for a bit. In the end I got a job in Buxtehude, a small town outside Hamburg. I worked in the

Halepaghen Oberschule. I was expected by the Herr Director to
teach Geography in English. A modern idea for 1957. I also taught
English and was fascinated by the level of text these children were
expected to read.

There was nowhere to live because with American occupation
you were not allowed to let accommodation. If you had a spare
bedroom it was requisitioned. You could only live in a pub or hotel.
It was a fascinating experience. For one thing my wife was half
Chinese and had long black straight hair. We got jeered at pushing a
pram through the street by white youths — she was jeered at as a
foreigner.

In the end living in Germany without being really able to speak
German and closeted in one room with two children became too
much of a strain. So we decided to come back to England and
Cambridge and I went back to language teaching. By then I had
decided that the world of theatre did not seem to be falling over itself
to attract my services. As I seemed to be enjoying teaching I would
try my hand at this on a more permanent basis. I first applied to a
secondary modern school in Kent and I remember being shocked by
a teacher there telling me that 'Provided you put it in them [the
pupils] you will get it out of them'. In another sense what led me into
teaching was reading Leavis and Thompson's *Reading and Discrimi-
nation* — I still have it. It interested me in the curriculum and the
teaching of English. Leavis had attacked the Oxford school of teaching English, largely on the grounds that it put too much emphasis on
biography — in place of this he picked up the I. A. Richards' point
about the words on the page.

In any case I applied to the school. The head, a good man,
seemed a bit surprised to get someone with a Cambridge degree
applying for the school. He said to me 'The job is yours but if you
have any doubts at all I would advise you not to take it'. I did have a
doubt so did not take it but applied instead to Simon Langton Boys
in Canterbury. The interviewing method was interesting. You
stayed the night with the head and his wife and had dinner with
them. Not a bad method.

PR: Would you employ it at North Westminster if you could?

MM: Yes. In teaching we put too much emphasis on the interview
and not enough on other kinds of interchange. The NFER study
supports this. At Simon Langton I taught English. The school was
located on a bomb site in the middle of Canterbury. I taught in a
HORSA hut. You would be teaching Wilfred Owen when the caretaker would come in to put more coal in the burner. I started
producing school plays including the *Government Inspector* in the old
hutted library, which was a huge success. Again I took a tour of the

children around Kent and Sussex. I was at the school for three years
and during that time first had a flat in Canterbury which was owned
by the Red Dean. We then moved out to a beautiful coach house
which we rented for almost nothing. We had another child who is
now Tina Turner's musical director. My wife had something of a
breakdown and the doctor suggested that we were too isolated where
we lived. So we came back to London. I was desperate for a job and
applied for all kinds of things including Head of Drama at Woodberry Down. I nearly got the job in a tough secondary modern in
Peckham. The head told me I had talked my way out of the job.

Then I was appointed to Abbey Wood, a new comprehensive
school in new buildings situated on an overspill housing estate. I was
appointed by one of the last non-graduate heads of a London comprehensive school to be head of English. She was a very good head in
every way. I was in charge of the Library as well as English and I
suppose this is where my experience in school libraries began. Working there was a powerful experience. The great majority of the
children were white working class. There had been no head of English before. Things had been run by a deputy-head. I recall teaching
what are now Year 10 pupils Stevenson's *Travels on a Donkey*
because that was the only set of books we had. I felt this was not
right. I am not against teaching Stevenson. I have been a strong
advocate of the earlier literature long before legislation. I have often
argued English courses in most secondary schools over the last
twenty-five years have been courses essentially in the post-1952
novel — starting with novels about happy families and ending with
novels about really miserable families. I was part of the move which
took up the work of working-class writers and did so first by getting
hold of thirty copies of Sillitoe's *Loneliness of the Long Distance
Runner* hardback direct over a shop counter.

I had three happy years at Abbey Wood. But Drama was in
another department and this was something I did not much agree
with. So I sought a move. At the time I did not like this separation
but have changed my mind. By the end I had got to know John
Watts who was then head of English at Crown Woods. He told me
that he was leaving for a headship and would I like to go there as
head of English. At the time Drama was run by the English department at Crown Woods. In career terms moving there was the best
thing that could have happened to me. It was a very large and very
successful school and the kind of school in which you could do
almost anything you wanted to in a good sense. Your back was not
against a wall the whole time so you could try things. I was part of
the early school bookshop movement whilst I was there. There were
also a lot of drama opportunities there. It was a banded 13-form
entry school — at the time I went they were banded into academic,

general, building boys and commercial girls. But it was a lovely place to be.

PR: Had you started your writing by then?

MM: When I was at Abbey Wood I realised that the educational publishers were not producing the things which schools and teachers really needed. I remember the first thing I wrote. We had taken our children to their first school in Islington and there we saw a note, badly typed and wrapped in cellophane which said 'Will parents kindly refrain from attempting to teach their children to read'. That was one of my first contacts with a professio-centric, we are the trained experts, we know better than you. The first thing I wrote was in *Forum* entitled 'At arms' length' in 1964. My first writing and editing was for the series which later became *Longman Imprint Books*. I think I simply wrote in to them saying I have a good idea and they ought to do it. I have never worried about doing this kind of thing. One of my very first books was *Following the News* and this came about because I had heard a talk on the radio by Merlyn Rees, then Home Secretary, complaining about the quality of newspapers. I wrote saying it is not surprising as in schools we teach nothing about newspapers. We ought to give lessons in how they work. I did not know he was a director of Chatto and Windus. He wrote back and said submit a scheme. I did. On the whole most of my writing was to fill a perceived gap.

The origins of the Heinemann management series is quite interesting. I found myself going around the country giving lectures on how to be a head of English. I wrote to Heinemann saying that 'I am tired of giving this lecture why don't you publish it as a book?' They sent me a contract. I had the thought that the book should be about the head of department rather than just head of English. They had some doubts about whether there was a call for such a book but I argued that any far-seeing publisher would realise that one of the big expansions of the next few years was going to be in management. They wrote back saying they were far-seeing. So I answered saying that what they wanted was a series and not just a single book. They agreed.

PR: What happened after Crown Woods?

MM: We were very broke but even so my wife and I thought we would move out of London. We now had five children. I applied for the headship of Cambridge High School for Boys, where I gave the prizes away last year. I got short-listed even though I was only a head of department at the time. I then applied for Eye Secondary Modern in Suffolk. Harry Ree, who was one of my referees and who I had got to know through our mutual membership of the York Nuffield

Committee chaired by Lord James enquiring into the education of socially deprived children, said this school will not suit you. He was probably correct. I was not even short-listed. At this point we bought a beautiful sixteenth-century house which we still live in in Suffolk. Its modern wing was put up in 1628. We moved in during the summer and on 29 December 1968 my wife was killed in a car crash.

The previous summer, Malcolm Ross the head of Crown Woods, had asked me to apply for the position of director of studies. There was only one deputy at the time. This was like a deputy's position but it was not paid as much. I said I would not take it because we were moving out of London. After my wife's death he wrote me a letter of condolence whilst I was in hospital. In it he said that he was stopping the advertising procedure to give me the opportunity to reconsider and to apply for the director of studies post. I started this in the Spring of 1969. He retired in 1971 and I applied for his post but with real doubts in my mind. To apply upwards in a school in which one had already been promoted can be difficult. Also, of course, I knew little about headship at the time. Furthermore, I had been invited to join the Schools Council's English Committee. I did apply but did not get it. I heard that one reason was that Malcolm Ross had the reputation of being an innovator and some saw me as another. He did innovate but I never really thought of him as an extensive innovator. For example he started a scheme in which he would take students from only two teacher training institutions and he insisted that they did seminars on various aspects of school life at the end of the day. In that respect he was twenty years ahead of his time. But those making the appointment wanted someone they saw as safe and secure.

The inspector advising the appointment's panel met me by chance some time afterwards and he said you should apply for Woodberry Down. So I applied and got the job. Curiously the man who had left and made the post vacant was the man who got the job at Crown Woods. Woodberry Down had been very well set up by Mrs Chetwynd. In those days governors tended to be worthy but not striking. But on this body there was one Dr Tessa Blackstone. I think she was an influential governor and I got the impression that she was looking for somebody from a rather different mould. In those days London heads seemed to roll slowly up the ladder and became heads through sheer stickability. I became head there in 1971.

PR: How far did you feel prepared for headship?

MM: Very little. At the time I did not feel unprepared but now I know I was not prepared. I had always observed and analysed organisational aspects, and brought that with me. I had a very good briefing from the outgoing head lasting all of half-an-hour. He gave me the keys and told me where the sherry was kept. I think initially I was regarded as a kind of decoration by the deputies who did the real business. I did not know much about educational management at that stage. I had not quite started the Heinemann *Organization in Schools* series — my book on the *Head of Department* had not quite been written. But the *Craft of the Classroom* was soon to come out. Those were the days of huge teacher turnovers and great unrest in inner London. There were some really difficult classroom conditions. I found myself dealing with a lot of young teachers who were not coping. I remember producing some notes for the young staff in which I said that what was necessary was to break down this thing called discipline into its bits. For example starting a lesson — how do you give out a set of books without chaos? In those days such things were expected to be 'caught rather than taught' by young teachers, as Margaret Peters said in another context. Worse than that there was the idea around, that good discipline was something which you had or you did not have. Soon after I remember sitting by a fire in Suffolk and beginning to write the notes up into a book. I first sent these to Penguin Education who sent them to their advisers who said don't take this, teachers do not want to be taught like this. So I sent it to Heinemann and they said yes. I had the gumption to reduce it in size since it was originally intended as a bigger book. It came out in 1975. Since then it has sold over 64,000 copies.

PR: How did you see your role as a head?

MM: Preparing for and supporting the work of teachers of course. I don't think I could then define the role of a head as I should now but I certainly saw it as centrally to do with scrutinising the curriculum. I was not satisfied with many aspects of the curriculum. At the time I saw the curriculum essentially as organised in subjects as discrete courses. Nowadays I do not use the word subjects for what happens in classes. Instead I use the word courses for this. The NCC has hijacked the word subjects as a planning division and neither Technology nor English can be delivered in one course so I prefer to use another word.

At the time I was very worried about the lack of something which we would now call PSE. So I introduced something like this. It was a set of themes which were rotated around the fourth and fifth year options. A kind of overlay, a way of getting it onto the timetable. I had been very influenced by Lawrence Stenhouse. By this time I was on the Schools Council's Whole-Curriculum Working Party. It published its findings in 1975. Whatever its merits I regard this as having been a failure. I learnt a great deal from it. But I believe our current curriculum messes can be largely explained in terms of the failure of that committee then. In my view the academics in this country had not and still have not, produced an analytical and conceptual framework or even a nomenclature to discuss the curriculum. I admired Stenhouse, he was on this committee and we became very friendly, but I think it was because people like him were writing the things they were writing, unlike our colleagues in the United States who were having what I see as worthwhile discussions about the curriculum, we were not. I was influenced by his great project on the Humanities which I had introduced as a compulsory subject when I was director of studies at Crown Woods.

So I certainly saw the curriculum as a head's task. I also saw the development of an appropriate ethos as a head's task. There is not much spoken about that these days but how people relate to each other is part of the education of pupils and of the mode of delivering the curriculum. At the time these were busy times just at an administrative level. With the turnover, just recruiting staff was a major task. Pupil grouping was also a big issue. Under my leadership, Crown Woods moved from banding, which is an elaborate system of streaming, to mixed ability. No easy task in a thirteen-form entry school. I did the same at Woodberry Down. I am not saying it was entirely right to do so but I did it. I failed in an attempt to get a primary/secondary curriculum liaison. I argued that Hackney should have a Hackney language policy so that pupils could work on the same path. I had visited America for the Bullock Committee and realised there that effective primary/secondary liaison need not rely on people being chatty with each other because there they would be working to a School Board Curriculum. When I returned I was determined to think about this. I saw the curriculum not only in subject terms but across the board. I may, in that context, have been the first person in the country to use the term 'whole-school policy' with respect to the curriculum. But I also saw this as involving curriculum continuity between primary and secondary school.

I enjoyed my time at Woodberry Down. It was a very workable school. It had inherited a good reputation from Mrs Chetwynd. The person after her was perfectly competent but this was perhaps a time in which the school marked time. But when I first came I frequently heard 'Headmaster you should do this or that. That was the way Mrs Chetwynd did it'. The senior staff treated the headmaster as a kind of functionary whose job was to do what Mrs Chetwynd had done. I was not very popular for a while because I had ideas on things. I had also always had an architecturual interest. At Woodberry Down I caused shock and horror by having offices built for the heads of houses. Jack Whitehead was a head of house there. He once said to me 'I will tell you headmaster how I learnt pastoral care. Mrs

Chetwynd had taken over music practice rooms to put in the four
heads of houses and their deputies. There was one desk in each. The
head of house had the side with the drawer and as her assistant I had
the side without drawers. Sitting there was how I learnt my job'. I
also built a careers interviewing room and a modest careers centre.
Building offices and waiting rooms for the heads of house and a
proper reception office were amongst the first things I did at both
Woodberry Down and at North Westminster.

PR: In what ways did you work differently when you took up your
second headship? What did you learn from your first headship?

MM: I came to believe that the prime task was to get the responsibility and management structure of the school right. At North Westminster the challenge was different. The history of comprehensive
schools in this area was a history of the 1947 plan as a dream which
never happened. As a result of falling rolls, after five years of rows in
the area, I had the task of taking over the closures of three schools.
Euphemistically, this was described as an amalgamation. Staff jobs
were ring-fenced. To create one out of four schools — almost everyone said that the new school could not work. You could not run a
school on three sites. Many did not want it to work. After all they
had been protesting against the idea for five years. It had been on
Shirley Williams' desk for three years. When Mark Carlyle took over
he agreed that it could happen if it could be done before a tight
deadline which he set. We had a term to plan things. So initially my
job in the two schools was very different.

The first thing I had to do at North Westminster was to create a
new structure. In a way this was a very good thing. Now I have the
problem I had at Woodberry Down which is adjusting an old structure. My second task was to tackle the serious recruiting problems I
was faced with. I was told one part of the school (Paddington School)
could go it alone — but it was not attracting pupils. I was told the
reason the schools had poor results was because there were no able
children in the area — nonsense. I did a bit of simple research. I took
the primary output figures of his planning area and compared the
measured output with the input of this school over a three-year
period and found that there were not many able children but they
were all going out of the area to the church schools or the single-sex
schools. I had a huge recruiting problem. In a sense coming to grips
with this was my major task for the first four years — no pupils
meant no school. The Conservatives did not invent parental choice
in London. Risinghill, for example, was closed on a fudge — the
truth was few parents would go there. I was chairman of Islington
State Education Association at the time. The LCC pretended it
wanted it for a college but what it really wanted to do was to get rid

of the school. One of the reasons they wanted to close Paddington School was because they reckoned it was not succeeding. So I had to attract pupils to us.

The curriculum was a third task. I got the staff to agree just one general rule — none of us were to say what we did last year. Rather we would take a blank sheet and ask ourselves what in the mid-1980s do we think pupils should have. This gave use great opportunities. For example, the performing arts department was set the task of making sure that all pupils did Dance, Music and Drama. The last HMI survey on this in the mid-1980s found that only 8 per cent of twelve-year-old boys have access to Dance. We made them all do it and we did not tell them this was unusual and so they loved it. That curriculum planning was a huge job. I failed in my ambition to introduce what are now called cross-curricular themes. I find this the hardest thing in education management to achieve. We are having another go now.

So structure, curriculum and public image were the key things I had to get right. Working with governors was important throughout that period. It had not been all that important in Woodberry Down where the governors tended to be pleasant and polite rubber stampers who saw their main task as supporting the head. By the time I got here that had changed for a number of reasons. Not mainly for national reasons but because the governors had lived through five years of rows. Those who were on the new body had become aware of their powers — they had created the school, they had named it, they had appointed me. From the beginning they wanted to be more involved and that suited me because this is how I think things should be. I now think that the prime task of the headteacher is to enable the governing body to work well. It is time-consuming but not as much as some other things. I think much national and local governor training has missed an important perspective. I think too much emphasis has been put on training the governors. After all when you put lay persons on a governing body in hospitals, schools or whatever you are not appointing them for their specialist knowledge but for their judgement and their knowledge of the outside world. If you teach them too much about education, for example, it could be they lose what is important.

PR: An OFSTED lay inspector in a recent training course put that point rather well. He said 'the problem for me is keeping my ignorance'.

MM: That is a nice way of putting it. In my view the headteacher should be the main trainer. For instance, I find the best governing body meetings are those in which the papers are very well prepared. This entails a number of things. First, that the issues are well defined and it is clear why the governors are being asked to look at them. Secondly, that any legal constraints are clearly and succinctly set out. Thirdly, the arguments and options are clearly presented. When you do that you can expect a really good meeting. I try to make sure that I am on the governing body of something or other in which I am not a specialist. It is very educative for me. There is the chief executive over there and here am I as an ignoramus asking the apparently daft questions. I am not sure enough senior staff understand that the paradox is that their power relies on the power of the governing body. If sometimes they over-rule me I should not complain. This is what gives me strength. At the last meeting of the finance committee they actually minuted a statement that I had not adequately prepared the budget submission — which was splendid. I am not happy about this, it makes me rather miserable but I have to accept it. I find all this a very important part of my job and so I spend a lot of time producing papers for meetings of governors. It is through this means rather than in formal ways that I can contribute to the training of my governing body.

PR: What do you expect of your senior staff? What should they be able to expect of you?

MM: I have currently quite a serious problem in terms of my concept of senior staff. Its origins are partly structural. First, working in three widely separated campuses is very different from the situation of a single campus where the head and senior staff see each other several times a day either formally or casually. Secondly, I set up a senior staff pattern which was initially meant to meet the serious worries which the communities and professionals had in this area. One of the reasons they said this school would not work was the trauma of the break between the lower houses, as I call them, and the upper school. It was believed that all the power would go to the upper school and the lower schools would not matter. To fight those two objections I built a senior staff structure whereby you could think of the school as two 'schools' which start their lives in lower houses and study as in a collegiate university in the upper school but still have their home/school liaison and pastoral care within the same line. So I put two deputies in who are heads of houses responsible for over 900 pupils each. But that makes it very difficult to work together. I have always been concerned that there may not be enough knowledge to enable effective pastoral care to take place. I therefore wanted specialists. It is more fashionable at the moment in all kinds of jobs that everybody does everything and that undoubtedly has certain strengths. But I worry that to know half of what you need to know to be an effective leader even in a typical school is really more than one person can achieve.

We are about to reconsider the organisation of senior staffing. I pushed for a lot of deputies because we are a big institution. So I got up to four. I saw them as a joint team in which we worked together on major themes but also each has specific responsibilities and speaking for that focus in our general discussions.

PR: What kinds of specific focuses?

MM: The first follows from my concern at a possible lack of coherence in a three-campus school. I am not the only one who worries about this. We have just had an LEA inspection, which they have not as yet reported, but the inspectors said to me that they feared they might find three schools but had, in fact, found one school. This is so because we have fought hard to make it one school. I have a director of curriculum, and I deliberately used the word 'director' because I wanted the curriculum to be 'directed'. It is very difficult to succeed in this because teachers very much want to be able to get on and do their own thing. His responsibility is for the curriculum across the school and for the work of the heads of department. He is also the time-tabler. The snag is the logistics of all this, especially after LMS, with all the calculations this entails. This means that we are always very heavily loaded with problems of logistics and this can make it difficult to find time for more fundamental thinking about the curriculum. Secondly, I have the two heads of house responsible for that continuity I talked of earlier. Thirdly, and this was the last to be put in, I have a director of upper school. The upper school has 950 pupils. It needs to be run by a head-type figure. This person does not have a specific focus but rather a general responsibility of all aspects of the life of a part of the school.

This pattern has certain snags. They all carry secondary tasks which entail school-wide responsibilities — appraisal, pupil reporting, community relations — but it is very difficult for someone who is a deputy head, say for Paddington House, timetabled to be teaching a lot there to really carry that Upper-School-wide responsibility. So we are probably going to have to restructure.

I have also reconsidered my views in another way. I had argued that I did not want a bursar or bursar-type figure because if this person is responsible for the non-teaching staff and the premises then she or he is spending a lot of money and I did not want the financial controller to be heading up a big budget as well. So I initially thought a separate director of finance and director of administration would be appropriate. I insist they attend every senior management team meeting because I have argued that everything in the management of the school interacts. For example, I view cleaning as an aspect of the educational responsibilities of the school.

In this context, I see one of my axioms of effective school management that, when things are not working as they should, I ask myself is this for personal or structural reasons or, as is often the case, for some combination of personal or structural reasons in which one is triggering the other. In all these cases you have to be very careful to get your analysis correct. If things are not working as well as they should and you alter the structure when the problem is really a personal matter then you are unlikely to achieve much improvement. It is just as bad to replace the person only to find that the job which they had been asked to do was impossible structurally. With this in mind, it seems to me that structurally it is very difficult for a head of house to lead the lower and upper house together. Not least for geographic reasons. Upper School is a long way from the lower schools. I walked it recently, using the quickest routes, and it took me twenty-five minutes.

I am partly a victim of the way in which the ILEA worked. I was a dab hand at playing the system. One of my greatest skills as a head was to know the 'Yellow Book' thoroughly. This was a directory of County Hall. And what you did was you played the 'Yellow Book' with different parts of the administration. You knew you were safe in this because there was little horizontal communication at County Hall. Take the case of the studio theatre we have in upper school. How did I get it? Well I went from one department to another and then another. The one thing you do not do is to put it all together. If anyone had costed the whole enterprise they would have told us we could not and must not do it. If you get a bit out of one budget and a bit out of another and so on you can achieve what would not be possible with a single budget. We run the thing as a small public theatre as part of community arts funded by the City of Westminster Arts with an outreach worker. Returning to our difficulties here, I think that I have put too many layers between myself and the staff as a whole.

PR: The trend in industry and elsewhere is to strip out layers of management. In schools, especially secondary schools, we do seem to have more layers of management than any other country I have seen. There are studies around which suggest that 60 per cent and more of staff in secondary schools ostensibly carry some kind of management responsibility.

How do you see yourself as the leader of the work of the staff as a whole?

MM: First of all there is a structural point of arranging what you are getting in terms of the sets of functions which you need to have fulfilled. Secondly, there is managing the border, by which I mean seeing people in and seeing them out. I play a major part in selecting staff. Give or take a very few occasions when the deputies take the responsibility I am involved in the great majority of appointments and there are many in a school of this size. Thirdly, I personally am responsible for specific professional development. By that I mean as opposed to that professional development which is part and parcel of being a member of a function group, such as the maths department. I like to see people and help them with this. I like to think I am quite good at this. There is a sense in which you can help people because you are not too close to them. If I sit down in this room and talk to them about their life and future and I have not had umpteen mini chats with them on this along the way because I have not seen them, the freshness was a definite advantage. I do not see staff very often. Given the size of the school and its three campuses, and that they may be moving around or I am moving around, that is not surprising. But I do think I may be too far away from the middle managers, especially the heads of department. This is partly due to logistics. But also I do a lot of individual case-work with pupils, including taking a lead on things like exclusions. I also do a lot of work connected with finance. For some of the other work, such as buildings, the administrator is responsible. But she, quite properly, will refer quite a lot to me.

There is a paradox about the large school. British people have a concept of the role of a 'headmaster', which means that many parents and outsiders don't much like dealing with other people. Sometimes I can make use of that by getting on to the right person for the enquirer. But it can have its problems in terms of how I manage my time. I spend a great deal of time talking to people. Firstly, I am interviewed by all parents enquiring about transferring their children to the school. You could argue this takes up too much of my time. You could equally argue that we would not have the level of pupil roll which we have if I did not. I think that I am one of the few heads who when I see them I usually see them singly. Sometimes I do see them in twos, threes or even fours if it is a peak period. They are shown around the school by a pupil. But I meet them and I explain things. There is a sense in which they are all asking much the same questions but they ask it in very different ways and the mode of answer, the detail, the level of sophistication has to vary according to the individual. I give every parent my home card with my home phone number on it and say that if they need to phone me please feel free to. This is used but very rarely improperly. Secondly, I do spend a substantial chunk of time on cases referred to me. Thirdly, I spend a lot of time on personnel issues. Fourthly, there is quite a lot of building matters. I imagine this is partly because I am particularly interested in and perhaps good at building matters. I used to know how to get work out of the ILEA. I also know how to commission architects and to get things done in a way that perhaps not many people in schools know how to. I put a lot of work into such things and when people ask why I say that the outcomes stay with us for quite a long time. Fifthly, I am not really much into management by walking about. I do not do much walking around the corridors. Sixthly, I have quite a significant public re-lations role. This evening, for example, I am at a meeting at 7.30 p.m. as chair of the City of Westminster Arts Council which I regard as having a largely educational function. And councillor Mare Louse Rosses, who is chair of the Arts Committee of City Hall is opening an exhibition. I regard being there as important.

What I do not spend as much time on as I would like to, is what you might call the warp and weft of the curriculum. I am afraid one of the problems in such a large organisation, particularly since the introduction of local management, is the amount of time we spend working things out.

PR: How would you describe your relationships with pupils and parents?

MM: I think I have a very strong relationship with parents. I meet them all when they first come in and I phone them up at their homes, I do a bit of home visiting. I have something of a feel for parents. I am quite personal with them. I tell them about my own family. I know you can argue that you should be professionally distant but when you have brought up as many children as I have, they quite like it when you draw on that experience talking to them. We also have a lot of events. We are a very active school, there are always things happening to which parents are invited. We have a very very strong parents' association committee. Not a PTA. I set it up as a *parents'* committee. I can hear the voices of the teachers on many other occasions. This committee meets regularly, every four weeks. They are in some respects rather like a mini governing body. I try to attend most meetings. The parent-elected governors are on the com-mittee. You could say, using the word not pejoratively, they are a cabal. There is no doubt that what the 1986 Education Act did was to put parents as the node of power. This is something I like and approve of. I get involved with them.

   Pupils, I don't see many of them individually. Unfortunately, when I do they are in difficulty of one sort or another. Not always. In upper school, the heads of year wheel in every half term some who have done well. We are a very personal school in the sense that one of the fears people had in the seventies was that such a big organisation would be impersonal. Of course, I do not pretend to know pupils by name — I know hardly any. But I always relate to them as I pass by them and they normally smile and say 'Hello Sir' if they see me out. I am quite strict. I tell them off if their shirts are not tucked in. But I try myself, and encourage the staff, to run a non-shouting regime. We have a uniforms policy in the lower houses but not in the upper school. I think this is important and if you walk around you will find it damn near perfect. I insist on it and encourage other staff to do so as well.

PR: That can be a problem with a big school. Some staff enforce such policies, others look the other way and some may even subvert it openly or covertly.

MM: I won that battle in 1980 in the face of opposition from teachers who did not want it. This is not an issue any more.

I have quite a few older students who get referred to me for special contacts and help. The staff think I have a great network out there to call on at such times. So I am always writing letters on behalf of such pupils. For example, we had a girl who came to us from another school into lower sixth having not done very well and did a one-year GCSE course and then a two-year Arts 'A' Levels and said she wanted to be a doctor. She was referred to me as an impossible case but I arranged for her to go to a medical school to meet the admissions tutor to talk about what she might do. On all these grounds I have a sprinkling of relationships with pupils.

PR: What of your relationships with the LEA?

MM: Westminster has only been in existence for three years. It was one of the earliest in the London area to go into LMS. This has changed substantially my relationship. I used to be a very successful networker in the ILEA. I used to know who to speak to about what. I was also rather good at knowing what level to go in at. So for some things I would not hesitate to go to Sir Peter Newsam when he was chief education officer. Of course I only did this rarely. Each time he gave me the help I needed. I liked and knew the Inspectorate very well although I did not find them as a system much help. When one says that a body is not much help it is usually because they do not know their stuff. This was not true of the Inspectorate. Most of them were highly paid and the role was a prestigious one. Most of them were people of distinction. I only have one criticism of them as professionals. You tend to get their kind of promotion by being a single-issue person. This meant that they were only prepared to give you their own particular line. I do not like that kind of advice and we do not buy that kind of advice now. We buy people who come and give us options. I did not think the Inspectoral Service worked very well. For a start it was incestuous in the sense that they said they would come in and advise you but what they then did was come in and inspect you and then ask you why you had not done what they had advised in the first place.

Even so I would say that I had a closer relationship with the ILEA officers and Inspectors than many heads. Partly because I have been around a long time and I have grown up with some of those people. Some I have even been teaching with. Partly, because I wrote lots of letters. In fact the Division Inspector once wrote me a letter which said would I please send him instructions as to which order he should read my letters. He now had to have a special in-tray on his desk which were just for my letters. I write letters quickly and this enables me to use a lot of professionals. A lot of professionals like being used. I find it strange that 'used' in such contexts is often regarded as a pejorative work.

The City started by trying to create what the divisional officer should have been if the Springett Report had been implemented by the ILEA. This was designed to devolve power to the divisions. If they had done that, the Government might have had a lot more difficulty than it did in breaking up the ILEA. But the new LEA set up a system which was characterised by too much interference from the centre. The second was the problem of the members. Whereas if, say, you were a member or an officer in Cambridgeshire and you saw the 1988 Act as a bill before the House, the things you would have homed in on was the central legislation on the curriculum and local management. If you were a London LEA you homed in on devolution. You either fought it, like Islington did despite the fact that in 1977 it fought for UDI on the grounds they were getting a poor service from the centre and they were right. But now, of course, the issue was seen in rather different political terms so they had to fight the other way. Or, like Westminster, you fought to get out. Consequently, the members had not tutored themselves on what an LEA is for in today's circumstances. I say an LEA in the new world of today is to do only those things which only the LEA can do. The members here had argued for years that left-wing ILEA made a mess of things and spent money profligately. This made them want to interfere too much. I have had to lead an attack on something called a business plan which the LEA has produced. I have argued that it is flawed in language, logic and law.

This serves to emphasise that when the school was first set up one of the objections which the NUT advanced was that the whole thing was being done for cheapness rather than to keep a number of schools going. The ILEA, daftly, said proudly that they did not cost such reorganisation schemes. In fact though because they made public promises that we would still have three librarians I was able to exploit that and get three librarians. I spend more money on librarian salaries than any school in the country — £46 per pupil per year.

When we went to Westminster, in the first year I sent them a long paper on the costs of working on three sites which I argued came to £500,000. Only now are they finishing consideration of that. And we are now trying to cope with a £400,000 deficit. So we have major financial problems. In the first years we found the individuals pleasant but the system not helpful. On the other hand the Inspectors have been superb. They, of course, have now been sacked.

Relationships are difficult. At one level I would put this very simply — LM is LM. If we need technical advice we can get this in various ways — not least by reading the relevant DfE circulars and other documents ourselves. Let me give you an example. The ILEA had the term holiday dates right across the authority. I am not saying that is unreasonable. Once we were into separate LEAs that was no longer going to happen. But the city put out a set of dates. I said, 'Hang on, you are not supposed to do that. Or rather, you don't have to do that'. The response was that 'Oh yes, we do'. The words of the Act are that the LEA shall 'determine' the dates of the holidays. I argued that this does not mean that the LEA has to determine them simultaneously. You could ask the schools what they want to do. A school like North Westminster might well want to work in a different way from a junior school. I do not want to go in late July when all the exam candidates have finished. I want to have time early in September. Now they have changed the system. There have been a number of times when I have had to tell them what the law is. They kept getting it wrong.

Now we have a delegated professional advice budget, that is even better. One general point about professional advice. This may not be true of a small primary school but in a school as big as this, and with the range of staff it has, much of the advice that can come from an ordinary inspectoral team is at the wrong level of generality. It is either not general enough or it is too broad. For example, when David Hargreaves was Chief Inspector, a man I respect, I said to him 'David, you have an excellent Dance inspector, Music inspector and Drama inspector but I have a head of performing arts and there is no one person to whom she can turn for advice at that level of generality. The advice she can get from your people tends to be too specialised'. On another example, we don't pay in to the local school library services — I am no longer convinced that the school library service is necessarily the best way for the future — we are all busy protecting it but what we should really be asking is what is the client need and are there other and better ways of doing things? Basically the SLS offers what is a book hire system. It might be cheaper to buy them or even to hire them somewhere else. We do not need their specialist advice. I employ three chartered librarians and I am a specialist in it myself. When we do need advice, the opposite generality point, on, for example, Moroccan literature, I cannot get it. I have Moroccan children here and to serve their needs on this I have to get advice from a real specialist.

PR: Do you think that LEAs have had their day?

MM: I think that if they work like, say, Cambridgeshire, then no. You must, in any case, have some way of establishing the money which is going to be allocated in the first place. This could be done by the central government. You must have somebody who plans the school system locally as a whole. You must have somebody who looks after children who are out of school. It is worth stressing that the law makes parents responsible that their children be educated either at school or otherwise. When parents choose to send their children to us we should see this as a privilege. They do not have to. Teachers tend to think that they must go to schools but they are wrong. As things stand the LEA has the task of ensuring that parents carry out their responsibilities for the education of their children. Some LEAs do this very well but others do not. I think LEAs should spend more time ensuring this and less time fiddling around trying to tell me and others like me what to do.

PR: How do you keep up with the pace of change?

MM: I dislike some of the National Curriculum and assessment changes because they were illogical. I am not against change but if you have to make so many and such fundamental changes to recently established policies then you could not possibly have done the thinking correctly in the first place. But I have not found trouble with reading the DES circulars. I like reading DES circulars because they give me freedom. Let us take one example. People are wandering around the country and saying that government are against multicultural education yet Section 1 of the 1988 Act for the first time in educational legislation contains the word 'culture'. Yet the DES Circular 5/89 on the curriculum contains a marvellous paragraph which stresses that schools must prepare young people for a culturally diverse society. I like knowing my stuff on this kind of thing. I must admit that I am not as up to date on everything and what I like in an SMT is for its members to take the lead on different things for the team as a whole. Other ways in which I keep up include the fact that I subscribe to a lot of journals and I read some of them. When I read interesting things in the *TES* I usually send off for the original documents. I enjoy reading but even so I have piles I have not managed to read. But I have no problem in reading in ways which meet my needs even if this means looking at things very selectively. I also read the stuff from the professional associations. This can be very useful. Also, if necessary, I do not hesitate to ring up DfE officers. For example, when I picked up just after term had ended that the Secretary of State did not intend to follow the assimilation steps on the pay scales I got on to the head of the salaries section of the DfE. I found that if you ask people like that a difficult question, they rather like it. I got a useful answer. I find I can cope.

PR: What do you like most and least about headship?

MM: What interests me most is not a single aspect but the interaction of all the aspects of headship. I really like the way all parts have to be made to come together. One reason I approve of local management is that there is no cut-off experience. This first came to me at Woodberry Down when I realised my Music teacher was inhibited by the fact that the Music rooms were filled by house heads and my pastoral care managers were very inhibited because their rooms were located in a very unsuitable position within the school. Also they lacked a waiting area and a reception desk. We got this changed. Later I was interested in what the schoolkeeper's office should look like. I sent to the ILEA asking them for their brief on the school-keeper's office only to find they did not have such a thing. I wrote another memo to the DE Branch saying will you please design and build a reception office for us. They wrote back asking what a reception office is. These are the kinds of architectural issues which I like dealing with. I can say the same for personnel issues. If you look at allowances — let's take an example. On one Sunday I found that the deputy head of Art here on an 'A' allowance had applied for a part-time post in another school. I rang him up and said I am sorry to trouble you but I am a bit worried about the fact that I am a bit late with your reference. In any case why do you want to move? He said he wanted to pursue his own art work and wished to go part time for that reason. This was the only part-time post he had seen. I said why not let us consider your going part time at North West-minster. Also why do you want to give up the allowance? He said I do not want to give up on the 'A' but he thought he had to if he went part time. I said it used to be so but it does not have to be any more. I also suggested to him, well I hope your venture is very successful but what if it is not? Why not apply for leave rather than part-time work? He was over the moon. I could never have done all that in the ILEA despite the fact that it suits us and it suits him. To try to do it you would have to ring up 33 people and each would have only known the little rules which they work to. The same can be said of the curriculum. You will remember my piece in your book on the pas-toral curriculum. I am not succeeding as well as I would wish but I like the curriculum to be delivered through a number of different modes. In answer to your first questions, it is this kind of interaction which I most like. Almost no decision in headship is made for a single reason. This is what I really like: creating coherence.

PR: What causes the greatest stress for you and how do you cope with it?

MM: The greatest stress comes from consultation. I approve of it. Indeed, it can be argued I have sometimes overdone it. But when you have parents and governors and the community and teachers and unions and the LEA you face pressures from many directions. As for coping with it, I do not seem to have been getting it right recently. I try and cope with it by putting out discussion papers and following them up in the proper way. I can do the papers quite well but I have not quite had the time to follow things up. My mode of doing things is very communication orientated and not much of it can be oral because of where we are. I therefore have a very hard job keeping up.

PR: How do you personally cope with stress?

MM: That is an interesting question. I do not do it by switching off. I don't indulge in displacement activities, unless you regard the following list as displacement activities — first, I have a busy out-of-school professional life. I like that range. One way of relaxing is doing things which give me a warm feeling and if they add to my understanding of this job that is a bonus. I am not sure I have any other answer. Reading books, editing them, writing them reduces stress — and teaches me!

I suppose one thing. My mother, who had no real education, had two or three outstanding characteristics. I will illustrate this before trying to generalise. Once after the dance band world had faded and my father was trying to make a living with radio broadcasting with his little orchestra. He went for a job one morning to do with conducting on television in the very early TV days. When he returned, my mother asked him how it had gone. He said: 'They offered it to me but I did not take it. I did not really know how to do it.' I can remember it to this day. She said: 'Get on that phone. Tell them you will take it and then find out how to do it.' That has remained in my mind. I never say no just because I do not know what I am taking on. I remember when I was invited to join the Bullock Committee my deputy Shirley Hase said to me but you know nothing about the teaching of reading. I said I know but I am going to find out. That attitude is one thing I learnt from her. The other is not to hesitate to ring people up no matter how distinguished. She thought nothing of doing this. I have become very good at writing to such people without being obsequious. The third thing I got from my mother is optimism. If you look back on the developments of the last few years we sometimes seem to do so without a sense of history. Of course the 1988 Act was introduced in a hurry but so was the GCSE and people said we could not do it and we did. We also said, when the school-leaving age was being raised that we could not do it, that it would be chaos, but we did. We look back and remember a wonderful Valhalla of peaceful times. They never existed. My first teaching job was in a bomb site. My next was in a new school which had just been built. You recall the Beloe Report: we said we could not do CSE although we had been arguing for something like it for several years. But we did and did it well. I have also found that things that people said could not be managed have been managed. They said this school could not work, that we could not introduce Dance for boys but we have.

PR: What do you do when things go wrong?

MM: I take the line that even racial violence is soluble. Not, perhaps completely and not overnight. We do not have toughness in this school. Rutherford School, when we took it over, was rough. We do not have much at all. I reckon there is a solution to every problem. It may be complex and I am willing to take as many approaches as are required to achieve my purpose. I am sometimes unorthodox. I sometimes make unpopular and unconventional decisions. You need to decide what you are going to fight on. I sometimes make decisions the staff do not like. For example, a boy who I have done a deal with not to come back, but I have not excluded him. It is legal but on the edges of legality. If there is a problem I try and get into it and sort it out. I like doing this I have come to love checking the facts. As a head I say about the school that half the things which people say about it are wrong but I do not know which half. I try not to jump to conclusions and to move too fast. But when necessary I can make a quick decision.

PR: How far do you see the school as your school?

MM: I see it very, very much as my school. More so even than Woodberry Down. It is not quite right to say I invented it. That honour must go to Peter Newsam, who thought up the idea. The scheme he produced was described as a federal school but I created it in the face of adversity and have invested more of myself in it than perhaps was sensible. I personalise it quite unashamedly.

PR: My wife, who as you know is also head of a secondary school, says that when she hears you on the radio or sees you on television that a minute will not go by before you work North Westminster into the conversation.

MM: She is absolutely right. My wife also teases me about it. I try and weave it in in such a way that they cannot easily cut it out.

PR: You have been a head for a long time. Does it still give you a buzz? Have you thought about doing anything else?

MM: For twenty-two years. Yes it still does give me a buzz. Just recently the sheer quantity of work is exceeding my hours. But the thought of being responsible in a sense for 2000 people does not really daunt me. What does is my lack of a really high-powered office and the way in which this inhibits my ability to respond as quickly as I would like. I have a fine personal assistant but she is swamped with other work. If you asked me what single thing would help me to be more effective in my job I would probably say that I would like to enlarge my personal office by one person, so that I can have an assistant who is doing all the organisation and following up.

PR: How far do you see yourself as a curriculum policy maker or manager still in the light of the National Curriculum?

MM: I very much see myself as still a curriculum manager. I do not see the legislation as having greatly affected this. Recently, I wrote a chapter on the whole curriculum. I am hoping to write a book on planning the secondary curriculum shortly. Essentially I think many people have got this wrong. I call this National Curriculumitis. I put it like this: The trouble with educational management in this country since the war, and this is a theory I have developed only in the last four years, is that unlike other organisations we have fudged where power lies. So nobody has known who is in charge of anything. Section 23 of the 1944 Education Act declared that the LEA should 'control the secular curriculum'. But it never did. Nobody has known where curriculum power lay. I was chair of English on the Schools Council. If you look back at the Schools Council it, of course, had some good projects but quite apart from the failure of that particular whole-curriculum working party its main problem was that nobody knew what it was for and therefore it put up a kind of buffer which held up curriculum management thinking or rather held up decision making on the curriculum for much of the period of its fifteen years of existence.

In my view the National Curriculum was, in effect, invented by Christopher Price, a Labour MP who was the chair of the Education Select Committee. You can see it happening if you read the appropriate page of the Report. They were questioning a senior DES officer and asked 'When would you take action under Section 90 of the 1944 Act because the curriculum of a school was patently inadequate?' I do not know Christopher Price well but I did meet him once and talked to him about that event. He said to me 'It was quite clear from that man that the DES had no idea about when they might act under that section'. In any case the discussion continued with a question which asked 'Supposing there was a school without modern languages?' The officer answered something like 'Well if they were clearly trying and the school was in a rural area we would probably let it go. Perhaps if they were in a city and did not seem to be trying then we might do something about it'. 'Oh' says the chair 'tries hard but could do better would be the report on such schools?' They ended up 'If there is a national consensus that every child should be able to learn a language other than English this should be for every child in every school'. That was an important statement.

The next major step was the 1986 Act which curiously nobody talks about. But Section 18 requires the Governors when they consider the LEA policy on the curriculum and have modified it, if they wish to, to settle the aims of the school. Few LEAs have checked up if governors have done this. But this should be the beginning of curriculum planning. It is the centre of the head's role to faciliate the governors and the staff and the parents to establish the aims of the school. Logically everything else derives from that. The next section of the 1986 Act says that the headteacher should be responsible for implementing, along with the governors, the curriculum of the school.

Then we get to the 1988 Act. This has a marvellous first section. How on earth can anyone argue with the idea of preparing young people for the opportunties, experiences and responsibilities of adult life? Only then does it put in what I have come to call the building regulations of the curriculum. The metaphor I use starts from the idea that if you and I were architects we would speak to our clients, work out what they want and how it would function and in proposing a plan we would have to meet the building regulations — the ceiling could not be less than and the windows could not be more than — the style and the ambience would be shaped to meet the particular requirements of our clients. That is how I see the present legislation. The governors are the node of power, which means the headteacher is essentially a curriculum manager whose key task is to facilitate their work. They should *use* the National Curriculum — I will give you some examples to illustrate what I mean. Before doing this we need to clear up a problem of nomenclature. If subject is now the word for describing the planning division of the curriculum regulations — I do not use it to mean course. That is out there, I have whole school policies which incorporate those regulations and then I divide it up into courses, tutorial programme and community life of the school. A course is a subject in all but name. I was talking to my head of Technology this morning. I said 'We are having a whole-school technology curriculum — it has to have a number of

things. First, it has to have within it the National Curriculum requirements but it is wider than that. Secondly, you are running a
course called CDT. In that course you will have to agree what parts
of the whole-school technology curriculum you will include but that
is not all. You will also have to include things like the occupations.'

Leading on things like that makes the head a curriculum
manager. Too many people have become too obsessed with the
requirements of the National Curriculum to see this. For instance,
the National Curriculum physical education working party plans
Dance. Some people think that means it has to be taught in Physical
Education. But it does not. We include it within the Performing
Arts. It is the same with our Languages curriculum. Some people
have been trying to tell me that it does not meet the requirements of
the National Curriculum. It does meet the requirements of the
National Curriculum. The fact that I am teaching other languages
does not alter the fact that they will be tested on one language at Key
Stage 3.

So I regard the head very much as a curriculum manager and see
the legislation as there to be used. Of course, as in architecture,
certain forms of architecture have resulted from bad drafting of the
building regulations. For example, our architect told me that certain
building regulations say that the sun has to get into the building at a
certain angle. One of the reasons why we have tall buildings is to
meet that regulation. Sometimes the style has inadvertently come
from the building regulations. I think that is also too often true of
the curriculum. However, I also think that Sir Ron Dearing is going
to have to thin out the regulations a bit.

PR: In what sense?

MM: He needs to make them rather less heavy in content. History
and Geography are too heavy and the set of books listed for English
looks too heavy for me.

PR: So schools still have important decisions to make on the curriculum? These have not disappeared with the imposition of the
National Curriculum?

MM: Schools and headteachers still have very important curriculum decisions to make. Heads have to be curriculum managers. If,
following Stenhouse, the curriculum is a description of a school's
intended learning outcomes then the school is about the curriculum.
Even if part of that curriculum are those aspects I call the pastoral
curriculum, for instance there was something going on today in a
discussion about Technology and Home Economics (which I call
Home Studies) and I said that this is not co-terminus with Technology. There is some Technology in it, that some of our concepts

like child rearing, and I gave the example of teenage violence which I said it is fixed by four, that has got to be taught for the next generation. I know this sounds like an old-fashioned comment. The Newsam Report had it, if only for girls, all those years ago. It is part of the curriculum. Take the case of racism. A sub-set of this is the way we masculinise boys. We have to discuss this and we have to teach the way in which it takes place as part of the curriculum. So I would say that heads not only can be, but must be, curriculum managers. There is a sense in which every word you have with pupils is part of the curriculum because you are teaching something. Even if it is only how to be a bit less unpleasant.

7 Brian Sherratt

with Peter Ribbins

PR: How did your background, early life and schooling shape your attitudes to education?

BS: I was born in Oxford. I suppose I was reasonably hardworking. Certainly, I was encouraged at home by my parents and grandparents to work and to be successful. It was at home with books, with music, with intelligent discussion. I was encouraged to read and use my brain and to be interested in cultural events — theatre, music, art. This was normal family life.

PR: What were the occupations of your parents?

BS: My mother didn't work and my father worked in industry.

PR: Few of the heads I have talked to have identified grandparents as an influence.

BS: I can't say that either my parents or my grandparents influenced me in terms of the kind of job I've ended up doing. I do not think they did. But they certainly were instrumental in creating the kind of climate in which I was brought up and it was a climate in which the importance of education was taken for granted. It was assumed one was going to work hard. I never knew any other kind of expectation.

PR: What kind of school did you go to? What were your feelings about it?

BS: Because I had a reasonable voice I was fortunate enough to be successful in voice trials for a cathedral choir school. I enjoyed it immensely. In a real sense one felt one was a professional musician. I must admit that I enjoyed all that went with being part of the Anglican tradition of cathedral music. It was tough. One was expected to do well in lessons and to pass exams and so on, but also to cope with the daily discipline of choir practice. In a way, hearing the liturgy of the church on a regular basis gave one not only a sense of language but also an appreciation of esoteric musical taste. My musical taste in terms of a classical, romantic and modern repertoire is quite wide, but I have a particular penchant for some forms of church music — Palestrina, Victoria, Anderio, Lassus, Monteverdi. I'm also interested in other music within the classical repertoire. I listen to as much of it as I can but of course this is mostly during the school holidays. During term time it's mostly what I can snatch from Radio Three or cassettes whilst driving the car.

PR: You remember it as hard work but that is not your main memory of it. It seems quite unusual to come across somebody who regards their first school as an almost unalloyed delight?

BS: Looking back, despite the work involved, there was also the sense, or the illusion, of stardom, in that people appeared to come along to hear the choir. I think we all knew we were rather good at what we did; we were professionals.

PR: I recently read Joanna Trollop's *The Choir*. Something that comes over very clearly is how very competitive the members of the choir are. There were stars amongst the stars and it was clear who they were — the soloists. Is this how you remember it?

BS: Yes. I enjoyed all that. In its way it was a very competitive environment. The competition began even before one became a member of the choir. Only a few made it that far. Survival required a degree of mental and physical toughness.

PR: Did you come from a background in which religion mattered?

BS: No. But at school it would have been surprising not to have been influenced by the cathedral tradition and what that involves. Later I became a server in a church which was much influenced by the ideas of the Oxford Movement. Looking back and thinking about the changes that have taken place in the Church of England, in particular in the light of Vatican II, I think of this period as the end of a golden era. You ask me about a religious background. I went on to read Theology. I suppose I must have been influenced by the experience of my early school life, by the cathedral tradition, and later by the ethos of Anglo-Catholicism.

PR: How old were you when you left home to be a boarder? What do you remember of your secondary school?

BS: To start with I attended a local preparatory school. I was about seven when I won my place at the cathedral choir school as a probationer and this was a boarding place of course. Then I went away again at thirteen to a traditional independent school. It too was extremely competitive with academic and sporting standards. I've always been conscious that I owe a great deal to both my schools and to my parents and grandparents who encouraged me. I should like to think that, in years to come, Great Barr pupils will look back with the same kind of affection on their school days. I also felt, in a sense, and this might seem a curious thing to say, that since I was subject to the influence of liturgical language of ritual, I must also acknowledge that I owe an important part of my education to the Church.

PR: Can you explain that?

BS: I think the the art of listening and hearing language, often very beautiful language, is something which, perhaps, young people today miss out on. I know that they hear the language of great literature in the formal context of lessons. What they miss out on is the art of listening and hearing — experiencing language — the symbolic language of religious mythology, arousing our deepest questionings and touching our deepest anxieties about ourselves as human beings, in the context of a ritual occasion, enshrined within a historical tradition. They have missed out on that sense of occasion; on experiencing the symbolic value of ritual; on the *mysterium tremendum et fascinans*. And despite the fact that my interest in matters ecclesiastical has become somewhat vicarious, I nevertheless believe that if young people miss out completely on this dimension of human experience, that they are somehow thereby emotionally impoverished.

PR: Were you successful, in your own mind, as a schoolboy? How was this defined?

BS: Success is relative. I suppose I was successful, but never as successful as I wanted to be. According to my headmaster, being educated meant having learnt to be at ease with all kinds of people in all kinds of situations and having acquired the skill to put others at ease — whether I've actually achieved that I don't know. There is a side of me which has always been suspicious of people who constantly talk about their successes, about how good they are. I think my parents taught me the importance of a sense of perspective in life; of the need to do one's best but at the same time not to take oneself too seriously; not to boast, not to crow about achievements or things that we might have which other people did not have. One simply didn't do that. And so I find it quite difficult, even now, to say 'Well, I was — or am — quite good at this, that or the other'.

At school I was reasonably average in the classroom, passing exams and so on. There were some highly gifted pupils there. I was not excellent in sport, although again we were encouraged, even if we weren't good, to do our best and I tried. I became reasonably

proficient at boxing. There were people at the school then, who
nowadays occupy high prestigious positions, which make my job
totally insignificant. In relative terms I suppose I was reasonably
successful.

PR: You carry the ultimate responsibility for the education of 2300
children. I find it hard to think of a job that would make that seem
'totally insignificant'?

BS: A relative of mine, I understand from a reliable source, was at a
wedding and was asked by someone who was sitting opposite during
the reception what I did. She answered 'I believe he works for the
Council'. Amusingly, perhaps, I think my job is considered by some
members of my family to be slightly suspect. After all, comprehensive schools have not always received favourable press and no doubt
a large comprehensive must inevitably be something to be avoided.
Perhaps it is my fault because I don't particularly want to be talking
about my job when I'm with members of my family. Perhaps I
should attempt to illuminate their misguided thinking.
    But you are making a legitimate point. Don't misunderstand me.
I am not saying that I don't consider being head of a large comprehensive school an enormous responsibility. Of course it is and I am
acutely aware of that responsibility. Perhaps it is that sense of responsibility and duty to pupils and staff that drives me and makes
me an enthusiast for the job. I love the school and think of it
somehow as an extension of myself. When things at school go well I
feel good; when there are problems I put all my energies into resolv-
ing them. But in the grander scheme of things I'm not at all sure
society ascribes great importance to the role of head of a comprehensive school, does it?
    You began by asking me if I think of myself as successful. I'm
trying to say that I can't answer the question without reference to
how other people might perceive the way I operate. I do not go
around asking them so the answer to the question has to be 'relatively' I suppose. Furthermore, I don't think it's the position you fill
that counts so much as how you fill it.

PR: What were the key values of the secondary school you
attended? How influential have they been on you as the headteacher
of two secondary schools?

BS: That is a very interesting question. I think the key values
would have included education for taking one's place in, coupled
with a realistic approach towards what one might contribute towards, society; there was an emphasis on the moral and spiritual
dimensions of life, a sense of duty towards one's fellow human
beings with stress on such virtues as integrity, trying one's best in

one's academic studies and in competitive sport, and, in particular, thought for others, and politeness. It was certainly expected of us that we should conduct ourselves responsibly and with consideration for all other members of the school community at all times. This, I recall, was the backdrop to the more formal aspects of the curriculum which, certainly, for those days, included, I think, a measure of balance and breadth.

I suppose one answer to your question is that I've been too busy to think about the answer because of the nature of my job. In so far as I admired certain characteristics of my own school, it must have shaped the way I think about education although I have never wished or attempted to run Great Barr as an independent school. I have never worked in the independent sector. I think that schools of that kind — that is, independent schools — can provide a good education for pupils and I've always wanted to provide my own pupils at Great Barr with the best education possible. In several respects I'm quite sure that we provide a better education than some of the independent schools. I want the best for Great Barr pupils. In short, my ambition in life — and all my efforts go into this — is to make Great Barr the best comprehensive in the country. Perhaps our examination successes, whilst good, can't compete with selective schools but I'd like to believe that the Great Barr values make an abiding contribution to the future lives of the majority of those educated here.

In thinking about the two kinds of schools I think there are significant differences and significant similarities. One thing I try to do is to create an environment at school within which it is possible for teachers to teach and therefore to gain the professional satisfaction they deserve. But, most importantly, because teachers can teach, it is possible for pupils to learn. That's a function of management and also a function of caring. If you care for an individual child you will want the best for that child and the last thing you'll want is for the child to be hurt in any way. I use this as an example when I am talking to pupils. I say 'If you're looking after your younger brother or sister and they slip your hand and run into a busy road, you will probably speak sharply to them and pull them back onto the pavement. If they do it again you might give them a smack on the leg, not because you want to inflict pain but because you love them, you've been made responsible for them and you don't want any harm to come to them. And so you discipline your brother or your sister because you care for them'. The idea of discipline as a function of caring is something pupils understand and relate to. It seems to me that schools in which teachers turn a blind eye, allow youngsters to get away with bad behaviour and poor work, are short-changing the pupils.

I sometimes describe to pupils a situation they can readily imagine in which there are a couple of pupils talking at the back of the classroom. The teacher doesn't intervene. It is not long before other pupils begin to show an interest in this conversation, start joining in themselves, and soon the teacher has lost the class. Occasionally, the teacher shouts for quietness but the pupils don't believe he really means it. It's not long before the rumour spreads you can do whatever you want in old so-and-so's lessons. He doesn't really care. A school where there is no discipline, in which teachers can't teach and pupils can't learn, is a school that does not care. I believe strongly that all children have a right to learn in an environment free of disruption.

PR: They are not caring.

BS: It's not caring and it's not long before those pupils understand that. If pupils form the opinion that a teacher doesn't care what they do, that is a terrible indictment. That is not what I want for the children of Great Barr. I want the school to be one in which pupils are not short-changed. I believe that they have a right to a good education. I would not want a child to turn round and say, with justification, 'Well, I had a great time chatting to my friends and generally wasting my time and other people's time. I didn't get any good grades in my GCSEs and I know I've done far less well than I should have done — it is your fault.'

Of course there will be some who will reject the system whatever we do. At Great Barr very few pupils reject the school and its values outright. We seem to have created the kind of environment in which even those pupils who perhaps don't adapt comfortably to our culture of learning, nevertheless feel that it's right to conform to the norms and expectations of the school, based as they are on caring for the individual. I believe the school I went to inculcated similar kinds of standard based on caring for the individual. In any event, parents choose Great Barr because they perceive it as a school with standards of work and discipline. We're very heavily over-subscribed. I believe the school I attended inculcated similar standards based on care for, respect for, the individual. I think the difference is that in a school like that the one I attended the parental pressure on the child can be very considerable. There was a powerful and shared culture. But it's not just that. I also remember quite clearly being told in no uncertain terms if I didn't knuckle down and get on with it that there was not a bottomless purse; that other priorities mattered. There was a definite expectation at home that I got good reports, that I got 'As' in everything. If I didn't they wanted to know why. There was an inquest. I believe that my own schooling has influenced the way I see things. Obviously, in a comprehensive we have pupils of all abilities and so the measure of success must be more sophisticated but some of the core values are the same. We want the best for all pupils irrespective of ability or the degree of parental support for the school's values in practice. There is a difference between being keen to obtain a place at Great Barr for your child and actively supporting the school's values as they're lived out on a day-to-day basis.

PR: When we last spoke you described caring for the individual as part of a broader civilising impulse. This seemed an honourable idea and one you held without being committed to a naïve view of human nature and unrealistic ideas of what makes pupils act in the ways in which they do.

BS: Many of us look for things to do which are interesting to do, but which may have little to do with the business in hand. Many children, unless they are pointed to what needs doing, and told to get on with it, won't do it. The first priority of the school is to make sure that the structures are there to enable it to be on task. Then it's basic things like staff being outside the classroom at the start of the lesson; overseeing the orderly entry of pupils into the classroom; settling them down within a matter of seconds so that no valuable teaching time is lost. If it takes five minutes and multiply this by the number of pupils in the class, by the number of periods in the day, by the number of periods in the year — you begin to get a real idea of what can be lost. Pupils can't put the clock back. You could lose a lifetime's education and that's wrong. So, yes, I hope that the school is a civilising influence. But I am not one of those heads who subscribes to the view that if you get the curriculum right then everything will fall into place. I think that's naïve. Nor am I one for just doing interesting things with the curriculum simply because it is interesting to do interesting things with the curriculum. You risk losing sight of the reason why the school is there in the first place. It's there for the benefit of the pupils. It's there so that we can develop professionally and become better teachers or administrators or managers. It's not there so that we can go home feeling that we have done something frightfully interesting, that we have indulged ourselves, but that we have done nothing for the pupils.

Going back to the comparison, I think that some, not all, independent schools, have a different climate; sustained by the staff but effectively created by the pupils themselves. These schools are often highly selective and their pupils bring great expectations and pressures from home. Such pupils tend to succeed in whatever context they find themselves. In many urban comprehensives those expectations and pressures from home are lacking. I've the greatest admiration for those schools whose teachers find ways of generating pupil self-motivation and the will to succeed, particularly when home values are not supportive of those underpinning the school's culture.

PR: Did any of your own teachers particularly influence you?

BS: There were several very good teachers there. One English teacher in particular I remember being outstandingly good at involving pupils, generating an authentic excitement in literature. I can remember several teachers who interested me in things that I might not otherwise have read. I have recently gone through a phase of reading French novels in French, basically because I did 'A' level French as a kind of hobby. We were encouraged to do additional subjects in the sixth form and, if appropriate, to take an exam in that subject. My voluntary subject was French and the master who took this class was a disciple of Proust. As it happened my grandmother, who was Swiss, considered *A la recherche du temps perdu* her favourite novel. I first started reading Proust in English and then in French. I was struck with his incredibly tortuous sentences which seemed short on punctuation. My interest in Proust goes back to that particular voluntary class but was nurtured no doubt by my grandmother's enthusiasm, and by the fact that she took every opportunity to speak the French language when I visited her.

PR: You read Theology at university. Why?

BS: Yes, I read Theology. I wanted to read Oriental Studies and I was offered a place at St. Andrews to do so. They wrote to me and noted that I had no German. It was pupils of lesser ability, would you believe, who studied German at my school. You studied Greek if you were thought to be any good. So I had no German at all. For classical Arabic many of the exegetical books were written in German. I did not relish spending a couple of terms working my German up to the required standard. And so when it was suggested to me by a member of staff that I should perhaps look at Theology, I did.

PR: What attracted you to the study of Theology?

BS: I had the necessary Latin and Greek. I suppose I was interested in ecclesiastical matters and at that stage I was sufficiently realistic or naïve or self-assured or whatever, to believe that one went to university to read a particular discipline for the intrinsic value of that discipline rather than for any extrinsic benefits that might accrue. That meant that one rather looked down one's nose at people who read, say, Law for a first degree. The idea was that one first read the subject that one wanted to read and then went on to read Law if one had to. But I do not really know what attracted me to Theology. I find it very difficult to answer that question. I have asked it of myself several times. I can't say that I took to theology like a duck to water: Theology's interesting but not that interesting. I think it was just a matter of expediency. I was worried about the German. It was much easier to read Theology because I had a bit of a head start there. I knew I could cope with New Testament Greek and I had the necessary Latin. In practice I found that side of it relatively straightforward. I just had nightmares over the Hebrew.

PR: To what extent did the things you stress from your religious experience and studies seem more to do with ritual and ceremony than with substance?

BS: I think you are absolutely right — I had liked the music, the cathedral kind of music, the ritual of the Oxford Movement, the colours, the ceremony, the drama, the smell, the incense. Then I went away to university, read Theology, and quietly drifted away from the Church, taking solace in what might be called contemporary theology — the work of theologians such as Tillich, Bultmann and of philosophers like Heidegger. My interest was an academic interest rather than one which sprang from an inner point of view. To sum it up, my interest in the church is now essentially voyeuristic. If occasionally I like dipping into it, I don't want to be involved. It's a dreadful thing to say. It is self-indulgent. Proust believed ostensibly inconsequential stimuli produced 'involuntary memory' and vividly recreated past experiences. Anglo-Catholic ritual often conjures up for me isolated memories of childhood or incidents long forgotten.

   Some time ago I attended the High Mass at St. Mary's, Bourne Street, just off Sloane Square. It is regarded as the hub of Anglo-Catholicism in London. A place where they still do things 'the right way'. The music was outstandingly good, the ritual elegant, the sermon scholarly and the building packed to capacity. Perhaps were I fortunate enough to live off Sloane Square, I would become a regular attender at St. Mary's, Bourne Street.

PR: But rather in the same spirit of going to a performance of *King Lear* rather than in the expectation of taking part in a profound religious experience?

BS: Possibly. But one has one's favourite plays and favourite theatres. If you were offering me a free ticket I'd opt for the opera. I can remember attending a performance of *La Boheme* which was a profound experience. The thing about profound experiences is that they don't necessarily affect the way you are or the way you will be. I can repeat the profound experience by putting on the Beecham, Bjorling, de Los Angeles recording at more or less any time but I can't claim that to any great extent it's changed my life in the sense that attending church is supposed to do. I like listening to Puccini when performed by Jussi Bjorling and Victoria de Los Angeles directed by Beecham and I like the kind of mass they do at St Mary's, Bourne Street.

I'm the sort of person who can look and not commit himself, who finds it difficult to do more. I like to think that having read Theology I have huge intellectual difficulties in grappling with what other people can swallow. Well, that's my story anyway.

PR: Presumably one of the problems with reading Theology is that if you don't want to become a priest the number of occupations for which it prepares you is limited.

BS: I am not so sure about that. I've been surprised at the number of Theology graduates who have become heads. One of my children once tried on me the well-worn question 'What's the point of having to do RE? What job will it get you?' The answer of course was, 'You could end up as head of a large school'.

PR: You could become an academic or a priest or a teacher. At what point was it clear that your vocation was not religious? When did you begin to think that it might be in education?

BS: I do not think I ever seriously considered a religious life. I don't think of myself as a religious person. The second part of your question is more difficult to answer. I think that I might have done some drifting. Even by the end of my second year at university I had no clear view of what I wanted to do. It did cross my mind to read Law. I was quite interested in going to the Bar. Even now my wife tells me that is what I should have done. She seems to think I might have made quite a good barrister but at the time I began to look at various things. My father introduced me to the hospital manager at the John Radcliffe Infirmary. That didn't appeal particularly. I then went for an interview at the Department of Education, Leeds University with the possibility of doing a PGCE. I didn't particularly enjoy that one-year course at all. The part I enjoyed least was the RE element. Stupidly, at the time I thought of it as a kind of Sunday School equivalent of the Theology Faculty. It was quite difficult to take. And this wasn't just my view. Other people with my kind of background found it that way. I suppose I was rather dismissive of it. My second teaching practice was at Normanton Grammar School just outside Leeds, and towards the end of the practice the head of RE, or of Divinity as it was called at the time, who was about to become the senior master of the amalgamated boys' and girls' school (when I was there on teaching practice it was a boys' grammar school) came up, took me to one side and said 'Sherratt, I'm not quite sure how to put this. We shall be having a vacancy here. I don't know if it's presumptuous of me to put it to you this way but were you to be interested in the vacancy the headmaster would like to know.' I then went through an interview at which I was the only candidate. The chairman of the governors, the local vicar, asked me if I had noticed anything about the station at Normanton? I had not. What I failed to notice was that it was the longest station in the United Kingdom. Having failed this key question in the interview, I was offered the post.

PR: A serendipity really?

BS: Yes. I went on to become head of department at Selby Grammar School after two years at Normanton. I wrote a textbook on comparative religion which was published in 1972 and only went out of print three years ago. Of course it was hopelessly out of date.

PR: At what point did you begin to realise you might want to be a head, and why?

BS: When we went to London I became a lecturer in comparative religion. I held a .5 post and for the other .5 I taught at Kidbrooke School. There was a very well-known head there — Dame Mary Green. My head of department followed Michael Marland at Crown Woods when Marland went to Woodberry Down. He followed Marland as director of studies. It began to occur to me I wasn't sure that people holding such posts had anything that I didn't have or couldn't develop. I suppose I took it for granted that with the passage of time I would just move on. In the event I went on to a deputy head post in Tunbridge Wells. I was there for six years. First as senior master, then I became deputy head. In 1979 I was appointed to my first headship. In 1984 I came to Great Barr.

PR: How did you prepare for headship?

BS: In a variety of ways. I followed the part-time Academic Diploma in Education course at the London Institute of Education. My options were Educational Organisation and Administration and the Philosophy of Education.

On completing the examinations I received a letter from Professor Peters telling me that I had done particularly well in philosophy and inviting me to take an MEd, either in Philosophy of Education or in Philosophy. I chose philosophy. Whilst I was away on this course I rang home and my wife, Brenda, said 'You've got another letter.' This time from Professor Baron. It said more or less the same. 'You did particularly well in the examinations. Will you consider an MA in Organisation and Administration'.

I didn't know what to do. My whole background lent itself to philosophy. On the other hand, I saw this as something of an oppor-

tunity. I think I made a conscious decision then that I was going to
do the MA in Organisation and Administration, in part as a preparation for promotion and because I was interested in it. So that is
what I did.

There were parts of that course which initially I found rather
tedious. I don't think I would now. They related to central government and administration and yet they were brought alive by our
tutor, Sir Toby Weaver. That was in the second year I think. He sat
in on our seminars for the last couple of terms. He had some wonderful anecdotes to offer of his experiences at the DES with quite
brilliant descriptions of the styles of various Secretaries of State.

PR: In retrospect did you find the course a useful preparation for
headship? In what other ways did you prepare yourself for headship?

BS: I think that it was useful at the time in that not many people
had a higher degree in Educational Management. It was useful, in
that it opened a number of doors. Also I met some interesting people
during that course. It put me in touch with the literature, with the
concepts of school management. At the same time I was writing the
school timetable. In fact I finished the school timetable as a priority
and wrote up my MA dissertation in the holiday. It was in 1976, the
summer of the great drought. I shut myself in the study and just got
on with it. It was hard. I worked non-stop. I work hard now but that
summer I drove myself. It was unbearably hot and I worked with the
curtains drawn to keep the room cooler. I was doing all the things
one does to move on — the timetable, the curriculum. I became
curriculum deputy whilst I was doing that course. I went on an HMI
organised COSMOS course, that sort of thing.

I remember a conversation with a colleague at the school in
Tunbridge Wells who had taken over my job when I was promoted
to the curriculum deputy post. He's now head of a school in Cambridgeshire. He said 'Come on Brian, you will be off soon'. It was
the end of a particularly hectic week and I said, 'I don't know. I can't
really ever see that happening'. He said 'What on earth are you
talking about. Everybody else thinks that you will go on to be a
head. After all you look like a head'. I think I might have asked what
heads were supposed to look like.

Although I didn't assume the headship was inevitable I think at
this stage I'd made up my mind that I should start thinking about
framing an application. *La distance n'y fait rien; il n'y a que le premier
pas qui coûte.*

PR: Did you apply for many headships?

BS: I applied for two, was interviewed for both, and was appointed
to the second. It was at Kirk Hallam in Derbyshire, an 11–16

community comprehensive school with about 700 pupils. It was a school very much at its heart of the community in a very large estate. It drew essentially from a council estate but there was some private housing development too.

PR: What do you remember of taking it over?

BS: It's interesting you should ask. Only the other day I was talking to Alan Cooper, the first deputy I appointed there, about how we tried to improve the school. He is now in his second headship.

Putting it as succinctly as possible, I picked up a fairly run-down small comprehensive school on the Nottingham/Derby border which had been a secondary modern. It was still in the process of going comprehensive when I took it over. I saw that it needed status and a sense of belief in itself that wasn't rooted solely in the sort of work-ing-class culture that people were seeing it as. I wanted to widen its horizons. In essence that is what I was trying to do.

PR: What did you do and how did you do it?

BS: I set about creating proper expectations of behaviour. I intro-duced school uniform. I worked hard at improving the examination results and widening the catchment to include children from a neigh-bouring village in addition to the local estate. It was a widening of the horizons job.

There were a significant number of parents who wanted to see the same developments I wanted to see, who wanted to see some more academic rigour, who wanted to see better results, who wanted to see smarter looking pupils, pupils dressing to come to work; I worked hard at image building and with some success. I made a number of strategically important appointments and gradually the ethos of the school began to show signs of coming into line with my starting point — that every child has the right to a good education; that we fail as teachers if we cannot provide the climate in which pupil learning can flourish; that all pupils, irrespective of ability or background, are entitled to experience a measure of success in their schooling and that to rationalise our way out of providing that cli-mate and that success on the basis of the pupil's background is deeply offensive and offensively patronising.

The school became somewhat more popular. Of the three depu-ties whom I apppointed at Kirk Hallam, each has become a head. So, yes, I had a job of work to do and tried to do it in the four-and-a-half years I was there. I then moved on to Great Barr.

PR: Why did you move?

BS: Essentially because I liked large schools. Although I valued my years at Kirk Hallam, I suppose I always knew that I was cut out to be head of a large school. In a large school one is more at the hub of things. I liked the size of Kidbrooke although, of course, there were some things about it I didn't take to. For me, there are greater possibilities in a large school for staff and for pupils than can exist in a smaller institution. I'm very much a large-school head.

PR: Had you been looking for some time?

BS: I'd been looking but not applying. We had a full HMI inspection. It was one of the very first to be published and although I hadn't seen it the indications were that it was pretty good in relative terms. I suppose I felt I had managed to do something worthwhile in the school. In fact I was beginning to settle into the school and made many contacts and friends within the local community. I remember thinking that although I was still relatively young I could nevertheless remain at Kirk Hallam and take it forward. On the other hand I had twenty-five years of working life ahead of me. In retrospect, I think I rationalised my situation along the lines that 'I'm not the sort of person who is naturally at home in a small school. I shan't be until I'm in a larger school'. I suppose that has possibly proved to be correct. I'm in my tenth year at Great Barr now. I haven't wanted to move on and I don't want to move on. I feel much more productive as head of a larger school; productive in the sense I work well in the context of the challenges and opportunities a large school provides.

PR: What struck you about Great Barr when you went for interview?

BS: Initially the state of the building, their relative dilapidation. The good order I saw in the school. The motivation of the staff. It was very much a school I would like to take over. Since arriving at Great Barr I have worked consistently at maintaining tone and order, the pre-requisites to learning and pupil progress. I say to people who come for interview, that the good order they'll observe as they make their way around the school is not something that just happens to be there: on the contrary, we work at it every day. You don't just create a certain kind of ethos or climate and leave it to look after itself; it needs nurturing. Climate can change.

PR: What did you take and what have you tried to make at Great Barr?

BS: Given the changes which have taken place in the late '70s, '80s and now in the National Curriculum, with their implications for the chemistry of teaching in the classroom and for the organisation of lessons, I suppose I've managed to maintain our sense of purpose as a learning institution. People tell me as they walk about the school that they gain a strong impression that the school has a sense of purpose, that pupils are on task and appear to be well motivated and working hard. They sense a feeling of order when pupils move around the school; a shared understanding of how one behaves at Great Barr. I think I've maintained that. In other respects I have moved things on significantly. I was a curriculum deputy and my main interest was the curriculum. Things would have moved on anyway — but it would have been much more difficult had the preparatory spadework not been done in terms of making fundamental changes with regard to curriculum organisation and planning. Had those things not been in place such as the curriculum areas, curriculum managers, the recruiting of good heads of department and deputies, school-generated as opposed to national, developments would not have been extensive. Indeed, the fact that new structures were in place has enabled us to cope more effectively with government-led initiatives such as the National Curriculum.

Then there has been the GM factor, of course, which has made a dramatic improvement in terms of the ability to get things moving, to get things done; to improve the school for pupils and staff. The motivating factor was to improve the school. Money has been spent on books, equipment, upgrading existing facilities and new facilities. Becoming grant-maintained has empowered us to move the school forward in a way I would never have believed possible. It has changed the school very much for the better.

There has been a continuing emphasis on broadening the curriculum and more recently a new emphasis on Technology which we are now in a position to take further. It's a difficult question to answer. I think, perhaps, it's for others to say but I believe I've maintained the essential climate and ethos of the school and that I have improved on what I found. I believe that the major steps have been taken in terms of the organisation and structure of the school and therefore (I don't like the word 'delivery') of the mediation of the curriculum to pupils. Also, there's been steady improvement in examination results, marginal improvement, year by year. That is true not only of GCSE but also of 'A' Level. More students are going on to university.

I think the school has a high profile. Since I came we have been heavily involved in LEAP1, LEAP2 and LEAP3. We have also been involved in a number of projects at the national level. The school has featured in the *Times Educational Supplement* on numerous occasions. Becoming GM has served to increase our profile in the media including television and radio. So we are now a well-known school nationally. We are also even more popular than we were in terms of first choices. Projecting the image of the school is perhaps something I do well. One of the things I am told I am able to do well as head is to communicate to all parents what Great Barr is all about, and they like what they hear. It's from the heart. As I said before, I tend to think of the school as almost an extension of myself. When things are going well at school I have a sense of well-being but when there are problems I cannot rest until I've resolved them. Of course, it's a large place and one can never, therefore, be entirely at peace with oneself all the time.

PR: You've been a head for fourteen years. Has headship changed significantly in that time?

BS: Can I attempt to answer in two ways? First, there's a temptation for heads to believe that the world about them is changing so rapidly and dramatically that somehow they have to become different people, to modify their views of what is entailed in effective headship. I am not sure that that's particularly helpful. My view is that one has to see these things in evolutionary terms. One changes throughout life, although in a sense one remains the same in terms of personality. I think to be a head you need to be adaptable. I have worked in a whole variety of situations. I suppose that I am adaptable. I can survive in very different circumstances. Kirk Hallam was a very different school from Great Barr. I believe that it's necessary for a head to, as it were, evolve personnel management and other techniques in accordance with the way in which the institution is developing, and to be aware that in many respects it's developing because of certain pressures the head is exerting. The clearer one's perception of the school — the realities of the situation — and where one wishes to lead it, the clearer one will be about how one is in fact leading it and the extent to which one has contributed to institutional change, not just to be passive in the process. If I know now where I am now I stand a better chance of getting to where I want to be. But I'm not convinced by the argument that because education is changing, we must therefore change our styles. No doubt, I have changed my style but it is something to do with the dynamic relationship between the institution which I happen to be head of and the way I am.
     Secondly, I think that as one grows in the headship role one develops a certain persona; one develops the ability to make judgements about the institution and about one's leadership of it; the ability to tell people, with evidence, what they may or may not wish to hear; the ability to get under the skin of the school — a gut understanding of what the school is about.

PR: Has recent legislation increased or diminished your ability to manage?

BS: I think I would say that I am conscious of much greater freedom. Many of the changes have been externally driven but I don't have too many hang-ups about most of those changes. I have hang-ups about Key Stage testing, not testing *per se*, but its introduction has been mis-managed. If we had been left to introduce it ourselves I think some of the difficulties could have been overcome — if the whole process had been teacher-driven. In our school many developments have been introduced successfully, in part because they have been properly managed. If you get staff involved, if they begin to perceive the advantages of an innovation for the pupils, for the school and for parents, for themselves as professionals, then I think there are ways of managing even the most difficult situations effectively. But politicians are not always managers. Here we have a situation where the idea in itself may not be flawed because parents are entitled, I think, to information about how their children are doing and perhaps they are even entitled to information about how a school is doing, with certain caveats. But if the change is managed in such a way as to alienate those very people who must facilitate the change, and if the press is not managed effectively in a way by politicians — who should be good at such things — then you are on a disaster course and I think that's what's happened.

So I'm not one of these heads who is over critical about recent legislation but I do have severe reservations about the way it is being implemented.

PR: What do you see as your key tasks? What is crucial to the exercise of effective and successful headship, reflecting?

BS: To me, it is the ability to develop effective teamwork; to work as an ensemble rather than to promote soloists. I do think that gone are the days of the really autocratic head. There are still some around of course and it could be that some people regard me as one. There are occasions when one needs to be autocratic. There are occasions when — even though I am the only one who thinks that something is right for the school — one must stick to one's guns. But this should happen only very occasionally. Generally speaking it's necessary to involve others. I don't mean simply to involve them in paperwork, but to enable them to understand the processes and to contribute towards the decision. The way we went about introducing teacher appraisal is an example of how this might happen in practice. Another thing I think is absolutely crucial in running a school is making good appointments. I don't make all the appointments myself because sometimes we may have up to three interviews running concurrently but I have confidence in the people with whom I am working intimately. I am confident that they will make the kind of appointment they know I'd approve of; that we'd all approve of. We think the same. The people who are working closest to me can, you might say, read my mind. They know what I would have said on

any particular issue. And that's good. Not that they are clairvoyant
or that there is an incredible level of predictability about what one
does or thinks; it's that we are on the same wavelength. That doesn't
mean we agree about everything. I look forward to the cut and thrust
in our debate of issues. I think that's another point — you need a
frank discussion of issues affecting the school at a variety of levels.
Even when you are used to consulting, one still needs to develop the
kind of antennae which read situations. You need to have your finger
on the pulse of what is going on in the school and what staff are
thinking. You need to be talking to people and getting around the
place and having those people who are prepared to talk, to feel at
ease in doing so. You can weed out the political gloss which they
might have added to what they tell you and get to the bones of what
they are saying about the institution. Absolutely crucial is building
the ethos of the school and maintaining it daily and working at it
daily.

PR: Is this ethos expressed in the aims and values of the school?

BS: And its procedures. Aims are pretty useless in themselves.
Because we have these *values* this is the way we do these things. It's
necessary to break aims down into manageable ideas and tasks. It is
necessary to get away from abstractions. On the whole teachers are
not very happy with philosophical talk. They tend to say 'Oh, that's
philosophy, its nothing to do with the facts, the realities of the job';
but it can be and if they can see the principles which drive the way
the institution wants to do things and if this can be broken down into
the things they do in the classroom, in the corridor, in the yard, they
will accept that this stress on values can be helpful.

PR: I know you find the mental model idea useful. What is your
mental model of the school?

BS: Let me begin by saying that a mental model is generally a
mechanism for getting away from words and having got away from
words one can, through the symbolism of the model, get to the truth
of how one actually feels about an institution. I'm one of those
people who's never conscious of having woken from a dream. I
imagine I never dream although I am sure I do, I understand everybody does, but I do not remember them. I find it very difficult to get
away from words in that sense, to perceive experience through symbolism other than language; or to be more precise, and despite what
I've already said about symbolism, I find it very difficult to generate
symbolic modes of communication other than the traditionally
linguistic. So my mental model is very much a spoken thing; I can't
get away from the words; all I can do is describe the words — this is
the way I see the school, think and feel about the school. Now the

feeling element comes over in the description I give and it would be
very artificial for me to launch into it now. If I were to present my
mental model of Great Barr to the staff — I've done it on a number
of occasions and it's different each time because the school is changing, and I'm changing — I would begin by explaining the nature and
purpose of the exercise before describing the mental model itself.

To manage a school effectively a head needs to face up to the
realities of the present situation, needs a sharp understanding of how
things are, needs to see the school as it is. If I'm to manage the school
effectively, I need to hold the complete picture in my mind; I need to
see the school as a unity. If I'm to have this overall picture, I need,
metaphorically, to rise above the school, to look down and see it in
all its interrelated complexity, to see the good points — the things I
feel proud of — and the things I feel less proud of; to see the school
working, its staff and its pupils.

But if I'm to see the complete picture I need to rise higher — to
see the school in the context of its community: parents, governors,
local residents, local employers, other local schools, the local political scenario. But that is still only part of the whole picture. So I need
to rise higher still — to see the school in the context of the national
scene, beyond our immediate circumstances to the significant
changes which have been part of our professional life for some years
and which will continue to engage us for some time yet; changes
which impinge upon our school at many levels.

Having risen above the school and being able to see it in the
wider context, I'm able to see the horizon, and having this height,
this vantage point, I'm more able to plan for what lies ahead. As I
look down on the school, as I see it in all its living, changing complexity — the dynamic of life — I must see myself in it. That can be
difficult — facing up to one's strengths *and* also one's weaknesses as
its leader. But isn't this self-indulgence? Not at all, because in working out one's mental model, one is creating a conceptual map. Maps
can be useful as long as they're up to date and accurate.

If I understand the school, and myself as part of it, I can understand how I'm leading it. I can plan to take it forward. But before I
can do that I must share my mental model with colleagues. Doing
the mental model is difficult, but that difficulty is nothing compared
with the task of enabling other staff, whose mental model might be
very different, to modify, to some extent, their perceptions of the
school, so that their mental model coincides to some measure with
one's own.

When you share the mental model, then it's much easier to plan
development, to establish a sense of direction and purpose, to sign-
post the way for the school because those who are leading it with you
— at whatever level — know that they are working from the same

conceptual map. *When the mental model is shared then the headship becomes shared.*

In talking to staff about my mental model I describe what I actually see — the pupils and their teachers; the teaching and the learning processes; the interactions which make the school what it is. I extol the virtues. Great Barr is my idea of what a good comprehensive school should be; it is the kind of school the community wants. I describe the sense of purpose, the tangible nature of pastoral care, the stress on standards, the parental support — all with appropriate evidence. I think it's necessary to feel good about the school and to enable staff to feel good about the school. *You* are part of this. *We* created this. *We* are sustaining it. *We* are working at it all the time. In other words I describe what I think is there and I try to do it as objectively as possible. I take ten or fifteen minutes to get to that point and then I describe the problems and how we're dealing with them. Then I come to the most uncomfortable part of all. Having risen above the school and looking down on it one is forced to see oneself, and that is potentially difficult to cope with because it entails coming to terms with not only what you think might be your strengths as the school's leader but also your weaknesses. The things you might have done for the benefit of the school. The things which for whatever reason you've failed to do. Having risen above the school, I'm seeing it in its entirety, seeing how I am leading it and facing up to the truth about how I am leading it, in terms of both the good and the bad. One is able to see things perhaps more clearly. If you face up to the realities, to the faults in your own leadership, it means you can do something about them. It is a powerful incentive to do something about them. To modify one's management of staff, perhaps to involve people more. It means taking stock. It involves knowing how other people are seeing you as a leader not just thinking you can see yourself. That is a useful exercise, it's useful to do it oneself and also to share it with others. It is relatively easy to talk about how one thinks and feels about the school. It is much more difficult to communicate that to people. If their mental model of the school is very different from yours it means that you may be living in cloud cuckoo land. From this perspective the task of leadership is not to impose on other staff but to enable them to see it your way. We should see our mental models as not just pieces of paper but as our maps. If we are all working from different maps, we won't be starting from the same point and we are certainly not going to end up in the same place. But if you are all working from the same map, the same conceptual map, it means that there are shared concepts, principles and ambitions for the school and the route one should follow in order to take the school forward becomes more evident.

The other thing about the mental model is that it can communicate far more than it seems to. I can stand up, as I will do later this month, when we have a new intake evening, and describe the school. I'll say things about it which I believe are right, which are factual. But when you offer your mental model to others you communicate more than factors, you communicate how you feel, you become very vulnerable. Coming back to what I was saying half-an-hour ago, there is a sense in which I feel that the school is a kind of extension of oneself. If people don't recognise what you are describing or if they feel that what you are describing is very much not to their liking, that can be crushing.

PR: That's eloquently put. The thing that you stress is the extent to which effective headship entails sharing your vision with staff and working through it with them.

BS: I think as head you have to know what you want. I don't have a great deal of respect for the sort of head that will go in and ask 'Well what are we going to do?' You might say that, but if you don't know yourself you are tending towards abdication rather than delegation in the decision-making process. That does not mean that you won't modify your position in the light of discussion. There's no point in having a discussion unless you are prepared to modify your views. You must have certain basic concepts of what makes a good school. Those concepts may be dynamic in a sense that in talking to my colleagues, in whose judgement I have considerable faith, I'm prepared to modify my position and hence the management line. Its rather like being able to change the lens of the eye, the conceptual lens of the eye so to speak. Or perhaps it's like using a zoom lens — in discussion with colleagues one sees a problem from a wider perspective and yet collectively we're able to zoom in on the detail too. If one is obsessive about consensus one isn't leading the school at all. You've got to have the courage of your own convictions, to be a leader of school.

PR: To be clear about what your ambitions are for the school?

BS: You've got to be able to communicate that vision and you've got to be able to communicate it to the people there and then. And the vision doesn't arise *sub specie aeternitatis*. You are working within a particular situation. You're working with people who are there at the time. It's no good saying 'Were things very different here this school could really take off'. You've got to try and create that reality in terms of the circumstances in which you find yourself. You will never make a new reality unless you face up to the present realities of the situation as it is. Only so much is achievable and one can only work through the people you happen to be with.

PR: Let's take up that issue of working through people. You have stressed the centrality of the staff in all this, especially the teaching staff. What do you expect from your senior staff, what do you expect from the middle managers? What should they be able to expect of you?

BS: I hope the people I have appointed, the heads of department and other senior staff, are the sort of people who have the potential, whether they wish to realise this or not, to do the job I am doing now. And I hope that I would give them, through good example and leadership, the passion to wish to do their job successfully. But also to have the ambition, the drive, to go on beyond that and to fulfil themselves professionally. I think that's terribly important. I would never want to appoint someone to a terminal appointment; so I owe it to them to provide them, through appraisal targets and appropriate in-service training, with the wherewithal to achieve, either within their existing job specification or beyond it, the necessary preliminary expertise to move on to other posts. I expect them, if they are heads of department, to manage their departments effectively. To do so within the context of the area within which they work and that includes even the physical environment. I expect them to take a very high profile in terms of their responsibility for the way in which pupils conduct themselves. That is, all aspects of the conduct of pupils whilst they are in their area including their corridor behaviour, classroom behaviour and attitude, effort, presentation of work, completion of homework on time, relationship with teachers. I expect all that along with a general responsibility for the quality of work in their subject areas. I expect them to ensure pupils are stretched. I expect heads of department to see beyond the confines of their own departments and in doing so to contribute in the cut and thrust of head of department meetings. I expect them to develop new and rejuvenating ideas at every level within the curriculum. Above all, I expect them to be successful. They are entitled to, and can expect my unequivocal support.

PR: You began with the heads of department rather than with the deputies. Am I reading too much into this? What do you expect of your deputies? What should they expect of you to?

BS: They should expect my confidence in them and my support, always my public support. They should expect leadership and professional guidance from me. Because I selected them, because in my judgement they are right for the school, because we are working from the same mental model the same conceptual map, they should expect me to have confidence in their decisions. In a very real sense when I am not around they are me. They are the head. They should expect that I will be happy with the decisions they make. If I am not, they would expect me to say so. They would expect me to be honest with them but in a professional way. In other words they should expect thorough-going delegation. Because I trust them and because we are working from the same map. My deputies and I form a team.

PR: They will be held responsible for how they exercise that responsibility?

BS: Delegated responsibility within an understood framework of accountability. We are not free agents. I too am accountable. I am accountable to the governors. I am answerable to all sorts of people for my actions. So are my deputies. Initially they are answerable and accountable to me. What do I expect of them? I expect their support, their loyalty. I expect them to work tirelessly. I expect total commitment to the school. I expect them to move things forward, to lead in their areas; they are very clearly defined areas. I expect them to be looked up to, respected as helpful people to whom staff can turn; to be sensitive to their colleagues as fellow human beings. But I also expect them to be able, on those rare occasions when it's necessary, to put a member of staff right; sometimes it is necessary to do that. I expect them to take a very high profile indeed in terms of the maintenance and improvement of the general ethos and climate of the school. I expect them to do basic things like lunch duty supervision, bus duty, being out on the yard, being on the corridors, on the staircase. I expect them to get around observing lessons, to look at pupils work, to look at what teachers are doing, to see that all is well, actively to support their colleagues. I expect them to do all these things in addition to undertaking the very specific jobs which they are appointed to.

PR: Are you more likely to be disappointed in your senior staff than in your middle managers?

BS: I think there is a greater possibility of a head being disappointed in very senior staff, in deputies, than there is in being disappointed in heads of department in general. For one thing, there are fewer deputies and they occupy positions of greater institutional prominence. Obviously, if you've got a head of Maths or a weak head of English that can be disastrous for a school. By 'weak' I mean someone who can't manage the department rather than academically lightweight. In a sense you can get away with — carry — an ineffectual deputy but you won't get away with a bad head of Maths or English. On the other hand, if you have got somebody with responsibility for the timetable and it becomes apparent they can't do it, then you have a potential disaster on your hands. Presumably, as head, you would have the foresight to ensure that the new appointee had the requisite training in timetabling. You would also make sure that you had the opportunities to discuss how the timetable was proceeding and examine what had been done thus far. You could judge the measure of departmental consultation from your heads of department meetings. As a last resort, you might have to enlist the support of another deputy or take on the task yourself. Fortunately, it's not a problem I have had to face. We tend to rotate roles periodically, anyway, and this represents excellent professional development: it provides deputies with an extensive repertoire of skills. Great Barr deputies have little difficulty in moving on to headships if that is what they choose. We're seen as a good stable to come from.

I imagine there is more potential for disappointment where a deputy is concerned than there is where other staff are concerned. Not least because in departments generally people support each other and so institutional weaknesses are not so institutionally exposed as they can be at a deputy level. Deputies here are very much members of a team and we work together to support each other every working day. In a large school such as ours there is a clear division of labour between the deputies. Where such lines of demarcation are clear, deputies tend to show a natural reluctance to trespass on each other's areas of responsibility without invitation. Because of this it may appear to the observer that support between deputies is not as evident as in smaller institutions where the responsibilities are less clearly divisible. The reality is that my four deputies are highly talented. Any one of them would be highly successful as a head of a large school.

PR: Do you bring a greater tolerance and understanding to middle managers who are not performing as you would expect them to than you would to a deputy in a similar situation? Are you more prepared to support them? Do you feel that you should not have to do this with deputies?

BS: I hope I'm tolerant of all staff in the sense that I can recognise achievement at all levels and provide support — bearing in mind that support can take various forms — to those colleagues requiring it. If a colleague is underperforming then it's my job to enable him or her to perform. If a teacher is bone idle, then it's my job to ensure that the work is done satisfactorily. There are times when one should not be, or appear to be, tolerant. As I said some moments ago, there are times when you need to tell people what they don't want to hear. That is a necessary aspect of headship, the same applies, irrespective of the role. It's a matter of professional integrity.

I can't pretend I have ever found sloth an endearing characteristic in any human being. If a teacher is experiencing genuine difficulty in performing his or her role, that's somewhat different. Our professional responsibility as teachers is to provide the best education possible for all our pupils. It's a matter of the greatest good of the greatest number — a *utilitarian* view, if you like.

Probably, my attitude to the deputies has been shaped by my expectations of myself. I expect a lot of myself. I remember how I performed my duties when I was a deputy. I worked with considerable commitment and I think I did the job well. I expect something similar from my deputies and no doubt were I to see them going off the boil — which I hasten to add they are not — or if they were not single-minded in the pursuit of what I — what we as a team — think the school is about then, yes, that would be a disappointment.

My interests are wider than the school and I suppose when people sit down and talk to me about my interests they are sometimes surprised: they seem to think that I live and breathe the school and that alone. But that is not the case and if it were there would be a sense in which I would be dead to the world; certainly not the kind of person who should be entrusted with the education of children. However, interested as I am in music and books, and committed though I am to my family, these interests and commitment are not such that they take over in such a way that makes me unable to carry out my duties properly. Nor should they be an excuse for not carrying out my duties on the grounds that they are more important than my responsibilities to Great Barr. As far as I am concerned in my professional life, the great thing is Great Barr and the pupils for whom we are responsible. I want to be creative in the role of headship, not a slave to the school: the same applies to the deputies. They would be strange role models indeed in an educational institution if they had no interests other than their school work. It is a question of balance.

PR: The deputies are closest to you within the institutional structure of the school. Does this make disappointment with their performance especially acute?

BS: It must be very, very hard when you have someone at that level who is simply not up to the job. Whose centre of gravity is self-evidently not the school. Who does not have the confidence of the staff. That would be incredibly difficult. And of course you are right. They are nearest to one and in that sense they're an extension of oneself. Indeed, we are known collectively as 'the management'. We are managing the school. If you have got someone who is ostensibly managing but is perceived to be mismanaging, then the management of a situation like that is very difficult.

PR: It reflects on you all?

BS: It could do. And one would have to be mindful in managing that situation that one's feelings of resentment do not get out of hand. It would require a degree of professional objectivity coupled with a sense of damage limitation. Some straight talking might help in rationalising the situation in the offending individual's mind. They would have to come to a conclusion as to whether they soldiered on and faced whatever might be the consequences or resolved the problem with some alternative stratagem.

PR: How do you lead the work of the staff as a whole?

BS: In a variety of ways. I hope I lead by example as, for example, in the setting up of the appraisal process. I went through the whole process myself first because I thought that was right. Not just going through it myself, but setting it up, reassuring staff individually in writing, talking through more problematic aspects and only then passing it on to a deputy having demonstrated that it can work.

Also I'm a great believer in never passing by an incident, never letting things go, never looking the other way. That is a slippery slope. Being out on the yard occasionally, stationing myself on corridors. Not just because it's good for staff to see you there, but because you perform a useful function. Gerald Haigh once came and walked round the school with me. He said 'You are incredibly "hands-on"'. It hadn't occurred to me that I'm around the school more frequently than he'd anticipated. And when I am I do not hesitate to deal with matters as I encounter them. I don't knowingly let anything slip. I suppose I am leading by example. I will deal with discipline matters myself by referring them. I'll say something myself but I'll refer them to the appropriate head of house or deputy but I will never knowingly let an incident pass me by. I suppose my mental model has helped in this. It clarifies how I think and feel about the school, being honest about it as far as I can be. In my appraisal, rather to my surprise, it emerged that I am thought of as a good listener. Somebody who can take on board other points of view. I am perceived as someone who is out there not standing any nonsense, but on the other hand, as someone who is prepared to listen. I think that what's come out of that is they don't just see me as a kind of office person, but as somebody who is out and about. There are times when I take a very high profile in terms of the management of the school. In doing so I try to give a very active leadership.

PR: You are not just an office-bound administrator?

BS: No. I'd hate either to be, or to be thought of as that. One of the bonuses of GM is that one gets rid of a whole area of LEA-generated bureaucracy and can concentrate on the things which one was appointed to do. Leading the school.

PR: How do you relate to pupils' parents, the local community? It must be quite difficult in a large school to know the pupils in the way which you might be able to in a smaller school?

BS: Where parents are concerned, we are quite a lot in the press. We have our own newsletter. We try to ensure the school is in the public eye in a positive way. Sometimes through the press, sometimes through radio or even television. There are, for example, photographs in the local newspapers this week covering the opening of our new technology centre. So there is plenty of communication in a formal sense — we put out press releases and so on. We communicate specifically through the newsletter which goes home, or we hope goes home, through pupil post. There is communication through the PTA, though it does not involve a large number of people. Governors also provide a channel of communication, at least seven of them are parents. I speak at various meetings in the school, curriculum meetings, departmental open days and so on. Obviously parents hear me and see me at Open Day and on intake days, and sixth-form intake evenings and similar events. I must be reasonably well known in this part of Birmingham. But how many people know me, or recognise me or say that they know me, I've absolutely no idea. If I drive my car down the road there are potentially over 2000 pupils and getting on for 4000 parents of existing pupils who might know me. There are also all those who've gone before. It would be very unlikely for me to go far without being recognised by somebody. It happens all over the country. If I go to a school in Bristol or somewhere, I get asked by a teacher, 'Do you remember me? I was a pupil at Great Barr'. I can't escape that but how well I interface with the local community is for others to say.

As far as the pupils are concerned, I don't know everybody. I know some and I think I probably know most by sight. If I saw them out of school I would know it was a Great Barr pupil. I am probably perceived as somewhat remote as a head and I think that this is a matter of choice in a sense. It is necessary to maintain a certain distance, particularly in a very large institution. I can't be everybody's mate. I have been known to be quite sympathetic and pupils want to talk to me. I quite like talking to pupils about their work and aspirations, but probably they regard me as a remote figure, but a sort of omnipresent figure because I get around the place. I'm never far away. I am doing my job.

PR: How would you describe your relationship with your governors? How do you seek to manage that relationship.

BS: Very good. I do manage it, of course. The art of headship is managing the interfaces and one of the most crucial interfaces is the school/governor relationship. I think that it's vitally important that relationships are kept good. There is nothing worse than fall-outs between the head and the governing body. The governors have got to have confidence in the head. I work hard at that. Most of all I have a lot of time for them; I actually like them; I get on well with my chairman. We have had our disagreements but they have been open and I find the chairman very supportive. She knows that I work all hours for the school. That I never give up. She recognises that. I know the vice-chairman socially. He has children at the school. I've been to his house several times for meals and so on. I get on very well with the responsible officer and chairman of the finance committee. I get on particularly well, I think, with parent governors who are great supporters of the school's values: they approve of the way things are and they look to preserve and sustain those values as they manifest themselves in the social and educational experiences of their own children as they pass through the school. There is a good deal of mutual respect between us. I work hard at keeping them informed. Not burdening them with useless or patronising information. I involve them in training, in the LEAP material for example. I regard myself as being very fortunate in my governing body. Several of them supported me through thick and thin during the debates on GM. I think that we have got to know and to respect each other.

PR: What are your feelings about the LEA in Birmingham and about LEAs more generally?

BS: As far as I am concerned there is no particular animus between myself and the LEA. We chose, and I chose, to leave this LEA. The LEA's policy was to adopt a certain position on the GM issue in relation to this school, and no doubt also to others. Certain individuals, to my mind, adopted postures and said things that made them look ridiculous. My view of it now is that it is water under the bridge. It was all a bit unfortunate at the time. By no means always an edifying spectacle for the head of an educational institution to become involved in. But that was not necessarily of my making. But all things pass. I'm far too busy and far to pragmatic to be in a position to devote time to think through how I feel about the LEA and certainly I'm not in the business of holding grudges. In fact I hardly think about the LEA at all.

PR: You don't much miss them? Perhaps some individuals were helpful? Your description earlier was that going GM has stripped out a level of LEA generated bureaucratic requirements and had freed you to be the kind of leader you wished to be.

BS: The LEA had certainly been a strait jacket. But I'm not now into the business of using every opportunity to slate this LEA or other LEAs. I'm running a grant-maintained school and I want to do it successfully and I don't want to divert my energies. I tend to forgive perhaps too easily. I find it very difficult to keep grudges. There were certainly some people who said some pretty unpleasant things about Great Barr and about me during the days when we sought GM status. I'm not particularly bothered by this now.

I still have friends in the LEA and still meet them socially. My friends are officers, advisers and fellow heads. With professionals you can argue about GMS and not fall out. You can't always say the same about some elected members. But I'm here to do the best I can as head of Great Barr.

PR: The job of headship, from the accounts we have of it, tends to be depicted as very demanding. Your headship must be as demanding as anything in the state sector. At a time when new requirements are being imposed on schools, almost every day, and thinking is shifting on what makes for effective schooling and learning and the curriculum, how on earth do you keep up to date?

BS: I am surrounded by colleagues who are expert in their own fields. There is no way I can pretend to be an expert in every aspect of the changes which are taking place. I cannot know in detail about every aspect of Key Stage requirements in Mathematics for example. But there are people on hand who do and I can get briefing there. I read journals and books when I can. I tend to read for relaxation. I never go to bed without reading. I prefer to read Jane Austin or Proust. So I'll read what I feel I ought to read for relaxation purposes, even the *Times Educational Supplement*, which I find a very unsatisfactory diet these days. So I keep up-to-date that way. I attend courses. I have recently been on an OFSTED course — who hasn't? I worried myself about that but attending the right course helps to sharpen you up. The more you know and the more you talk with colleagues the less worrying it becomes; perhaps it's not daunting after all; you feel that you are getting to grips with the challenge. And if it is capable of being done it's capable of being done well. It is a question of managing and structuring your time and delegating to the right people at the right time. Having confidence in them. Working as an ensemble.

I am not aware of pressure. I've been asked about the pressures of the job before and I'm not sure that I know that I experience — or recognise — pressure. But let's assume I do. I think the answer has to be that I cope with it by working. I work quite long hours by virtue of necessity. During the week my life is Great Barr and at the weekends what I try to do is to be a good husband and father.

PR: In one sense you live a curiously contained existence. Headship during the week and a large family and house fifty miles away which you retreat to at the weekends?

BS: The reason we live there is because before I came to Great Barr in 1984 I had been a head in Derbyshire. At the time Nottingham was a convenient place to live. Our oldest boy had just started 'A' Levels, then our next child, a girl, was in her second or third year and had settled in a comprehensive school in Nottingham. The next one, a boy, had just started primary school and the youngest one was at nursery school. My wife was quite content to live there. I already had a headship. I was moving to another one. It seemed incredibly self-indulgent to up-root the whole family, although my wife would have been prepared to do so, just because I wanted to move from one job to another. Originally I commuted every day but now I stay over from Tuesday to Thursday most weeks. On those evenings I work. I shift the work because of that; I am able to do quite a lot.

PR: Are you disciplined in the way you work? Do you manage your time well?

BS: People say I do, but sometimes I think I could manage it better. If I could sleep less I could do more.

PR: You seem to be saying two things. That it's possible to exaggerate the extent to which you feel under pressure. That in so far as you do feel pressure, you cope with it by embracing it.

BS: Athletes require an element of nervousness if they are to summon up the adrenalin they need for a good performance, especially if they engage in explosive or short distance events such as the shot putter or the sprinter. Without it they would be useless and I think there are many situations like that. You need a bit of adrenalin. I am not conscious about being up-tight about the job. Obviously there are times when something happens when you react to it but I'm not conscious of being under great pressure, or strain or stress at all. I don't think I could do the job if I was.

PR: What do you like most about headship? Is there any aspect you really do not like?

BS: That is an incredibly difficult question. Let me start by saying that because of the nature of my job and my involvement in things happening about me, perhaps, I have become less introspective, less reflective than I might have been at one stage. I am not conscious about thinking about those elements of the job I like or those I dislike and I'm not sure that I can categorise them because things happen on a daily basis and one is dealing with situations as they arise. Some of those can be predictable situations, such as making appointments and so on, which is a serious business and one doesn't want to make a mistake. Others are less predictable. Nobody enjoys seeing a difficult parent who seems on the verge of getting up, coming across the room and punching you on the nose. Nobody can claim to like that situation. Although, apparently, it seems I am quite good at handling such situations, bringing them in and calming them down, but I don't like it. Who would? Some people apparently like confrontation and cannot exist without a bit of aggravation in their lives. I'm not like that; I do not look for it. I do not like huge amounts of papers. I detest paper and wish we could do without it. I have to discipline myself to shift it, to read what I need to read, not to read those things which I do not need to read but to pass it on to those people who need to read it. I hate work lying around for longer than it needs to. Where possible, I try and shift things within twenty-four hours. There are a number of frustrations I suppose. I like efficiency. This goes back to what we were talking about earlier on. I find inefficiency, and anyone can be inefficient at times, in colleagues, particularly senior colleagues, frustrating. Perhaps I'm not always as understanding as I might be. Perhaps something intervened to prevent them from achieving some task or goal. Perhaps I'm not as forgiving as I should be in such circumstances. I find it irritating to have to sort out problems created between two other people, which have nothing to do with me apart from the fact that I happen to be head of the institution which forces me to try to sort it out for them, to bring them together, to enable them, even though they might dislike each other intensely, to work professionally. I sometimes find the foibles of individuals hard to take. People who are on their high horse, who are pretentious, who have an over-rated view of their ability, importance or contribution to the school. I sometimes find the position adopted by the unions unhelpful and not altogether in the interests of the pupils as clients or parents as the principal stake-holders. Sometimes I wonder whether unions always serve their members well.

PR: You are not the only head I've spoken to who said that.

BS: Generally speaking, I think that if you were to ask the union representatives here, or their union officers, for example, they would probably say the approach to the unions and to union business at Great Barr is professional. We do business properly, but there are times when I find it a bit irritating. I expect I find it irritating because it intrudes into what I might otherwise have been doing, not because I feel the unions go out of their way to irritate. At the end of the day, I appreciate that unions are there to serve their members who are also my professional colleagues. I don't look for confrontation with unions and I'm not anti-union.

But I don't think there is anything in particular I dislike about headship. There are times when one goes home and thinks 'There must be other ways of making a living'. But I imagine everybody feels like that about their job occasionally. I have never thought this in a serious way.

PR: You are a round peg in a round hole?

BS: That I don't know. I think that one has to be sensible, down to earth, pragmatic. There is no point in thinking about doing something else now. I know people do make major career changes at my age, 51 in politics is nothing, not that I want to go into politics, I hasten to add. At one stage I wondered whether, when I was at the London Institute, if I should read Law. I went so far as to make enquiries about the possibility of doing that on a part-time basis. I had noticed that a number of people, some CEOs and some academics, seemed to have LLBs. I wondered if that would be an interesting route and whether I should take it. But there I was, a deputy head, and the obvious thing was to become a head. I think it's been more a case of 'the spirit blowing where it listeth' and finding myself in situations rather than having a major scheme, a planned critical path, designed to take me from being a teacher at Normanton Grammar School to the headship of Great Barr.

PR: How do you cope when things go wrong?

BS: I cope by trying to put them right. Things go wrong — mistakes are made, or people say things they should not have said — there are times when it's necessary to react immediately. There are others when it's necessary to distance yourself from the problem and take a weekend to live with it. I've come to the conclusion — and this may sound ridiculous — that because I'm busy and I haven't got time to say to myself, 'Well, I'm going to sit down for the next half an hour and think carefully through this problem', that, somehow, when I am asleep, or when I am working on something else, that the problem is somehow worked on at the back of my mind, and something useful happens as a result of all of this. It is a curious phenomenon. I get up the following morning and quite often the solution seems to be there even though I have not consciously thought about it.
    To cope when things have gone wrong you need to make sound judgements. You need to have your own view. You need also, and this is the great advantage of having a team like mine, to take advice. To say 'This has happened, we've got a real problem here. What might we do? ' We bounce ideas off each other. That is very useful. Often the solution to a problem is not just my solution, or a particu-

lar deputy's solution, but a team solution. I enjoy arriving at a team solution.

Part of being able to cope with things going wrong is to anticipate potential problems as early and as far ahead as possible. Also when people make mistakes it is unfortunate, whoever they are, if they cannot bring themselves to acknowledge this. When you upset a member of staff you should be able to say, 'Perhaps it's my fault you misunderstood me', or 'I didn't say what I wanted to very well', or 'It is the end of a long week, I'm sorry'. It is important to try and patch things up at a one-to-one level. I don't think I am noted for upsetting people. Nobody is perfect. I am certainly not perfect. Because I am the head does not mean every decision I make has got to be the right or the best one. There are occasions when its necessary to say 'Look, I made a mistake'. Where it is very difficult is when you've got somebody who has made a mistake and does not, or will not, acknowledge it: yet as head you have to bring them to face it. I will give you an example suitably anonymised — of that in practice. What do you do when somebody goes right over the top in chastising some girls who apparently had not really done anything at all? On the following day I received calls or complaints from all the parents of these girls. The first thing I did was to see the girls individually, to find out precisely what happened. I also discussed it with the parents. I then had to see the individual who clearly thought that I was being unhelpful but I was quite convinced that what had been done was not appropriate. I felt I had to ring up each parent. All of them said that having got things off their chest, they wanted to thank me for taking the trouble to make contact. They had got back from work, they had their supper, they were sitting down, and they thanked me for taking the time, at that time in the evening, to be in touch with them. They were very appreciative. I had taken this in hand, the matter was being dealt with. It went away. I was able to solve the problem. When I called the member of staff in and said that I had looked carefully into the problem, that I had spent a great deal of time talking to each parent, that they were now happy and had thanked me — the look of relief on that member of staff's face was very evident. Even so, this member of staff later told a deputy (he/she) thought it was weakness on my part because I had not supported (him/her). It was not a weakness. The problem was dealt with in an appropriate way. It's difficult when as a head one is compromised by other colleagues.

PR: Can we consider one last topic? Given the reforms of the last few years, how far can and should heads exercise significant curriculum leadership?

BS: There is some truth in the claim that powers over the curriculum have been redistributed in such a way that the ability of heads to shape things has been circumscribed. Gone are the days in which heads could dabble in curriculum issues. We've all known schools in which, in the past, heads could take an idiosyncratic view of the curriculum. This may have been very interesting for the heads who promoted it, for some of these staff who were involved, whilst others might have felt disenfranchised. But pupils in such schools might have been short changed — particularly in cases where they moved from one school to another and when they were applying for jobs. So the National Curriculum has brought about a degree of uniformity but that uniformity is not necessarily a cost. My own view is that its introduction has been to the advantage of pupils in general and has sharp focused the minds of heads and staff on those things which they should be doing — which is managing and delivering effectively a curriculum for pupils.

In such a context I see my role, as leading professional and chief executive, as creating the climate in which the curriculum can best be delivered. I certainly do not see it as simply implementing the National Curriculum. The ethos of the school in terms, especially, of positive forms of pupil behaviour and attitudes to learning are things which we have worked very hard on over a number of years and well before 1988. If you can bring about a state of affairs in which teachers can manage the teaching/learning process effectively then I think they can take the kind of planned risks which are necessary if worthwhile developments are to be achieved. Without this, teachers cannot take those risks because they are spending so much time and energy on the management of pupil reaction in the classroom rather than in pupil reaction to the curriculum itself. I think it is critically important for heads to be instrumental, and to be seen to be instrumental, in creating the right climate for learning. This is so that not only in terms of pupil reaction but also of professional expectations of staff, their own expectations of their teaching and of pupil performance. Any head who forgets all this is in trouble.

Related to all this is the head's role in setting up and reviewing the structure within which the curriculum is delivered. At Great Barr we base this on areas of experience — on broad curriculum areas. In structural terms this is represented by the responsibilities of curriculum managers working with heads of departments. This can mean that from time-to-time individual subjects move from one curriculum area to another. So it is not just a matter of setting up a structure that works at a given time: you have to keep reviewing the structure and revising as necessary. It has to have continuing credibility as far as staff are concerned and they need to have an understanding of what gives it coherence. This is also a key function of headship in this area. The head must take a lead on this. It is all a question of creating the culture and the structure which enables the curriculum to be managed at all levels including, and most especially, within the classroom. No head can abdicate all this, and despite the fact that recent legislation has brought in many changes, what remains immutable is the teaching/learning process. It could be that the way in which teachers present in classrooms, the way they expect pupils to react, may be shaped by aspects of the National Curriculum and its assessment but some of it will have been shaped by things we have done which significantly predate the introduction of the National Curriculum.

In any case, what goes on within the school and within the classroom is part of the professional function of teaching and its relationship with pupil learning. This is what must remain uppermost in a head's mind. If a head starts to see himself or herself as just an administrator rather than as a manager of the learning process; if you see yourself as an administrator then it will not be surprising if you find yourself bogged down in administration. It is seeing the trees rather than the wood. It is a myopic approach to the job. If you do this you will appear to staff not to know what is going on; you'll seem unsympathetic to what's going on in the classroom and to the teacher, appearing not to understand what is going on in the curriculum and in curriculum change. As a result all kinds of tensions will occur, not least for the head.

PR: Your staff expect you to have a comprehensive grasp of all aspects of the curriculum?

BS: They expect me to have a comprehensive grasp of what the school is about but not precisely what is to happen within a specific Key Stage. That is their job. I should not be meddling in that. I should not be seeking to manage how teachers tackle a particular aspect of the curriculum at that level. I should be listening to them and through my curriculum deputy and other seniors managers I should be creating the environment in which they can work effectively. I should not be restraining them by insisting on inappropriate requirements or structures. I should be offering support where it is needed and doing so in particular through the targets identified in the development plan and through the appraisal process.

To become trapped into an administrative role is a road to isolation. It sets up barriers. If you see yourself essentially as an administrator you can hardly hope to be the leading professional as well. Heads who see themselves as administrators are almost forced to act independently of the staff.

PR: Few heads express any desire to be seen essentially as administrators, but what several do say is that recent reforms have forced them to give greater attention to this aspect of their role. They are also forced to spend more time managing the interfaces.

BS: This is so but it is also one of the most interesting parts of headship. It is what makes being a head enjoyable. You do need to be aware that these interfaces exist and are important. Some heads do not seem to be aware of this. Managing the interface with the local community, with the complainers in the local community, with the press, with the LEA and with the governors. There are also internal interfaces — with, for example, your deputies, other managers, the staff in general and the pupils. The head who is successful is sensitive to those interfaces. In some schools, the most difficult interface can be between the head and the governing body. This is uniquely the head's task; you can't delegate the head's special relationship with the governing body to a deputy. It means cultivating governors, working with people with whom, perhaps, one does not have a natural affinity. I knew of one fairly senior teacher who wanted to be so financially secure before taking a headship that, if necessary, he could tell the governing body to take 'a running jump'. As far as I'm aware, he is still doing the same job. It seems to me that this is excessive. You need to learn to see other perspectives and where necessary to manage the compromises.

PR: How as a head do you exercise control over the curriculum?

BS: Ultimately by establishing what the core values of the school are. By articulating aims which reflect those values. They must be achievable in the sense that they help to relate purpose to practice. Say, for example, you want to provide a higher standard of support for people in the classroom which might be based on a value which emphasises the need to improve the learning of pupils at all levels. This entails being critical about your own classroom practice, being aware of relevant school policy, planning the lessons carefully, keeping up with the marking of work, making sure that the pupils keep their homework diaries up to date, making the time to do it, insisting on good behaviour and not leaving it to someone else. All this may sound trivial and mundane but ultimately these are the ways in which one can best enable improved learning.

My job is not to have a direct influence on the specifics of the modern languages curriculum in German for Year 9. I can't do that across the board. What I *can* do is to influence the ways in which the pupils relate to the teachers and the teachers to the pupils. I can create the mechanisms to ensure that staff properly prepare their work and that pupils do it. In this context I see my influence as agreeing with the staff what the values of the school are and determining with them what this means for the curriculum in terms of teaching and learning. All this then needs to be put down in straight-forward language which nobody can misunderstand. You specify these things by agreeing that we set, collect, mark and record work properly and that we do so according to the timetables which are agreed. I would be seeing the trees not the wood if I set out to control, for example, exactly what was to happen in every aspect of the work of the English and every other department. It would not be possible anyway. Of course, I have a general responsibility to see that the national requirements are met and that their application in practice is monitored. That is the job of the head and the curriculum deputy. Once areas of weakness are identified I suppose I am into the job of staff management as it interacts with that of curriculum management. But both ultimately have the same aim. In practice I'm not sure I can make a useful distinction between the two.

PR: In summary, a great deal of control over what happens in the curriculum is still down to the school to determine and deliver, despite what some say about the centralisation which has taken place as a result of the detailed requirements of the National Curriculum and its assessment.

BS: I might be out on a limb on this but I think this has not happened for a variety of reasons. One of the things I have found since we've become grant maintained is that I'm not faced with the increase in the bureaucratic pressures I was warned about. Without the requirements of the LEA some non-productive bureaucracy has disappeared and if I'm not able to have direct control — not that I would wish to — over what teachers are teaching in the classroom I do seem to have a greater influence over how they are teaching. I do go into classrooms. I sit in there and I listen. I talk to pupils and look at what they are doing and what they have done. I would claim to know the climate which individual staff have set for themselves and their pupils. It's monitoring on the hoof of management by walking about, if you like. It is a bit *ad hoc*, and perhaps I need some kind of a formal timetable for visiting individual members of staff. The head's job is to be about the place.

PR: How much flexibility remains for schools in the way in which they package the curriculum? It has been argued by some that this has been determined by the specifications of the National Curriculum, amounting, in practice, to the setting of a detailed syllabus.

BS: I don't see it like that. We still have considerable flexibility. I think it is important to see and present the curriculum in a humanis-ing way. It is possible to do that as things stand. The curriculum should be more than just a set of separate subjects. It must have coherence. You can achieve this in various ways — for example by identifying themes across the curriculum. In a sense, areas of experience can be seen as an alternative or as a supplement to subjects as a way of delivering the curriculum. Also you need to see all this in terms of a school having a clear interest in enabling the personal development of the pupil through the curriculum and in other ways. In some areas of experience, such as PSME, this is at the forefront. It is there within the pastoral curriculum also which in this school is intended to have a civilising impact by establishing certain norms in the way in which we treat each other. It is all part of the civilising impact of the curriculum.

I am not one of those heads who says that if you get the curriculum right everything else will automatically fall into place. Rather you need to get these other things into place in order that the curriculum can become a civilising instrument. You need to do some civilising by laying down benchmarks which shape the way in which we live together. I am not one of those who believes an interesting curriculum will necessarily get the interest of the pupils. Many pupils are not naturally interested in such things; they need to be helped to become interested. For example, they need to be encouraged to become hard working — partly out of necessity. Once this has happened work can become a habit. You need to create the environment which enables all this to happen. Of course, some pupils may still choose to reject the civilising influence. Fortunately, the vast majority of pupils here do accept it and support it. If they didn't, it would be hard to see how individual progress and self-fulfilment could be possible.

PR: As legislation has sought to circumscribe the control schools have over the curriculum, there has been a growing interest within schools in whole-school curriculum planning. Do you agree? It has been suggested that national legislation on the curriculum and its interpretation in practice has had a good deal to say on breadth and balance but much less on coherence. What do you think?

BS: It could get lost. To avoid it schools need to make a judicious use of the time available to them to ensure that those value-added elements of the curriculum we have talked about earlier are given their due attention. If they're there, presumably they pull together in a way which enables pupils to feel they are experiencing a coherent package rather than a number of separate packages. Where schools plan the curriculum in such a way then coherence shouldn't be a problem. Where schools take what they see as the injunctions of the National Curriculum too literally there might well be a problem: where they feel their freedom to interpret things in terms of their own circumstances and needs has been taken away. Where they feel that the National Curriculum has determined exactly how much time they can devote to various aspects of their work. With more creative management it is still possible to include within the curriculum those things which help to humanise it.

PR: So coherence is something which the school needs and can sort out for itself. It has not been set out as part of the National Curriculum as such?

BS: You couldn't describe the National Curriculum as a coherent curriculum package. Rather it covers a whole range of areas of experience, of knowledge, of skills which are generally thought necessary for a person to be aware of in order to function intelligently in today's world. So it is coherent in that sense but I think you can have coherence in a deeper sense — the sense in which a school organises its curriculum, in fact organises itself, in such a way that pupils begin to grasp that the development of human understanding and the appreciation of human values is still there and still at the heart of their experience within the school and the curriculum. Ultimately the test is whether this is what the pupil experiences rather than what the curriculum planner intends.

Achieving all this can be very demanding. Some heads are more comfortable simply retreating into their administrative duties as a defence from the hard intellectual and personal effort required to make sense of the curriculum. But one illusion is to believe that this is something new. To achieve the things we have been talking about has always been difficult and there is little evidence that the last few years have seen a significant retreat from breadth, balance and coherence when compared with the past. On the contrary, whatever the difficulties, these are things which are more on the agenda now than they have been during my years as a teacher let alone my years as a head.

This is not to say that heads shouldn't be interested in administrative matters. In particular, it would be a very strange head who did not have an intense interest in budgetary matters. It is the budget which virtually drives everything. But you need to be clear as a head what your task is within in. Some heads seem to enjoy becoming a kind of financial clerk. It is hard to defend this. At Great Barr we have budget managers for major areas of expenditure. We have agreed, authorised and notional budgets. In other words you agree part of the budget. All that is very interesting because it helps you in terms of the school development plan to prioritise. As such, school development planning has really come into its own since heads have become real managers of the school budget. Any school development planning is worthless unless it is linked into a four- or five-year financial plan, a four- or five-year staff development plan, a four- or five-year buildings development plan.

PR: And a four- or five-year curriculum development plan?

BS: That should be the key feature of the school development plan. But it would be meaningless if it were not linked to the other development plans I've identified. You need to have your financial plan in place. I can see some heads throwing up their hands in horror at all this, usually because they don't know the technical issues or how to use a computer. It's not about using the computer, unless you want to make it so. Unless you want to retreat into this or to use it as a convenient excuse. Or if you have so little confidence in the people around you that you feel you have to do it all yourself. If so, maybe it is time for you to look for another school or, better still, for another job.

8   Harry Tomlinson

with Peter Ribbins

PR: Can you say something about your childhood and schooling and how these experiences have influenced your life and career?

HT: My father was a teacher which may be of significance and my mother was one of those people who was denied a proper education by her circumstances. She was always very ambitious for my brother and myself and put a high value on education. In fact she achieved an Open University honours degree at the age of seventy-two. That kind of spirit was an important part of what drove us on to succeed. I actually got an under-age scholarship at 11+ and therefore went to a grammar school at the age of ten. I think that probably was not a very good thing to do. I was a youngish young boy and I met the oldest old boy on my first day there and he was a hundred! So I was picked out on the very first day, I was there as somebody who everybody knew about. I left the school, it was a West Riding grammar school, for a state scholarship and then got into Oxford to read Chemistry on the basis of my double Maths, Physics and Chemistry at 'A' Level. I quite quickly realised that I was not going to be very happy with the Chemistry course, or perhaps I was not doing as well at it as I had hoped, and so I changed and did a degree in English instead having not done the subject since taking my 'O' Levels.

I suppose the other influence in terms of my early background was that my brother followed me all the way through. He is about three years younger than I am. In the end he did not take his degree and that was a source of much family trauma not least because he was brighter than I was. Looking back we were a traditional Yorkshire family but I achieved what I have, I think, because of the kind of ambition which our parents, and especially my mother, had for us.

PR: So it was a home in which education was important?

HT: Yes it was. My father was working under Sir Alec Clegg whom he admired immensely. So my early education and my ideas about its importance took place not only in my school but also within my home. My mother was always trying to learn. This was even so when she went into an old people's home recently, She wanted to take *Macbeth* and a book on teaching yourself German in order that she could study them there. So it is that kind of commitment to education which I associate with a traditional working class. My mother was always a great influence. I was always closer to her. My father was a bit distant. He was not a warm person but very ambitious for us to do well. I remember the first time I played cricket, which was something he encouraged me to do, I knew that batsmen carefully watched the ball go past the edge of their bat. The first time I played I was out first ball because I carefully watched the ball go past my bat on to hit the stumps. He was furious with me. It was that kind of relationship. He was essentially a class teacher in a secondary modern who carried responsibilities for Technical Drawing and Careers. Towards the end of his own career he achieved a Scale D. I think he looked back with much greater affection to the small secondary modern in which he spent most of his teaching life than he did to the large, multi-racial comprehensive in which he ended his career.

PR: What do you remember of your primary school days?

HT: I remember two teachers in my primary school. Miss Turpin who taught the first year juniors and Mrs Rhodes who taught top juniors. The image I have of them is of women who I wanted to work with and to work for. They were both very strong and firm but that was necessary for that sort of primary school in those days. Both were to some extent family friends as well. It was Mrs Rhodes who made sure that I got the under-age scholarship. My father was so proud of that. I think I was on the 'A' list as well. Nobody from our school was on that list, and to be so under-age as well. He was almost aggressively proud of this.

PR: What do you remember of your secondary school years?

HT: I think as I hinted earlier when I was talking about being one of the youngest I was bullied a certain amount and I responded rather aggressively to this. By the time I had reached the top end of the school I had built up a useful reputation of being an aggressive footballer. In a way that is one of the worst things about sport. A kind of showing off of aggressiveness. I remember being in trouble with the head, I was a prefect at the time, we were playing in a gym corridor. He said 'Stop doing that. You might break a window.' I thought he had left and I said something like 'Silly old sod' and kicked the ball and did break the window. But he was still there. He then took my prefect's badge off me. But when a few months later he heard that I had got into Oxford he came padding down a corridor and said 'Harry, now that you have got into Oxford you can have your prefects badge back.' It was a boy's grammar school and I was not really happy being in a boys' grammar school. It was an aggressive place full of boys acting in macho ways. There were teachers there whose behaviour was unacceptable. It was at times an unpleasant place to be.

It was a highly selective grammar school and was essentially working class in its clientele. Perhaps I should correct that. All the evidence I read suggests that absolutely everybody who went to grammar schools was middle class. It seemed working class but in the way in which we define these things in this country I suppose my background was really lower-middle class. I do remember the contempt with which other pupils and teachers alike regarded and treated the third stream. This was in the context of a highly selective and very elitist grammar school. But even there the third stream were made out to be idiots by the teachers. That group must have had a better chance of prospering in a comprehensive school.

Some teachers acted in quite unacceptable ways in terms of violence and homosexuality. There were a number of teachers who behaved like brutes. They were really quite disgusting. There were also some who were an influence for good. One I recall was the Chemistry teacher and it was his influence and support which led me to go to Oxford. The fact that proved a mistake was not his fault. I suspect I was simply doing what I seemed to be good at rather than thinking hard about what I would like to do. George taught not only Chemistry but also Ballroom Dancing. It was in one of these lessons that I recall first meeting with the girls of the girls' grammar school. So there was that kind of social background.

Three teachers at Oxford influenced me. The first was a chemist, Ben Brown, who I think got me into Oriel. I remember when I went for interview there he seemed to be persuaded because I was a good footballer, college football teams of that time were pretty poor, that I ought to be admitted although my subject grades were not quite what they might have been. He was the England amateur goalkeeper at the time. He was a very nice man. Then there were my two English tutors — Brian Miller and Elizabeth Mackenzie who were both wonderful people. I had a great sense of liberation with them. That seemed to me to be what Oxford, at its best, was all about. We were encouraged to think and feel in a way in which I had never experienced before. I was there from 1958–1963. This included one year of Chemistry, three years of English and one year doing the PGCE. I remember Oxford with some affection. Although I resented, in the early days, the kind of mimicry of my accent that went on. I learnt to adapt and became sufficiently bourgeois in my accent to get by. In fact many of my friends were from independent schools. The one who influenced me most was from Charterhouse. I think that he went back to be a teacher there and I did actually play football for Charterhouse Old Boys once when they were short.

I found it reasonably easy to switch from Chemistry to English. My father was not pleased because he saw Chemistry as offering better career opportunities. I would be able to work for ICI. He saw English as wishy washy and creative in a soft way. So there was a lot of anger at home about my decision. But Ben Brown, as my personal tutor, was helpful in enabling me to make the change.

PR: At what point did you decide to become a teacher?

HT: I was predicted to get a first. My teachers thought this likely. I was assuming that I would do an MPhil so I was not even thinking about what I might do if I did not get a first. When I did not get a first I almost did a Diploma because it was too late to think about anything else. I wanted to stay in great part because I had already decided I would produce Ibsen's *The Master Builder*. I had previously acted in it and it has always been a play that I think about quite a lot. There is a marvellous phrase in it in which the Master Builder is trying to build real castles in the air. That is the kind of thing I have often thought of doing throughout my life. The PGCE was, I fear, an opportunity to stay in Oxford for another year and to do this.

The idea that I might become a teacher came partly through the influence of a couple of friends who were interested in travelling the world. They were quite interested in doing their PGCE in East Africa. We talked it over and eventually I got a job teaching there. They also went there to do their PGCEs. Once I had started teaching I found myself enjoying it. I had done the PGCE almost because I could not think of anything better to do. I went to East Africa because these friends wanted to. But that turned out to be a tremendously valuable experience. When I hear today of teachers who are anxious about doing this because of the damage it might do to their careers in the long term I think it very sad. It was a very exciting experience. It certainly helped me to grow up and to begin to understand teaching.

PR: What happened next?

HT: I did two years in East Africa and then came home. I still was not terribly clear about what to do. I had a relationship which had gone wrong in East Africa which was one of the reasons I came home. Even so I was not quite clear if that relationship was going to resurrect itself and if the girl involved was going to follow me to England. But it did not work out. I then went to teach in the Middle East in Kuwait for a year and had some exciting experiences there. That was a time in which the British were alleged to have bombed Cairo during the Arab–Israeli war. I recall two experiences there. In the first the caretaker literally held a knife at my throat in the headteacher's office and in my panic I recall saying something like 'If you do not put that down I will have to tell the British Ambassador.' Fortunately he did. The second had to do with the fact that I was teaching a primary school teacher GCE English. She was in her early twenties and very pretty. Her parents actually allowed me to teach her in a room on her own which was very unusual. She was a Palestinian, very hard working and clearly going to do very well. When the war started she asked me to go around and to collect the money owing to me. When I went there she was angry. By then the Israelis had won the war, it was a bit like watching *King Lear* in a primary school teacher — 'I will do such things — What they are yet I know not; but they shall be, The terrors of the earth.' I next saw her on an aircraft carrying two bombs in her hands. She was Leila Khaled. I suddenly realised that this woman whom I had been so patronising about actually meant what she said.

In a sense you might argue that the first four years of my career involved a degree of messing around. I came back because the contracts were not renewed and again had to find a job. With great good luck I became a lecturer at Kesteven College of Education teaching teachers, having done virtually no teaching in England. I was there for three years. John Kirkham who was head of the English department and Norman Bishop who was head of Drama both much inspired me. I think that was really the point that my career in teaching became a career in a real sense. I began to see what education could do. I was visiting lots of primary and secondary schools and seeing what teaching was all about. I learnt an enormous amount in those years. Then I got married in 1970 and was once again so lucky with the job I got. It was with Arthur Lingard at Billericay School. I was appointed straight out of a college of education to be head of Humanities. Within a year I became a senior teacher. By this time I was working very hard. I was doing all I could to use all my potential. I think Lingard recognised that. Within a year of teaching in England in a position which carried some management responsibility I was appointed to be a senior teacher. That established my career and made what I have done since then possible. Arthur Lingard was the kind of head who was willing to take risks.

As a senior teacher I did all kinds of jobs in the school. This included setting up all kinds of systems — a new library, a new Humanities curriculum which brought together English, History and Geography. So I was involved in curriculum development. The head gave me the chance to develop the range of pastoral, academic and administrative skills which are required for senior management. So when I applied for deputy headships I was well prepared. I was appointed as deputy head (curriculum) to a comprehensive school which was opening in Walsall. It was an open-plan school. I believe only two or three such schools were built in the mid '70s. They were of variable success. That was an interesting learning opportunity for me in a new purpose-built building. The first learning experience which I had there was in 1973. The secondary modern staff stayed and a number of us from outside were appointed to senior positions. That created a degree of managerial tension. But, if I am not maligning him, the head produced a timetable that did not work and therefore the other deputy and I, over the first half term had to reproduce the whole curriculum because the timetable really was in a state of chaos in the new comprehensive school. As a consequence I had to learn very quickly how to do a timetable. I had been planning to do this in the following year anyway. I think it was the year in which the school leaving age was raised. The kids that I taught were amongst the most difficult in the school — we had to show that we were capable of doing this. Many were very unhappy at having to stay on for a further year. This was a fairly deprived area of Walsall and, therefore, as a teacher you had to earn your reputation. I was there between 1973 and 1977. Although the head did not do the timetable very well he was willing to let me get on and do the things which he felt I could do. I remember him with some affection but I do not think he was as effective or as imaginative a thinker as my previous head.

In 1977 I started to apply for headships. My recollection is that I made over forty applications and was interviewed six or seven times before I got the headship which I did get. At that stage an interesting thing happened at the interview. Perhaps I should say first that I have always thought that interviews are a very unsuitable way of choosing people. There were five or six of us who got through to the final round and the other five had all been called for interview elsewhere in the following week. In a sense I felt that this job had to be mine. I believe that was an important factor in getting me the job. I think that is often how things happen. I felt unusually confident and so controlled that I was not surprised when I was offered the post.

PR: Why did you want to be a head?

HT: I think it was simply because I had to do that to achieve the things which I felt I ought to achieve. I think it was that I could help children and teachers but I should not emphasise that too strongly.

It was also very tied in with an ambition to become what I thought I was capable of becoming. I do not think I ever thought seriously of anything other than headship. I have continued to feel that as a head over the last sixteen years. I have vaguely flirted with the idea of applying for a post as director of education but even this is nowhere near as fascinating as being a headteacher. Therefore I really did get the job I most wanted in 1977 and I think it is the most interesting and useful job there is.

PR: How well prepared did you feel when you were first appointed to a headship?

HT: I had had quite a varied career by then with a number of years as a senior member of staff. In preparing for this interview I have tried to look back on my career. It is easy to impose an *ex post facto* rationale which was less evident at the time. I have recently taught an Open University course on educational organisations and administration and the first thing which people are asked to do in this is, without reading any of the course material, to look at their own career and to try to begin to understand what they mean by the word 'career'. In reading these you come across all kinds of rationale. There are people who clearly wanted to be teachers from the age of seven and there are the people who drifted into teaching as in a sense I did. For my own part, I did the PGCE in 1963. I did an advanced diploma, mainly on secondary education, in 1973. It was a very broad three-year course which Arthur Lingard supported at the Cambridge Institute. Then whilst I was in Walsall I did the Diploma in Business Administration and in doing so looked at things like organisational psychology, personnel and financial issues. So I was all the time, I think, training myself for headship. In fact the dissertation I did at Aston University was on the selection and training of comprehensive headteachers. I was researching theoretically on what I was doing practically.

PR: It sounds like you took on your first headship with some confidence in your readiness and preparation. Was that confidence well founded in practice?

HT: Broadly yes. I should begin, though, by saying I went to an absolutely wonderful school. It is easy to be overly romantic about it and the staff in retrospect. It was Birley High School and it was in Manchester. I remember before I was appointed we were taken outside the school and shown these dreadful council high-rise flats — there were four murder charges pending and we were told that most of our pupils came from those flats. People wanted us to know what kind of school it was. It was actually a tremendous school because, in contrast to one of the schools down the road, all the teachers there had chosen to come and work in the inner-city. They were not people who had simply been left or drafted into an inner city school as a result of a reorganisation. They were deeply politically committed to multicultural education. I think the thing I did most successfully in that school and I really believe that it was the best multicultural school in the country by the time I left, was that I allowed highly intelligent and committed teachers to explore issues related to multiculturalism. HMI in a report said that they were the most professionally articulate staff they had met. The report was sent direct to the chief education officer in Manchester. The Rampton Report, if you read it, in its section on secondary schools, talks about one school which it said had got things right. By the documentation that was used it was clear that they were referring to Birley High School. The performance of the pupils was very much evaluated and carefully measured and monitored. The levels of attendance and punctuality improved a good deal over those five years. Examination results improved over those five years. Their results in terms of added value was quite magnificent. We had visitors from over fifty counties to come and see what we were doing. To have the opportunity of leading a staff like that was wonderful. Leading is a strong word, it was more a question of gently directing. It was an incredible experience.

PR: What was the balance of the pupil population?

HT: It was about 35 per cent Afro-Caribbean, 5 per cent Asian and 60 per cent whites. Significantly the racists in the area always assumed that it was about 80 per cent black. I was there for only five years and during that time I was able to measure the performance of one year-group all the way through and one of the nice things with that group is that I was able to take six of them to Jamaica. They had never been out of Britain. They got a tremendous welcome in Jamaica.

PR: How did you see headship at that time?

HT: Having told you all the wonderful things perhaps I should tell you that, for me, it had to be a very fast learning experience. There were two things that went quite badly wrong. One of which was a result, I think, of misinformation, I alienated the black women's co-operative. That was something which I was never really able to get over. More interestingly for me, in terms of learning what headship is about, was another issue which I need to get in context. There were two other heads who were appointed in Manchester in September 1977. It was agreed that we would meet at some time in the Spring of the following year to talk about settling into headship.

They arrived at Birley on a day in which a riot was taking place. I had been trying to tighten up on punctuality. I think there was some fomenting of discontent by some elements of the community but at break time the television cameras arrived and the kids erupted. They ran across the road, there was chaos. Subsequently, the *Daily Mail* accused me of being right wing. Quite a surprising and original position to find myself in. But I had then the most difficult decision which I ever had to make as to what to do. I had only been at the school for six months. I seemed to have created a situation in which the whole school was in chaos. The staff were wondering what I would do. The kids were wondering what I would do. I was wondering what I would do. I decided that the only thing I could do was to go out and tell them to come back into the building. Slowly, over a period of time, I got most of them to do so. Slowly, over three or four days I began to calm things down. That was the most dangerous and difficult thing I have ever done. It could have all gone so wrong. But also if I had not done it I would have failed then and there. I am not suggesting everything was wonderful there or that I did everything well. As a head you sometimes cannot help creating situations. I remember once saying to the staff, as all good heads do, that I am not going to make any changes in the first year. I am going to listen and learn. But it seemed to me that some changes, particularly in the assessment system, were so obviously necessary. I did make changes in the first year. That too created ructions. This time with the staff rather than the pupils. I made mistakes early on but what I think I did do is to learn very fast from my mistakes. So that kind of mistake, of trying to force teachers to move too quickly, which is something new headteachers may be given to, is something I have learnt to avoid. I certainly have not had anything to deal with as tense as all this. I did have at Birley to cope with individual kids who carried knives in the classroom. I have not provoked in any other school I have worked in that kind of anger from the staff and rebellion from the pupils and opposition from groups of parents.

It was an interesting few months. When you first become the head of any new institution there is allegedly a honeymoon period when you can get things done in part because you are not seen by anyone as part of the established culture. There is also the idea that you should not make decisions which require significant change too quickly unless you are very sure of them. It could be that the idea of a honeymoon period was always a bit of a myth or perhaps it has become much briefer in recent times. Look at what has happened to Clinton. Looking back, despite all my attempts, I never quite regained the confidence of the black women's group. It could be that as a leader you sometimes have to go through periods when everybody seems to be against you if you are to get things changed.

Perhaps with experience I have learnt to minimise the risks of doing things which might alienate.

PR: I know you are interested in ideas to do with multicultural education and things like value added. It seems as if such interests began to develop in those years?

HT: I was writing about multicultural education at the time and subsequently taught about it. I became, for example, the secretary for the Society of Caribbean Studies which is the academic organisation in the area. Once I recognised that there was an issue, and looking back it was so obvious that multicultural education was an issue, we encouraged people to come and undertake research within the school. We learnt from them as they learnt about us. We had a working party on multicultural education and a television programme was made about the working party. I came to be seen as somebody who was seen as sympathetic to research on the issue and was involved in DES research on factors associated with effectiveness in multiethnic schools. We had black and white kids in the school and I doubt if any school in the country provided a more appropriate curriculum given our circumstances. Looking back what we were trying to do seemed so obvious but it was clearly not so obvious to others. If you are seen to take new things seriously then you seem to become a person who is thought to know about them.

Much the same happened with the issue of value added. I wanted to know if we were doing the black kids justice. Geoffry Driver's research showed black girls were vastly overachieving, white kids were achieving slightly more than might be expected given their home background and black boys were underachieving. We were interested to try to explain why all this should happen.

PR: How would you describe your philosophy of multicultural education?

HT: What Birley High School had was multicultural education. In trying to move it on to the antiracist education agenda, where I think it really needed to get to, I am not sure that we developed as fully or as quickly as others. The attempt in Manchester to get into antiracist education in the way in which they did was one reason for the problems which emerged at Burnage and elsewhere subsequently. There is a real difficulty for heads in deciding how far they will become publicly, politically involved, as opposed to educationally involved. But I think a number of schools did try to take antiracist education on and did so rather unsuccessfully. For me multicultural education means giving equal validity to different relevant cultures in the curriculum and behaviour within the school. The things that we did in our history curriculum meant looking in an appropriate way at what had happened in the Caribbean, Caribbean culture and history and its relationship to British history and culture. In English this means looking at Caribbean literature and giving a place within the syllabus to a study of Afro-Caribbean writers rather more than is the norm in schools.

PR: To what extent is that replacing one dominant culture with two dominant cultures — bicultural education as opposed to multicultural education?

HT: There is a problem. Last Saturday night on Radio Lancashire, we heard of a case in which a school had introduced Moslem prayers at the school on Fridays. I was asked to comment on this for the Secondary Heads Association. I raised precisely that issue. It seems to me there is absolutely no reason not to have Moslem prayers in the school if the parents and pupils wish this to happen. But there are so many routes which one can take in considering this issue. I recall one parent arguing that we were giving too much prominence to Jamaican culture. She was from Guyana and believed that her children should be exposed to this culture within the school. It could be that what we were doing was bicultural but if in looking at British and Caribbean culture you can encourage people to recognise the need to look beyond their own cultures and in doing so to develop a level of sympathy and tolerance to the views of others, this is worthwhile.

PR: How would you distinguish between multicultural education and antiracist education?

HT: I have talked about multicultural education. Antiracism, in my view, is trying to deal with the political aspects of societies which make racism sustainable. It is about enabling kids to understand why and how society is racist and what can be done about it. This leads you inevitably into political issues and the politics of change. This can have implications for schools. For example, there was a number of evening schools which were organised by the local communities which had implications for the curriculum. We did bring examples of Afro-Caribbean culture into the school in terms of poetry, writing, dancing, music and other things. When there was a film of the school some people accused us of giving too much prominence to these cultural activities.

PR: You were five years at Birley. What happened then?

HT: Manchester had a reorganisation. A number of schools were seen to be undersubscribed. At Birley we had always had a small sixth form. In the reorganisation I applied for the new headship at Birley but so also had my deputy. He had been at the school much longer than I had and probably had a fuller understanding of the multiracial issues than I did. The Education Committee decided which heads they were going to appoint and then they discovered that nobody had applied for the headship of Margaret Ashton, a proposed sixth-form college. It was very small college so they invited two of us back for another interview for this before the whole Education Committee. We were asked 'If you were appointed to the sixth-form college would you take it?' I said 'yes' because it seemed an interesting job and in any case, after five years at Birley, perhaps it was time for a change. I was appointed to set up the college but starting off with a school made up of 800 girls of 12–16 and an expected sixth form of 300. It was a very odd sort of situation. Before the college had even opened the LEA was already making proposals to close it. They had never really been reconciled to the idea of sixth-form colleges. They had wanted tertiary colleges but Sir Keith Joseph had made it clear that he was not going to allow them to do this. The other interesting thing about that reorganisation is that I only discovered which teachers I was going to get a few weeks before the college was to open. It was an interesting situation trying to manage an institution on two sites with 70 people who hardly knew each other and who did not know me. In the event the whole situation was so absurd that we pulled together remarkably well. A lot of the women teachers who had been recruited to look after the girls as that part of the school was run down year by year, chose to stay with us afterwards. We all knew that we were in a situation which was unlikely to survive and this was quite difficult. Even so we did some interesting curriculum development. We were, for example, involved in the early days of City and Guilds 365 in schools. We also tried to so some thinking on special needs but we were never really able to make much progress with this.

I was there for three years in all and it closed after four years. Whilst there I managed to get into trouble with the politicians. Reflecting back on our earlier discussions about race, it seemed to me that within the community too many girls were leaving school at sixteen mainly because they had lost access to single-sex education. I proposed a course, in consultation with the girls, which would in certain ways entail a degree of racial and sexual stereotyping but would have meant that they could stay on beyond sixteen. There was support for the idea from amongst the girls and amongst their mothers but it became a major political issue. The CRE, EOC, City Council and others became involved and I ended up having worked on something which I thought was of value to the girls being shouted at as both racist and sexist. Several city councillors made it quite clear to me that because of the trouble I had caused over this they thought it would be in my interest to get out as soon as possible.

I then started to look for posts elsewhere. I remember being interviewed in Doncaster where the first question was, 'Mr Tomlinson there are no miners' children here but if there were how would you handle the miners' strike?' I was interviewed in Cornwall trying to present an image of relaxed confidence but being so tense that I got cramp in one leg and had to hobble out of the room in considerable pain. I was interviewed in Derbyshire where in the feedback I was told that I did not smile often enough to get the job. But when I got my present job, once again, at the interview I felt certain that the job was to be mine. I was able to make the right kind of joke early on and in doing so to develop the right kind of atmosphere.

It was an interesting school. When I went there in 1985 I remember saying at the very first staff meeting, because there was an issue about sixth-form reorganisation at the time, that I had not come to create a sixth-form college but to run an 11–18 school. But two months later the Education Committee decided that they wanted sixth-form colleges and the institution which I said would not be a sixth-form college would be a sixth-form college. I had managed to cut my own throat but I think that the staff did forgive me. I arrived at the school in 1985 and was told in 1985 that the school was going to close in 1991. So there was to be a six-year closure period whilst Stockport carried out its reorganisation policy.

PR: You are an experienced head. What do you see as your strengths and weaknesses?

HT: I have had so many and such varied experiences that when difficult issues arise I have developed a number of techniques for dealing with them. Also I have spent a great deal of time working on the area between practice and research in education. I have done a lot of teaching about education at master's degree level. I have also been involved in the management of schools which have been the subject of research and I have been involved in that research. I have been the treasurer of the Secondary Heads Association and chair of the British Educational Management and Administration Society. So I have had both a good deal of experience in managing schools but also, and more than most heads, I have a good idea about what researchers are saying. I see myself as recognising major issues before others. This has always helped me to focus my efforts in managing change and development more effectively than I think would have been possible otherwise. I think my weaknesses are in areas like, not having and seeming to be unable to, develop a sense of humour that I can manage all the time. I am also conscious that one of the dangers of working too closely with children is that the staff possibly think that I am very much better at managing pupils than I am at managing staff.

PR: How do you see yourself as a manager?

HT: I think the important thing to keep in mind as a manager is the idea that everybody else has something potentially valuable to contribute. One of the things which has become clear to me as a result of my teaching with the Open University is how many teachers are frustrated by inadequate management. I would like to be able to create conditions which enable the highly intelligent and dedicated people we work with to achieve what they are capable of. I am not wanting to underestimate the power of the role of the headteacher, but what I would like to achieve is a situation in which people of very varying strengths can flourish. That means taking their purposes and values seriously particularly those of women and not just trying to impose my own.

PR: What do you expect of your senior staff and what should they expect of you?

HT: In my time here I have tried to set up a management model which draws upon the best theoretical ideas but also works in practice. I have a senior management team made up of six heads of faculty three of whom are vice principals and they are the single line managers. Thus the head of Business and Technology Faculty manages all the work of all the teachers in the Business and Technology area. Not just their teaching but also their responsibilities as tutors and the rest. It is a very simple structure: I manage about twelve people and they manage about twelve each. The vice principals also have a general responsibility for marketing, the whole of the pastoral system and personnel. In addition to these, there is the head of management of information services, the head of adult and community education, the bursar, etc. They all work to very clear job descriptions. My senior managers know of me that I will trust them to be getting on with their tasks because I know what they are capable of and they have clear responsibilities. They can expect me to support them in the decisions they make within their areas of delegated responsibility. You should not be too ready to take things back when you have delegated. Also if people are not making mistakes it is usually because they are playing things too safe.

PR: How do you manage the staff as a whole?

HT: We have two ten-minute staff meetings every week. This means that there are opportunities for me to pick things up which are not being identified by other parts of the system. We do also have a termly staff meeting. It is totally inappropriate to try to use this as a forum for decision-making. But it does mean staff have an opportunity to put things on the agenda and talk things through. In

addition I have a full, hour long meeting with every member of staff
every year and the agenda for this is theirs entirely. It is an opportunity for them to say how they think things are going and what they
think I should do.

PR: How do you relate to pupils, parents and the local community?

HT: With individual students I think I work very well. I am not
sure that all the thousand will feel they have as good a relationship
with me. I understand my predecessor worked hard to know as
many students as possible quite well and could name almost all of
them. I could not claim this. But I do relate to individuals quite well.
I think that parents know me quite well. I have been around now for
quite a long time. I go to all parents' evenings. I go around the hall
talking to parents. We also have a group of parents who have constituted themselves as a Friends of the College group and I see them.
We have parents on the governing body. They are almost always
very supportive of what we do. We do have contacts with the wider
community. There is the Adult Centre with which we have just
amalgamated. This has 6000 on its lists. So, as with pupils and
parents, there is the issue of determining what is the right kind of
relationship to try to develop with them. I think I am widely seen as
knowing what concerns education. Because of my role within SHA I
appear on local television fairly often. I think parents and the community conclude from that kind of thing that I am respected in
educational circles. Certainly, whenever parents want to see me I am
open to them and will see them. Even if it is better that they see
somebody else who has a closer grasp of what they are concerned
about. Getting parents of sixth forms to be involved and to come in is
an interesting new problem for us to come to terms with. There is
less tradition of this amongst parents than there is with younger
children. Our young people tend to have a different relationship
with their parents than do those under sixteen. It is important to
develop these relationships with parents. They are in a sense our
clients but we should remember that our real clients are the
students. This is true for those under sixteen and it is even more true
of those over sixteen.
    This leads me to think of our relationships as teachers with
parents and pupils. Some teachers seem to make claims about their
professionalism which amounts to the claim that 'They (parents and
pupil) ought to know what we know to be right.' In my view that
notion of professionalism has all too often been used to disadvantage
our clients.

PR: How important are your governors?

HT: Manchester was an old-fashioned authority where, whilst I was there, the Education Committee was the governing body for all schools. I do not recall often attending. One I do recall attending was the one in which they considered a report from HMI on the school. That was my situation at Birley. When I went to Margaret Ashton things had changed and there it was a case of the nominated Labour councillors coming along to the first meeting, voting the chair and it was then assumed that he or she would look after us. My recollection there was that the governing body certainly did not create any problems for us but also did not seem to be able to contribute to what we were doing. As a group of people they were generally supportive but not particularly helpful or useful. When I came to the Manor School one of the first things which struck me when I arrived was that my Conservative chair was proposed by a Labour member and seconded by a Liberal. In that way Stockport was very different from Manchester. But the then chair knew his way around the education world and the local authority. He saw his role as supporting the head and he ran the governing body very tightly and in a way designed to prevent any criticism of me or any of the teachers. But he came to adapt to the changes entailed by the Education Reform Act of 1988. I now have a very interesting governing body because when we reorganised there were a number of governors, many of whom had been members of the previous governing body, who had stayed on as well as some parents. But the people who came in included a former HMI in FE, a former principal of a sixth-form college, a former tertiary adviser, a head of department of a poly. So suddenly we got this large group of extremely knowledgeable highly sophisticated people who were able to ask very perceptive and intelligent questions and who saw their role as questioning constantly and constructively. I have never had any problems with a governing body but for the first time I now have one which is very knowledgeable and thoughtful. The presence of the kind of people I have been talking about seems to have encouraged the other governors to be more confident in taking part in the work of the body as a whole.

The governing body wants to be involved and to know what is going on but they have delegated a great deal of responsibility to me. In terms of staffing, for example, I could appoint anybody up to deputy head level. But what we do, in order that the staff do not feel that the whole thing is decided by the senior management is involve local authority advisers where we can and also the expertise of the governing body. It is not just my decision.

PR: How would you describe your relationships with local education authorities?

HT: I was heavily involved with the NUT earlier in my career and therefore I usually had a good idea of what was going on in Walsall. I also had a fairly good idea of what was happening in Manchester. I am now less heavily involved in the work of the union with the local authority. I suppose in Manchester, because I was so heavily politically involved, particularly in the reorganisation, since I was president of the NUT in Manchester in the year before the reorganisation, that I was seen to be somebody who knew what was going on and therefore had a relationship with the officers. But there was always a tenseness to the relationship in Manchester. I think I can explain what is symptomatic about what is best about Stockport by illustrating a particular case. The building work for reorganisation had not been agreed at the time that the decision was made about incorporation of sixth-form colleges. There were preliminary plans for building projects at the college. Stockport could have said, because we have to pick up the bill for this for the next forty years and because you are going to be incorporated, we will not go forward with any of the building proposals. But the authority through its chief education officer made it quite clear that this was not the line they were going to take. That shows the LEA at its best.

Whether there will be LEAs in the future and whether they are necessary is rather more difficult to answer. I think there will be a continuing need for something like the LEAs to support primary schools. It already seems to be that the delegation of responsibilities to primary schools is proving difficult and has been highly problematic in some areas. I gather increasing numbers of primary schools are beginning to try to cluster together to provide mutual support in place of what LEAs could once offer. Whether we need LEAs in the present form I am not certain. But in terms of the local accountabilities which the existence of LEAs to some extent made possible, I do not see how this can be achieved with the quangos currently being proposed. We may end up with a system characterised by highly centralised control over secondary education and this could mean more and more decisions being made by bureaucrats who are not really accountable to anybody.

PR: What do you enjoy about headship? Are there any things you dislike?

HT: I enjoy being able to be idiosyncratic. I am the kind of head who enjoys research. Perhaps significantly, my appraisal this year focuses upon whether the college does actually benefit from this research and my interest in it. One of the principals of a local sixth-form college who I much respect is undertaking my appraisal along with the local authority adviser. We agreed what they would do. The principal of the college would talk to the three vice-principals and bursar about what they saw me doing outside the college and the ways in which this might or might not benefit the college. They thought the benefits much outweighed the costs. The adviser would talk to other people about the same issue. They have done this and fed their perceptions back to me. Their central suggestion is that I ought to try to communicate more effectively to the staff exactly what it is I am doing. So since I have been involved in editing three books we discussed how this should be presented. Some might think this is a good thing whilst others might believe I would have better occupied my time on business more directly connected with the college. One of the things I did at Birley which people thought very brave at the time was that all the teachers were asked to comment anonymously on the performance of the head. I have sought very strongly and positively to hear the view which staff have about me. A head's central role is staff development.

PR: How do you keep up with the pace of change?

HT: Through the whole range of things I do. I do a great deal of reading about educational issues particularly reviewing. Also the kind of feedback I have sought from staff has been very helpful. My membership of various bodies and especially SHA and BEMAS has kept me in contact with things and with many people who help me to keep up to date. SHA keeps me in contact with others who are struggling with some of the things that I am and helps me to identify friends who can be at the other end of a line if I need information or assistance. I should also stress that I get a lot of support from staff at all levels. I am always conscious that some of the most useful advice and feedback I get comes from the staff with whom I am not particularly close or friendly. Also after sixteen years of doing the job I have a large number of friends and good acquaintances whom I can call upon when I need help or advice.

PR: How do you cope with the pressures of contemporary headship?

HT: I do sometimes feel stressed and I do sometimes seem to get tired at the end of the term. I react in a variety of ways. Sometimes it is necessary simply to catch up on some sleep. I hope that this does not sound like I am not taking all this seriously but I find that my job is actually to prevent responsibility for managing too much change landing on my desk. We have some superb staff and they need to be involved. The last five years have been tough but I have not felt under impossible strain. I have heard of heads who feel they are going under given the rate of change. I think there are two other things which have helped me to cope. The first is that I do make a real effort to try and understand myself. So, for example, I have had a number of anlayses done of myself. I have tried hard to understand what I am and what I am trying to do. It may sound pretentious but all this helps you to develop a proper understanding of what your strengths and weaknesses are and therefore you learn to understand and cope with them. For example, I know in Belbin's terms that I am not a completer/finisher so I try and have a personal assistant who will fulfil that role for me.

The other thing that has been quite important throughout my life has been the theatre. That helps me to prioritise. The things that I remember most having been involved in were that I played the leading part in *Who is Afraid of Virginia Woolf?* and I have produced *The Three Sisters*. About once every two or three weeks I try to go to the theatre. I suppose that is about trying to understand what life is like. I am not as interested in the other arts. Because for me the theatre is the art that most relates to real life. It is in a sense about education and it is about education in the best way. I like the psychologists to tell me about myself and I like to learn from the dramatist about myself and life.

PR: Can heads still be curriculum leaders? Do you see yourself as a curriculum leader? What are you going to tell Ron Dearing when you see him?

HT: One of the things we were doing at Birley in 1977 was that everybody was on broadly the same curriculum and I have tried to achieve the same thing in the other posts I have held since then. I believe that we ought to have a National Curriculum. I think if it is to have any real worth it will need to be relatively prescribed. That is not to say that it should have been prescribed in the way in which it has been over the last few years or by the people who have been given the task of determining what should be prescribed. If we had a very clear, agreed and coherent curriculum for those between five and sixteen then I think this would enable children to develop much greater skills than at present and we would be able to focus available resources much more effectively. This would enable us to provide a higher quality education for everyone. So I am very much in favour of a coherent, prescribed National Curriculum for all.

As a headteacher I have been very involved in curriculum planning and development. I recall in my first term as a senior teacher my curriculum development experience was that we did Nigerian History, Nigerian Geography and Nigerian Literature. That was the kind of idiosyncratic curriculum development which took place at the time. Every single school in Basildon at the time had its own curriculum. It seems to me that there is a lot of evidence which suggests that all was not well in the past. For example, the Oracle project seemed to suggest that kids were going backwards in Maths during their first year in secondary schools. So I am quite happy to sacrifice a degree of the curriculum control which teachers have allegedly exercised in the interests of their children. It seems to me this has all too often been exercised more in theory than in practice as teachers have gone about doing their own thing in their own interests. I do not want to be a curriculum leader if this means somebody with the responsibility for creating the curriculum. Rather I see my job as ensuring as best I can curriculum quality. It has to do with the delivery of a coherent quality curriculum.

PR: How much flexibility has the National Curriculum left schools? Some argue that it has become overprescriptive. Others claim that considerable discretion remains for individual schools if they choose to exercise this. That the National Curriculum identifies a number of things which must be done but it does not specify how.

HT: That may be true but I do think that there is a good deal of prescription even in this. It is the assessment procedures which increasingly prescribe the how. These are being altered but I still think we are some way from determining how all the bits of Key Stage 4 can be fitted into a sensible curriculum. As things stand probably nobody should do more than eight GCSEs. And there are probably ten or eleven subjects which need to be provided. So I think there is still a good deal of room for KS4 to be revised. But apart from the sheer amount of content within the National Curriculum at this stage the other key issue is its implications for teachers in primary schools. My wife is a primary teacher and she is in effect required to be a graduate in all subjects because one year later, for the pupils, the teachers are graduates in these subjects. I think the primary school curriculum has not been thought through beyond the vague assumption that you can build it all in and assume the teachers will either already have or will somehow develop the required subject expertise. There seems to me to be three possible solutions. First, to recognise that there is too much content and to reduce this. Secondly, once the assessment procedures are simplified, I think the view you expressed about a high level of flexibility will apply. But there is a need to concentrate on the primary school curriculum and on KS4. I doubt if anybody really thinks this has been got right. I think that what SHA is saying is 'Do not rush at things. Think about what is involved and try to convince us about the solutions which are proposed.' I think it is absurd that John Patten is already signalling what he sees as solutions before Dearing's review has taken place. I think the decision to try to force the present round of assessment is absurd. I suppose it is politically easier for him to go ahead and for them not to happen than for him to be seen to give up at this stage. I doubt very much if they will happen.

PR: What do you think is going to happen on assessment?

HT: I do think we need to think hard about assessment. What we have had has never really been designed to meet the needs of up to 80 per cent of pupils — those who do not do 'A' Levels. I think the continuing influence of 'A' Levels on the structure of the curriculum and how we assess is at the root of many of the problems we have faced in education. My book on *Education 14–19* is saying that that is the area which most needs reform. There are lots of alternative models all of which would be an improvement on 'A' Levels. We need to think more of the curricular and other needs of the 14–19 year cohort as a whole. That is the first thing we need to have. The issue is not really what we should do about assessment. On the other hand there is that hard line view that we need ways of assessing which can be used to measure school performance. There is no easy way of doing this and I am sceptical of the validity of ways in which this is being done now. But I am not against this in principle. It seems to me that parents do have a right to know how well an individual school is performing. In that context I am not in principle opposed to the idea of performance-related pay. I would like to be able to pay teachers who have performed particularly well. I am not suggesting that this can necessarily be done easily. I think it is possible to do but we are never going to do it on the basis of statistics alone there will also need to be an element of judgement.

If you did this I think it would have a beneficial effect on how teachers feel. I was reading recently that one of the things which causes teachers who want to leave teaching actually to leave is the whingeing of the teachers who remain. I think if we tried to be positive and constructive then we would probably enjoy our work rather more. I think recognising and rewarding teaching of quality would go some way towards enabling this to happen.

PR: Can we pick up one or two final issues on the curriculum? Do you see yourself as a curriculum developer? If so how and in what way? Thinking about what you have said and having read some of what you have written you almost seem to be more interested in how we might assess the curriculum than in how we might develop it. Is that fair?

HT: I think there is a changing perception. There is a curriculum developer amongst my senior teacher posts. In the past I have certainly been a curriculum developer but since we now have a National Curriculum I think there is less need for this and also one can become too concerned with developing the curriculum and not concerned enough about examining the quality of the learning that goes on. To put it another way the curriculum development perspective seems to be often more concerned with what it is we should teach and is not concerned enough with what it is they learn. Unless you can assess effectively then how can you possibly know what it is that they have learnt? That may be where my emphasis has changed.

PR: How do you cope when things go wrong?

HT: When things go really spectacularly wrong, as at Birley, you have to succeed in doing certain things or you will not survive. But I do not think that things go wrong as much now. Partly because I think I have learnt from experience. But when I get very angry at the way things might go then I tend to go away and lick my wounds. I tend to try to manage this on my own although sometimes I lean on my wife and daughter. But I also find that I am quite resilient partly because I now have so much experience. When things go wrong I tend to see this in context and do not exaggerate the magnitude of what has happened. And in any case I would be hard pressed to think of anything significant which I have been responsible for which has gone badly wrong for some considerable time. In any case if you build up a fund of success upon which you can fall back it helps you to cope with the failures which must sometimes come.

PR: Do you think headship is still necessary?

HT: I think that it is increasingly necessary. *Ten Good Schools* came out just as I was becoming a head and it made clear that headteachers really make a difference. Pretty well everything I have read since then confirms that this is the case. One of the things one has to be conscious of is that does not mean that as a head I am or have to be a wonderful person. What it actually means is that the ideal head recognises and enables others to contribute to the best of their ability. If you are successful as a head it is almost always because of the work which others do. But it is the headteacher more than any other who makes this possible.

PR: How do you think the next generation of headteachers should be prepared?

HT: I think those who wish to be heads ought to take it upon themselves to prepare for headship much more thoroughly than some do. We talked about all the things I did in preparing for headship but after that I continued to study. I obtained a master's degree in organisational psychology. Anybody interested in headship ought to so some of the things I have done in order to enhance their knowledge of education and its management. We have just appointed at the college a Scale B assistant curriculum co-ordinator for English who has already got a masters' degree and others are going to have to do that kind of thing in the future. I think people are going to take responsibility for their own development and not wait for it to be done for them. On this, recent developments in

NVQ, particularly at Levels 4 and 5, are going to be an important way forward. I think increasingly people will use the resources of their own institution to underpin training. This might well lead to a developmental culture within the institution and the creation of a cadre of staff who both sustain and benefit from that culture.

PR: What do you feel about the prospect of several more years of headship?

HT: I feel very good about it. It seems to me that much has already happened over the last few years and there are so many interesting things which are likely to happen over the next few years. If I had been faced with the prospect of doing much the same thing over the next ten years as I am doing now then I would probably want to go. Happily there seems to be very little prospect of this happening. I am sure there will be plenty to keep me going and growing as a person and as a professional. There is plenty to look forward to with excitement.

Appendix 1: interview schedule

1. To help us get this conversation in context, it would be helpful if you would say something about your background?
2. How and why did you become a teacher?
3. What made you interested in headship? How did you prepare for it?
4. What are your memories of taking over your first school? How did that experience affect your subsequent management of the school? What did you or will you do differently next time?
5. What do you expect of your senior and other managers and what can they expect of you? How are their roles divided and how did this pattern of responsibility come to be devised?
6. How do you lead the work of the staff as a whole?
7. In what ways do you relate to pupils, parents and the local community?
8. How do you manage your relationship and working practices with your governing body?
9. What are (or were) your relationships with the LEA?
10. How do you keep up with developments in understanding of what makes for effective teaching and learning and with the seemingly ever increasing pace of demand for change?
11. What do you enjoy most about headship and what interests you least? Has headship changed significantly in your time as a teacher and a headteacher?
12. Who or what has most helped you in coming to terms with headship?
13. More personally, how do you cope with what is expected of you? How well do you manage your time? What gives you most stress and creates most tension? How do you cope with these stresses and tensions?
14. How far is your school still able to determine the nature and shape of the curriculum and its assessment: How is curriculum planning and development organised and managed within your school? What part do you yourself play in all this?
15. How do you cope when things go wrong?
16. In what sense is the school, your school?

References

Baker, K. (1993) *The Turbulent Years: My Life in Politics*, London: Faber and Faber

Ball, S. (1980) *Beechside Comprehensive*, Cambridge: Cambridge University Press

Baron, G. (1956) 'Some aspects of the headmaster tradition' in *Researchers and Studies*, **14**

Barry, C. and Tye, F. (1975) *Running a School*, London: Temple Smith

Berg, L. (1968) *Risinghill*, Harmondsworth: Penguin

Best, R., Ribbins, R., Jarvis, C. and Oddy, D. (1983) *Education and Care*, Oxford: Blackwell

Burgess, R. (1983) *Experiencing Comprehensive Education: Study of Bishop McGregor School*, London: Methuen

Busher, H. and Saran, R. (1994) 'Towards a model of school leadership' in *Education Management and Administration*, 22(1), pp. 5–14

Castle, E. (1967) 'Thomas Arnold and Edward Thring: Great Headmasters?' in Lucas, E. (Ed) *What is Greatness*, London: Oxford University Press

Coleman, J., Campbell, E., Hobson, C., McPartland, H., Wood, W. and York, R. (1966) *Equality of Educational Opportunity*, Washington: US Government Printing Office

Creemers B. (1992) 'School effectiveness, effective instruction and school improvement in the Netherlands' in Reynolds D. and Cuttance, P. (Eds) *School Effectiveness: Research, Policy and Practice*, London: Cassell

Creemers, B. and Scheerens, J. (1989) 'Developments in school effectiveness' in *International Journal of Educational Research*, **13**, pp. 691–707

Dawson, P. (1981) *Making a Comprehensive Work*, Oxford: Blackwell

DES (1977) *A New Partnership for our Schools*, London: HMSO (Taylor Report)

Dyhouse, C. (1987) 'Miss Buss and Miss Beal: gender and authority in the history of education' in Hunt, F. (Ed) *Lessons for Life*, Oxford: Blackwell

Elton Report (1989) *Discipline in Schools*, London: HMSO

Greenfield, T. and Ribbins, P. (1993) 'Educational administration as a humane science: conversations between Thomas Greenfield and Peter Ribbins in Greenfield, T. and Ribbins, P. (1993) *Greenfield on Educational Administration: Towards a Human Science*, London: Routledge

Gronn, P. (1986) 'The boyhood, schooling and early career of J. R. Darling, 1899–1930' in *Journal of Australian Studies*, **19**, pp. 30–42

Gronn, P. (1992) 'Schooling for ruling', *Australian Historical Studies*, 25(98), pp. 72–89

Hall, V., Mackay, H. and Morgan C. (1986) *Headteachers at Work*, Milton Keynes: Open University Press

Hargreaves, D. (1967) *Social Relations in a Secondary School*, London: Routledge and Kegan Paul

Holmes, G. (1993) *Essential School Leadership*, London: Kogan Page

Hughes, M. (1972) *The Role of The Secondary School Head*, University of Wales PhD (unpublished), University College, Cardiff

Hughes, M. (1973) 'The professional as administrator' in *Educational Administration Bulletin*, 2(1), pp. 11–23

Hughes, M. (1990) 'Institutional leadership: issues and challenges' in Saran, R. and Trafford, V. (Eds) *Research in Education Management and Policy*, Lewes: Falmer

Jenks, C., Smith, M., Ackland, H., Bane, M., Cohen, D., Grintis, H., Hegus, B. and Micholson, N. (1972) *Inequality: A Reassessment of the Effect of Family and Schooling in America*, New York: Basic Books

John, D. (1980) *Leadership in Schools*, London: Heinemann

Jones, A. (1987) *Leadership for Tomorrow's Schools*, Oxford: Blackwell

Kogan, M. (1971) *The Politics of Education: Edward Boyle and Anthony Crossland*, Harmondsworth: Penguin

Kogan, M. (1971) *County Hall LEA: The Role of the Chief Education Officer*, Harmondsworth: Penguin

Lacey, C. (1970) *Hightown Grammar*, Manchester: Manchester University Press

Lyons, G. (1976) *A Handbook of Secondary School Administration*, Windsor: NFER/Nelson

McKenzie, R. (1970) *State School*, Harmondsworth: Penguin

Morgan, C., Hall, V. and Mackay, H. (1983) *The Selection of Secondary School Headteachers*, Milton Keynes: Open University Press

Mortimer, J. and Mortimer, P. (1991) *The Secondary School Head; Roles, Responsibilities and Reflections*, London: Paul Chapman

Mortimer, P., Sammons, P., Ecob, R. and Stoll, L. (1988) *Schools Matter: The Junior Years*, Salisbury: Openbooks

National Commission on Education [Chaired by Lord Walton] (1993) *Learning to Succeed: A Radical Look at Education Today and a Strategy for the Future*, London: Heinemann

Neill, A. (1960) *Summerhill*, New York: Hart

Pedersen, J. (1975) 'Schoolmistresses and headmistresses: elites and education in nineteenth century England', in *Journal of British Studies*, 15(1), pp. 135–162

Pedersen, J. (1981) 'Some Victorian headmistresses, a conservative tradition of social reform', in *Victorian Studies*, 24(4), pp. 463–488

Poster, C. (1976) *School Decision Making*, London: Heinemann

Rae, J. (1993) *Delusions of Grandeur: A Headmaster's Life, 1966–1986*, London: Harper Collins

Reynolds, D. (1994) 'School effectiveness and quality in education' in Ribbins, P. and Burridge, E. (Eds) *Improving Education: Promoting Quality in Schools*, London: Cassell

Reynolds, D. and Parker, A. (1992) 'School effectiveness and school improvement in the 1990s' in Reynolds, D. and Cuttance, P. (Eds) *School Effectiveness: Research, Policy and Practice*, London: Cassell

Ribbins, P. (1993a) 'Telling tales of secondary heads: on educational reform and the national curriculum' in Chitty, C. (Ed) *The National Curriculum: Is It Working?*, Harlow: Longman

Ribbins, P. (1993b) 'Towards a prolegomenon for understanding what radical educational reform means for principals' a Keynote Paper given at the *Annual National Conference of CCEA/ASSP* held in Adelaide in September 1993 (unpublished)

Ribbins, P. and Sherratt, B. (1992) 'Managing the secondary school in the 1990s: a new view of headship' in *Educational Management and Administration*, 20(3)

Richardson, E. (1973) *The Teacher, the School and the Task of Management*, London: Heinemann

Rutter, M. et al. (1979) *Fifteen Thousand Hours: Secondary Schools and their Effects on Children*, London: Open Books

Secondary Heads Association (1993) 'Conference Report' in *Headlines*, 12 June

Toogood, P. (1984) *The Head's Tale*, Telford: Dialogue Publications

Watts, J. (Ed) (1977) *The Countesthorpe Experience*, London: Allen and Unwin

Weindling, D. (1990) 'Secondary school headship: a review of research' in Saran, R. and Trafford, V. (Eds) *Research in Education Management and Policy*, Lewes: Falmer

Weindling, D. and Early, P. (1987) *Secondary Headship: The First Years*, Windsor: NFER/Nelson

Index